What Jesus' Crucifixion Accomplished For Us

CRUCIFIXION:
A Multidisciplinary Investigation of the Death of Jesus of Nazareth

Many fine books on the subject of crucifixion are available today, but no in-depth, multi-volume investigation of Roman crucifixion and Jesus' death has been available, until now. CRUCIFIXION: A Multi-disciplinary Examination of the Crucifixion of Jesus of Nazareth consists of seven volumes, each dedicated to an integral subject related to Jesus' crucifixion. *The Day Jesus Died* identifies the year, date, day, and hour of Jesus' death. And there's *From the Upper Room to Joseph's Tomb* which examines each location on Jesus' journey to Calvary. Other titles include: *Probing the Trials, Crucifixion, and Burial of Jesus of Nazareth*, *What Jesus' Crucifixion Accomplished for Us*, *Roman Crucifixion and the Death of Jesus*, *Watching Jesus Die*, and *Take Up the Cross*. With the CRUCIFIXION series, every aspect of Roman crucifixion and the cross is explored with specific reference to the crucifixion of Jesus. The scholar will appreciate each book's depth of research, often reflected in each chapter's extensive endnotes. The nonprofessional reader will enjoy the thoughtful and readable style of each book in the series. Every reader will quickly find value in each volume of this seven-book series.

What Jesus' Crucifixion Accomplished For Us

A Theological Examination of the Purpose and Meaning of Jesus' Death

WOODROW MICHAEL KROLL

Foreword by Craig A. Evans

RESOURCE *Publications* • Eugene, Oregon

WHAT JESUS' CRUCIFIXION ACCOMPLISHED FOR US
A Theological Examination of the Purpose and Meaning of Jesus' Death

Resource Publications
An Imprint of Wipf and Stock Publishers
199 W. 8th Ave., Suite 3
Eugene, OR 97401

www.wipfandstock.com

PAPERBACK ISBN: 979-8-3852-6959-4
HARDCOVER ISBN: 979-8-3852-6960-0
EBOOK ISBN: 979-8-3852-6961-7

VERSION NUMBER 03/09/26

Contents

List of Tables

Foreword

In most investigations of the death, burial, and resurrection of Jesus, we are treated to detailed studies of historical context, archaeological matters, and a myriad of interpretive questions and objections raised by skeptics. Less often are we treated to the question of what Jesus accomplished in his death on the cross. This question is, of course, of vital importance, and it is the question that veteran Bible teacher Woodrow Kroll has addressed in this, the latest volume in his Crucifixion series.

The historical event of the crucifixion is of enormous importance, and the reality of the resurrection even more so. But why? Why was the death of Jesus so important? And what did it mean? Jesus died on a Roman cross, to be sure, but what changed? What did it accomplish? Kroll probes this question in a deeply satisfying way, first by defining the biblical concept of atonement and then inquiring into what at first strikes us as a strange teaching: the curse of the cross. Why is being hanged on a cross (or tree) a "curse"? What does that mean? And how can Jesus becoming a curse benefit humanity in any way?

Kroll teases out this vital question in several chapters, addressing human sin (what it is and what its consequences are), divine wrath (its nature and how it relates to justice and mercy), the righteousness of Jesus (how Paul explains it and how it is applied), and how Jesus satisfied the requirements of divine justice (above all in the incarnation), and how Jesus accomplished redemption, forgiveness, restoration, and the final defeat of Satan.

The beauty of Kroll's study lies in how he ties together these important and complex themes, showing their logical connection, moving from the problem of a broken Cosmos to its glorious reconciliation with God, made possible by the crucifixion of Jesus. Readers will appreciate the theological nuance combined with perceptive exegesis that makes every effort to be fair to the sacred text. Kroll's wealth of knowledge, formed over decades of study and teaching, is in evidence on every page.

Craig A. Evans
Distinguished Research Professor
The Bible Seminary
Katy, Texas

Preface

People read the Bible for different reasons. Some read it for comfort and hope. Others are looking for loopholes to excuse their sin. Still, others read God's Word with a critical mind, looking for mistakes or contradictions. We will read the Gospels to gain a deeper understanding of the last hours of Jesus of Nazareth's life. We want to read the Scriptures to enrich our minds and sharpen our focus on the Bible's message.

In this book, we are seeking to address some serious questions. "What did Jesus' crucifixion accomplish"? "What benefit was gained by the bloody execution of an innocent Nazarene"? And, "What does Jesus' death on the cross mean for you and me"?

As you read this book or any of my works, you will quickly notice that I often appeal to the four Gospels for accurate historical information. That's because I believe these writings are the earliest, most accurate, and best documents to inform us of the life and times of Jesus of Nazareth. I accept the Bible at face value, and while I incorporate the valuable insights and research of other scholars into my own, I also draw common-sense conclusions that are often not evident in much of modern liberal scholarship today. As the final authority, I appeal to those "men [who] spoke from God as they were carried along by the Holy Spirit" (2 Pet 1:21).

Now, some technical information. The Scripture references in this book are from the English Standard Version (ESV) of the Bible unless otherwise noted. The ESV is based on the Greek text in the 2014 editions of the Greek New Testament (5th corrected edition), published by the United Bible Societies (UBS), and *Novum Testamentum Graece* (28th ed, 2012), edited by Nestle and Aland. The Hebrew words in the text are from the Masoretic text of the Hebrew Bible, as found in *Biblia Hebraica Stuttgartensia* (2nd edition,1983). Words in Greek are taken from the 1993 editions of the Greek New Testament (4th corrected edition) and *Novum Testamentum Graece* (27th ed).

Since multiple words in the Greek language may be used for the same word in English, wherever I have highlighted a Greek word, and there is more than one Scripture associated with it, I have always used the Greek of the first Scripture listed, as found in the 28th revised edition of the Nestle-Aland *Novum Testamentum Graece.*

Some decades ago, many scholars adopted the designations B.C.E. (Before Common Era) and C.E. (Common Era) to indicate dates on the calendar. I completely understand why this change was made. The B.C.E. and C.E. designations are more inclusive because they do not specifically relate to Jesus Christ or Christianity. However, most of the Western world is steeped in the use of BC and AD; even many highly influential scholars have chosen to retain these designations.[1] But I use BC and AD for a strikingly different reason.

Greek scholar Vincent Taylor said it best:

> We are bound to consider how we think of time, whether past events are only isolated points in a series, or whether God invades history with abiding consequences. This issue is of serious concern to theologians today. It is best considered by reflecting upon (1) events as points in the time series; (2) events with permanent significance; and (3) events as divine invasions in time."[2]

I do not believe the advent of God's Son was a mere point-in-time series. I see the birth of the Messiah and Savior as an invasion of time by God himself. Thus, despite scholarly arguments that Christians should adopt the BCE/CE dating system, I will use the designations BC and AD to reflect the incredible moment when God changed the world forever by invading time, not simply staging a timeshare for multiple religious communities.

> "The death of the Incarnate Son of God on a Roman cross marks the central point in the history of mankind."—F. W. Mattox

Jesus was very clear about why he came to Earth. He was not at all confused about his mission. In his own words, he declared:

John 6:38, "For I have come down from heaven, not to do my own will but the will of him who sent me."

Luke 19:10, "For the Son of Man came to seek and to save the lost."

John 12:46, "I have come into the world as light, so that whoever believes in me may not remain in darkness."

John 10:10, "The thief comes only to steal and kill and destroy. I came that they may have life and have it abundantly."

Others in the Bible also knew why Jesus came.

The Apostle Paul wrote to his young protégé, "The saying is trustworthy and deserving of full acceptance, that Christ Jesus came into the world to save sinners, of whom I am the foremost" (1 Tim 1:15).

The Apostle John said, "These are written so that you may believe that Jesus is the Christ, the Son of God, and that by believing you may have life in his name" (John 20:31).

And John the Baptist proclaimed, "The next day he saw Jesus coming toward him, and said, 'Behold, the Lamb of God, who takes away the sin of the world!'" (John 1:29).

It is impossible to overstate the significance of Jesus' crucifixion, for without his death on a Jerusalem cross, there was no reason for his birth in that Bethlehem stable or opportunity for the miraculous resurrection. Consider what we know about the Savior's life and ministry to others.

- As a baby, Jesus was visited by shepherds.
- As a young infant, he was worshiped by wise men.
- As a lad of twelve, he astonished the religious leaders of Jerusalem.
- As a man severely tempted by Satan, he proved himself to be unshakable.
- As a teacher, Jesus revealed truth that no one had ever heard.
- As a friend, he drew others to him like a magnet, both children and adults.
- As a leader, Jesus earned the loyalty of hundreds more than just the Twelve.
- As a paragon of kindness, he healed the sick, gave the blind sight, and hope to the hopeless.
- As the point man for God's salvation, Jesus set his face like a flint toward Jerusalem.
- As the long-awaited Messiah, he was adored by those along the Palm Sunday street.
- As a human being, he agonized in Gethsemane, knowing what atrocities awaited him.
- As an honorable citizen, when arrested, he complied with the Temple police.
- As a truth-teller, he refused to answer the false accusations of the Jewish religious leaders.

- As one who knew God's eternal plan, he did not stop those who were crucifying him.
- As a lamb led to the slaughter, Jesus was silently led to Calvary's Cross.
- As the victor over the grave, on the third day, Jesus rose from the dead.
- As God the Son, he ascended into heaven to sit on the right hand of God the Father.
- As the only one worthy, one day, before him, every knee will bow and every tongue will confess that Jesus Christ is Lord, to the glory of God the Father.

All these things tell us something about Jesus, but being aware of them does not save us from our sin. That required crucifixion. That required the shedding of Jesus' blood. That required Jesus' righteous death. Had Jesus not been crucified, there would be no blood to cover your sin or mine, like the blood of the Passover lamb covered the doorposts of the Jewish homes on the night of the first Passover. Everything leading up to the cross is meaningless without Calvary.

> "Either [Jesus] was what he said he was or he was the world's greatest liar. It is impossible for me to believe a liar or charlatan could have had the effect on mankind that he has had for 2000 years."
> —President Ronald Reagan

The eternal plan of God was for Jesus to die so that we might live. The question is: "Did Jesus' death accomplish what God intended?" Perhaps a more fundamental question is, "What did God intend for Jesus to accomplish while being crucified?" These are the types of questions we explore in the pages that follow.

You don't have to be a theologian to understand what theological accomplishments were achieved when Jesus died at Calvary. All you need is a reliable source of information and the Spirit of God to assist you in understanding (John 14:26). Armed with this information and anxious to know the truth, let's explore together what exactly Jesus accomplished on Calvary's Cross.

Woodrow Michael Kroll
Ashland, Nebraska

Abbreviations

BIBLE TRANSLATION ABBREVIATIONS

ASV	American Standard Version
CEV	Contemporary English Version
ESV	English Standard Version
GNT	Good News Translation
HCSB	Holman Christian Standard Bible
JBP	J. B. Phillips
KJV	King James Version
TLB	The Living Bible
NASB	New American Standard Bible
NCB	New Catholic Bible
NET	New English Translation
NIV	New International Version
NKJV	New King James Version
NLT	New Living Bible
NRSV	New Revised Standard Version
RSV	Revised Standard Version

SCHOLASTIC ABBREVIATIONS

AASOR	Annual of the American School of Oriental Research
Ant.	Antiquities, Flavius Josephus
BA	Biblical Archaeologist
BAR	Biblical Archaeology Review
BDB	A Hebrew and English Lexicon of the Old Testament
BibSac	Bibliotheca Sacra

BW	Biblical World
CE	Catholic Encyclopedia
CH	Church History
CT	Christianity Today
DSS	Dead Sea Scrolls
EBib	Études Bibliques
EH	Ecclesiastical History, Eusebius
EQ	Evangelical Quarterly
ExpTim	Expository Times
HTR	Harvard Theological Review
HUCA	Hebrew Union College Annual
IEJ	Israel Exploration Journal
ISBE	International Standard Bible Encyclopedia
JAAR	Journal of the American Academy of Religion
JBL	Journal of Biblical Literature
JETS	Journal of the Evangelical Theological Society
JJS	Journal of Jewish Studies
JQR	Jewish Quarterly Review
JRS	Journal of Roman Studies
JSNT	Journal for the Study of the New Testament
JTS	Journal of Theological Studies
LXX	The Septuagint
NHL	Nag Hammadi Library
NTA	New Testament Apocrypha
NTS	New Testament Studies
NTG	Novum Testamentum Graece
OTP	Old Testament Pseudepigrapha
PEQ	Palestine Exploration Quarterly
RevArch	Revue Archéologique
RB	Revue Biblique
RevQum	Revue de Qumran
SBLSP	Society of Biblical Literature Seminar Papers
ST	Studia Theologica
SWJT	Southwestern Journal of Theology
TalBab	Babylonian Talmud
TalJer	Jerusalem Talmud
TDNT	Theological Dictionary of the New Testament
TS	Theological Studies
TZ	Theologische Zeitschrift
War	Wars of the Jews, Flavius Josephus

Introduction

Unfortunately, so many people today—too many—get their theological understanding from movies, podcasts, and (*μὴ γένοιτο*—God forbid) the Internet. They interpret theology through the posts they read. They judge what the Bible says by the "scholarship" they find on Meta, X, or TikTok. As a result, some people, not all, have come to the mistaken belief that the cross demonstrates something dark about God's personality. They see on the news what a sick and demented father did to his daughters. How could parents do this to their own?

Even some theologians equate that abhorrent behavior with God's behavior at Golgotha. They ask, "How could a Father do that to his Son? How could God allow Jesus to suffer so and then be crucified on Calvary's Cross? How could he let this happen?" Unfortunately, and incorrectly, they see the Father sending his Son to the cross as something akin to "cosmic child abuse." When they learn of an abusive human father, seared through with sin, mistreating his child, with no discernment, they transfer that guilt to the Father in heaven. In God's most significant expression of love (John 3:16), they only see a God of hate.

Some feminist theologians have expressed similar interpretations of the cross of Calvary and Jesus' crucifixion. One feminist theologian claimed, "Christian theology with atonement at the center still encourages martyrdom and victimization." She protests loudly that "divine child abuse is paraded as a sacrifice" and "to argue that salvation can only come through the cross is to make God a divine sadist and a divine child abuser."[3] The cross means something different to this woman than it does to mainstream Evangelicals. One wonders why she is so angry at God.

Another reported, "The published comment by a feminist theologian at the 'Re-imaging' conference a few years ago was, 'I don't think we need a theory of atonement at all. I don't think we need folks hanging on crosses and blood dripping and weird stuff.'"[4] I beg to differ. That "weird stuff" is the stuff of our salvation. It would be unjust to place all theologians, especially female theologians, in the same camp as these extremely radical ones. But we must ask if these feminists and left-leaning theologians are correct. Is there any basis for their conjectures?

Various traditions within the Church differ significantly in their perceptions of Christ's atonement. One denomination or church tradition may emphasize an aspect of the atonement that is not emphasized here; I'll accept that and wish them well. However, orthodox denominations and their theologians do not generally refer to the divine atonement as "weird stuff."

Let me say at the outset that if you're looking for a theology textbook, this isn't it, for several reasons.

First, the doctrines of the Christian faith that you typically find in a theology textbook are not addressed here. You will not find areas of theology, such as Pneumatology, Ecclesiology, or Eschatology, in this volume. These have been left for others to write about. This book inquires into those things accomplished by Christ's death that others have either not thought of or decided not to write about.

Second, those doctrines that are examined are not exhaustively treated. This is a theological examination of the purpose and meaning of Jesus' death. It is an investigation into what Jesus Christ achieved at the crucifixion, not an in-depth theology of salvation or propitiation. We will always focus on the cross and what Jesus specifically accomplished there.

Third, my approach differs significantly from theological texts. The Lord's achievements addressed here may not be those you would choose. I have made these choices out of my appreciation for Christ's death. Some of the things I address will not even make the list of others, but I see them as significant accomplishments related to Jesus' crucifixion, and they speak to me. I pray they speak to you a well.

Fourth, my approach is more conversational than you would find in a textbook of theology. While various features of Christ's atonement are addressed, each one is subordinate to the fact that, "For our sake he [God the Father] made him [God the Son] to be sin who knew no sin, so that in him we might become the righteousness of God" (2 Cor 5:21). Everything must come back to the cross and the One who died there for us.

The cross was the dominant theme of the four gospels, especially in the final chapters. The cross enjoyed a rich history in Paul's letters. The apostle often used the word "cross" to mean the totality of the mystery of our redemption. God's one and only Son "humbled himself by becoming obedient to the point of death, even death on a cross" (Phil 2:8). Here we focus on the cross, on the Christ who died there, and on some wonderful things that Christ did for us when he was crucified at Calvary.

In Paul's writings, Jesus' crucifixion was treated as a multi-significant event. Since Christ's sacrifice, every culture in history has been touched by the effects of Calvary's Cross. Think with me of the characteristics of the cross upon which Jesus died.

- *Jesus' cross has content.* "For Christ did not send me to baptize but to preach the gospel, and not with words of eloquent wisdom, lest the cross of Christ be emptied of its power" (1 Cor 1:17). Paul knew that God had saved him and called him for one purpose—not to baptize, but to preach the gospel. The preaching of the cross has power because it has content.

Paul also knew he did not need to speak eloquently of the cross, for the content was simple. We have disobeyed and disrespected God. Still, God loves us. God sent his Son to be crucified at Calvary so Jesus would secure a pardon for our sin. By believing in Jesus as God's Savior, he will become our Savior. God's salvation is not complicated, and the wisdom of the world must not be allowed to bankrupt it. The cross of Christ's content was about God's wrath against sin, his love for the sinner, and Jesus' sacrifice to save us from divine wrath and sin's penalty, which is death.

- *Jesus' cross has a message.* "For the word of the cross is folly to those who are perishing" (1 Cor 1:18). If there were no message of salvation in the content of Jesus' cross, there would be no debate about that message. However, the discussion of the meaning of the cross began shortly after Jesus rose from the dead and continues today in seminary classrooms, Bible study groups, chat rooms, and around the kitchen table.

To those whose lives have been changed by God's grace, the message of the cross makes perfect sense and is both understandable and believable. But to those who believe there is no truth in the pages of Scripture, to those who reject the message of the cross and consequently perish without God's salvation, the cross seems to be a terrible and unwarranted tragedy. "Whoever believes in him is not condemned, but whoever does not believe is condemned already, because he has not believed in the name of the only Son of God" (John 3:18). If this statement by the Apostle John is true, Calvary's Cross was anything but an unnecessary tragedy. The message of the cross is the message of salvation.

- *Jesus' cross has power.* Not the wooden cross itself, but the content of the message of the cross has the power to change people's lives. It has the power to make the message real to people. "For the word of the cross is folly to those who are perishing, but to us who are being saved it is the power of God" (1 Cor 1:18). The contrast could not be drawn more graphically or sharply. Those who are perishing, those who believe the mind of man is more likely to hold truth than the mind of God, to them, everything the Bible says about the cross is foolishness.

Nonetheless, for those who trust the record of Scripture, to those whose spiritual eyes have been opened and the scales of human blindness have fallen away, to them, the message of the cross has the power to save from eternal hell. To us today, to us who believe that Jesus died for our sin and have placed our faith in him, we are the ones whom the power of God has saved.

However, there is another side to the cross of Christ, other than the saving side. Paul also knew these truths about the cross.

- *The cross would be an "offense."* Those who believe Christ-followers are fools and the Bible is an unreliable historical source, the cross offends them. Paul questioned the Galatians, "But if I, brothers, still preach circumcision, why am I still being persecuted? In that case, the offense of the cross has been removed" (Gal 5:11).

The apostle had been accused of preaching a gospel that required Gentiles to be circumcised before they could become followers of Jesus. In essence, Paul was accused of teaching that if you were a Gentile, you had to become a Jew before you could become a Christian, which has never been true. This offended the Galatian believers because they viewed their salvation as freeing them from all restrictions, which was never true either. But the message of the cross does offend those who reject it, those who will not be humbled by it and give up on the risky idea that if you are a good person, you will somehow gain heaven automatically.

- *The cross will also be a "stumbling block" for many others.* "For Jews demand signs and Greeks seek wisdom, but we preach Christ crucified, a stumbling block to Jews and folly to Gentiles, but to those who are called, both Jews and Greeks, Christ the power of God and the wisdom of God. For the foolishness of God is wiser than men, and the weakness of God is stronger than men" (1 Cor 1:22–25).

The apostle must have been a brilliant man. He was a trained rabbi, educated at the feet of the great Gamaliel (Acts 22:3), who was "a teacher of the law held in honor by all the people" (Acts 5:34). Gamaliel was the son of Simeon ben Hillel and grandson of the most famous teacher in Jewish history, Hillel the Elder. Gamaliel was the leading authority among the Sanhedrin in the early first century AD, bearing the titles *Nasi*, "prince," and *Rabban*, "our master." The Talmud speaks of Gamaliel as the president of the Great Sanhedrin in Jerusalem, although this is disputed.[5] Gamaliel has a reputation in the Mishnah as being one of the most outstanding teachers in all the annals of Judaism.

Becoming Gamaliel's student was then like gaining admission to the most prestigious university in the world today. Saul of Tarsus was automatically respected for his learning and dedication to the Mosaic Law.[6] Yet this same man, after his Damascus Road experience, is known as Paul the Apostle of Jesus Christ. He wrote that for highly educated people like him, the cross would be a stumbling block. Sometimes, education gives a sense of superiority over all who are not fortunate enough to obtain it. Often, the higher the level of education, the greater the sense of superiority. It's that presumption that usually makes the cross a stumbling block to the most educated among us. Often, however, the message of the cross breaks through that artificial shield of self-importance, and the cross humbles many educated people, causing them to receive Jesus as their Savior.

The concept of a "stumbling block" is frequently found in Scripture. It is applied to anything that causes a person to stumble or lose control. One of the Levitical laws was, "You shall not curse the deaf or put a stumbling block (Hebrew: לוֹשְׁכִמ; English: *mikshôwl*) before the blind, but you shall fear your God: I am the Lord" (Lev 19:14). The prophet Jeremiah warned the Jews of Jerusalem's impending disaster because of their sin. He conveyed, "Therefore thus says the Lord: 'Behold, I will lay before this people stumbling blocks (*mikshôwl*) against which they shall stumble" (Jer 6:21).

The prophet Isaiah also spoke of the Lord as a cause for Israel's stumbling due to sin. "And he will become a sanctuary and a stone of offense and a rock of stumbling (*mikshôwl*) to both houses of Israel, a trap and a snare to the inhabitants of Jerusalem. And many shall stumble on it. They shall fall and be broken; they shall be snared and taken" (Isa 8:14–15; see also 57:14–21). A stumbling block was never perceived as a good thing. It always implied a downfall. And yet when God the Father becomes a stumbling block to us, to trip us and thus prevent us from running headlong into devastation and destruction, that's a very good thing.

In the New Testament, Jesus spoke of a stumbling block in Matthew 16:23. He turned and said to Peter, "Get behind me, Satan! You are a hindrance (Greek: σκάνδαλον; English: *skandalon*) to me" (see also Matt 13:41; 18:7 [3x]). Consider Luke 17:1, where Jesus reminds us, "Temptations to sin are sure to come, but woe to the one through whom they come"!

The Apostle Paul also used the concept of a stumbling block in Romans 11:9; 14:13, 1 Cor 1:23; 8:9, and Galatians 5:11. Peter confirmed that for those who rejected Jesus, the Lord was "a stone of stumbling, and a rock of offense (*skandalon*)" (1 Pet 2:8). And John advised, "Whoever loves his brother abides in the light, and in him there is no cause (*skandalon*) for stumbling" (1 John 2:10). In each case, the word for a stumbling stone (*skandalon*) is used.

The cross is a stumbling stone, causing people to stumble—not physically, of course, but spiritually, psychologically, philosophically, and, yes, even theologically. The crucifixion of Jesus makes no sense to those who are educated in the wisdom of the world, but not in the wisdom of God. The problem is that so many who are educated in the world's wisdom almost uniformly judge the wisdom of God to be inferior to their own. Nevertheless, the cross of Jesus was a spectacular demonstration of God's wisdom. As a spiritual stumbling block, it triggers all who are unwilling to receive Christ to fall into more profound unbelief and greater suspicion of God.

- *Jesus' cross meant whoever put their faith in its message was at risk of severe persecution by those who refused God's wisdom.* To the Galatian believers, Paul said, "It is those who want to make a good showing in the flesh who would force you to be circumcised, and only in order that they may not be persecuted for the cross of Christ" (Gal 6:12).

To the Christ-followers of Thessalonica, the apostle wrote, "We ought always to give thanks to God for you, brothers, as is right, because your faith is growing abundantly, and the love of every one of you for one another is increasing. Therefore, we ourselves boast about you in the churches of God for your steadfastness and faith in all your persecutions and in the afflictions that you are enduring" (2 Thess 1:3–4).

And, "To those who are elect exiles of the Dispersion in Pontus, Galatia, Cappadocia, Asia, and Bithynia, according to the foreknowledge of God the Father, in the sanctification of the Spirit, for obedience to Jesus Christ and for sprinkling with his blood," Peter wrote, "In this you rejoice, though now for a little while, if necessary, you have been grieved by various trials" (1 Pet 1–2, 6).

And who could forget the horrendous litany of persecutions that Paul himself would face as a follower of Jesus Christ? To the Corinthian believers, he wrote that he had been through:

> More imprisonments, with countless beatings, and often near death. Five times I received at the hands of the Jews the forty lashes less one. Three times I was beaten with rods. Once I was

> stoned. Three times I was shipwrecked; a night and a day I was adrift at sea; on frequent journeys, in danger from rivers, danger from robbers, danger from my own people, danger from Gentiles, danger in the city, danger in the wilderness, danger at sea, danger from false brothers; in toil and hardship, through many a sleepless night, in hunger and thirst, often without food, in cold and exposure. And, apart from other things, there is the daily pressure on me of my anxiety for all the churches (2 Cor 11:23–28).

More than half a century ago, one of my seminary professors "baited" the students in his Pauline Studies class. He asked us to identify each of these incidents of Paul's suffering and persecution. One said, "We know he was shipwrecked," to which the professor said, "Yes, but that was on his way to Rome. This is 2 Corinthians, far too early to be included in this list." Hesitantly, I offered, "He was stoned at Lystra." The professor said, "That's right. That one we know. And we also know that he was imprisoned at Philippi. What else?" Everyone was fearful of answering. The professor then opened our eyes to the fact that, because 2 Corinthians was written around 57 AD, we know almost none of the things Paul suffered. By and large, all the apostle's sufferings occurred after he wrote 2 Corinthians. See Table 1.

Despite persecution and suffering in our own lives, all who correctly understand the accomplishments of Jesus Christ at Golgotha's Cross are capable of behavior that corresponds to what the cross stands for. "We know that our old self was crucified with him in order that the body of sin might be brought to nothing, so that we would no longer be enslaved to sin" (Rom 6:6). It was through his actions on the cross that Jesus reconciled everything in the heavens and on Earth, "making peace by the blood of his cross" (Col 1:20). The cross brought an end to the enmity between Israel and the Gentiles (Eph 2:16). It also brought an end to the enmity between God and us. That's the power of the cross. Humankind knows no other power like it.

> "The cross itself, maybe more so than any book written, has had a profound impact on how Christians think about their religion and their religious experience."—Jonathan Reed

Table 1: Paul's Sufferings for the Cross

Scripture	*Paul's Suffering for the Cross*	*Location or Event*
Acts 16:23,24	Many imprisonments	Philippi, Greece
No Scripture Location	Countless beatings	No Known Location
Acts 14:19	Often near death	Lystra
No Scripture Location	5x received 39 lashes	No Known Location
Acts 16:22	3x beaten with rods	No historical account of this
Acts 14:19	Stoned	Lystra
Acts 27:41–42	3x shipwrecked	Off the coast of Malta
Acts 27:43–44	Adrift at sea	Off the coast of Malta
General Sufferings		
Acts 15:36–51	On frequent journeys	Antioch, Syria, and Cilicia
No Scripture Location	Dangers from the rivers; dangers from robbers	No Known Location
Acts 17:5; 20:3; 24:1,2	Dangers from the Jews	Thessalonica, Macedonia
Acts 19:21–41	Dangers from the Gentiles	Ephesus
Acts 23:12–22	Dangers in the city	Jerusalem
No Scripture Location	Dangers in the wilderness; dangers in the sea; dangers from pseudo-Christians	No known location
No Scripture Location	In toil and hardship; many sleepless nights; in hunger and thirst; often without food; in cold and exposure	No known location
2 Cor 11:28; Phil 1:8	Daily pressure from the Church	No known location

The grandeur of the cross, as the New Testament conceives it, lies in the fact that here the Son of God offered himself in the place of sinners. But what did the cross achieve? What was specifically accomplished when Jesus bled and died on Calvary's Cross? "The cross achieved expiation, propitiation, reconciliation, justification, redemption, forgiveness, and victory; and even this list is not exhaustive."[7] Indeed, it is not.

Writing of Jesus' theological accomplishments on Calvary's Cross is a little like seeing beyond the stars for the first time through the James Webb

Telescope. There is just so much more "out there." What Jesus accomplished on the cross is far more than we ever realized or can realize this side of heaven.

While the list of what God accomplished through Jesus' death is long, we have narrowed our focus to just twelve impactful achievements. However, the theological topics in some of the chapters that follow will not be found in a theology textbook. That's intentional.

We will investigate some of the many astonishing accomplishments that are paramount in my mind; others may be paramount in yours. Regardless, every follower of Jesus Christ should rejoice in each achievement, for they not only changed our lives but also our eternal destinies.

ENDNOTES

1. Witherington, "Biblical Views," *BAR* 43.6 (2017): 26.
2. Taylor, *The Cross*.
3. Brown and Bohn, eds, *Christianity, Patriarchy and Abuse*, 2–3, 23.
4. Quoted by Heim, "Christ crucified," March 7, 2001.
5. Schechter and Bacher, "Gamaliel 1," *Jewish Encyclopedia*.
6. Köstenberger, *The Cradle, the Cross, and the Crown*, 389.
7. Macleod, *Christ Crucified*, 101.

Chapter 1

Jesus Made Atonement for Us

When Jesus died at Calvary, he did not simply stand in solidarity with sinners; he stood in place of them. His death was a substitution, not a show of unity.

Because it is frequently mentioned in conversations about salvation, we begin our investigation with a concept that encompasses a variety of different topics. This makes it something of a catch-all or all-encompassing concept. In English, what Jesus accomplished on the cross is frequently referred to as "the atonement," a term often used to describe God's salvation of sinners.

The book of Revelation speaks mysteriously of "a beast rising out of the sea," and "all who dwell on the earth will worship it, everyone whose name has not been written before the foundation of the world in the book of life of the Lamb who was slain" (Rev 13:1, 8). Jesus is the Lamb who was slain, whose death brings atonement to those whom God will save. However, our primary understanding of atonement comes not from the Church councils or the Church Fathers, but from the four Gospels themselves.

Robert B. Steward aptly observes, "Nicaea was further from Jesus than we today are from George Washington. One benefits from reading patristic theology, but the earliest written Christian theology is found on the pages of the New Testament."[1] This prompts us to ask a fundamental, almost constitutional question.

> "The four Gospels are the primary witnesses, not just for the events of Jesus' life, but also for the meaning of his death. It is astonishing to see the extent to which the four Gospels have been marginalized in discussions of atonement."—N. T. Wright

WHAT IS THE ATONEMENT?

Before God could save sinful people such as you and me, his holy nature required that he first do something about our sin. God had to satisfy the demands of his divine nature against sin and the sinner. In other words, before God the Father could do anything for us, he had to do something for himself. This is where Christ's atonement comes in.

The role of God the Father

God the Father gave his Son to appease his wrath against the unholiness of sin and the sinner. Jesus did this by paying our sin debt for us. The Apostle John wrote, "In this is love, not that we have loved God but that he loved us and sent his Son to be the propitiation for our sins" (1 John 4:10).

God's nature is perfectly balanced. His wrath against sin is balanced with his grace in dealing with it. His holy need to remain pure is balanced with his mercy for the sinner. Most of all, his need to punish disobedience is balanced with his love for those who have disobeyed.

Perhaps the most famous verse in the Bible, John 3:16, also speaks of the Father's role in the atonement. "For God so loved the world, that he gave his only Son, that whoever believes in him should not perish but have eternal life." The Father knew only divine love could satisfy divine wrath against the crown of his creation—humankind. The Father knew that the only acceptable sacrifice that could dispel divine wrath was a divine sacrifice, and that meant sending his Son to Calvary for us. Think about this. God the Father initiated your salvation. You didn't reach up to him; he reached down to you. Keep that on the sticky side of your mind as you read this book.

The role of God the Son

The Son, in total obedience to the Father, went to Calvary's Cross, suffered, bled, and died to atone for our sin. It was Jesus' death, not his healing, teaching, or raising the dead, that paid the price for our redemption (Rom 6:23). The holiness of God could not be sustained if the punishment for sin was inferior to that holiness. Thus, the price of the sacrifice for sin had to equal the holiness of the Most Holy Being, or it would be inferior and unacceptable.

The only way to offer a sacrifice equal to the holiness of the Father was to provide a holy sacrifice equal to the Father, and that meant a member of the Godhead had to be offered. In the eternal plan and wisdom of God, God the Son was charged to be that holy sacrifice. The Father accepted the Son's death to appease divine wrath and atone for sin and the sinner. This acceptance was ratified by Jesus' resurrection on the third day.

The role of God the Spirit

The third member of the Holy Trinity was also involved in our atonement. God the Father's wrath against sin and the sinner was appeased. God the Son gave his life to accomplish this. And God the Holy Spirit enabled the Son to do all that the atonement required to free us from the wages of our sin (Rom 6:23).

"If the blood of goats and bulls, and the sprinkling of defiled persons with the ashes of a heifer, sanctify for the purification of the flesh, how much more will the blood of Christ, who through the eternal Spirit offered himself without blemish to God, purify our conscience from dead works to serve the living God" (Heb 9:14, 15; see also Rom 8:11).

The power to make a perfect sacrifice and the power to defeat Satan came from the Holy Spirit, the most significant source of authority and strength in existence. The Holy Spirit was the medium by which the sacrifice of God the Son was made.

An overly simplistic explanation of what transpired at Calvary is this. Adam and Eve and their posterity, including you and me, disobeyed the Godhead and severed our relationship with God. We joined Satan's rebellion against the righteous God, and his wrath against sin was the result. To appease that wrath, God demanded a blood sacrifice, the taking of a life, but not just any life. It must be a life sufficiently worthy to assuage divine wrath. The holy God would only be satisfied with the perfect sacrifice, and that's why neither you nor I can supply it. The only sinless, spotless, perfect sacrifice worthy of the Heavenly Father would be God's Son, Jesus Christ.

So, to appease the wrath of God the Father, God the Son died on the cross, God the Holy Spirit enabling his perfect sacrifice for you and me.

Thus, all three members of the Holy Trinity were active that Friday at Calvary. In the background, the Spirit of God acted as the power to accomplish the atonement. In obedience, the Son of God was the payment for that atonement. And in holiness, God the Father was satisfied with Christ's atonement. And your part? Nothing. You and I receive the gift of God's atonement, but we have no part in achieving it.

The word choice for "atonement"

Even those who are not Jewish have heard of Yom Kippur, Judaism's holiest day of the year. In Hebrew, the word כִּפֻּר, English: *kippur,* means "atonement," so Yom Kippur is the "Day of Atonement." Almost always translated as atonement, *kippur* appears ninety-four times in the Hebrew Old Testament.

Yom Kippur Shofar

The word "atonement" does not occur in the New Testament.[2] However, the concept is frequently represented by synonymous terms.

Sometimes in the New Testament, the word (Greek: καταλλάσσω; English: *katallássō*) is translated to mean atonement or reconciliation. It comes from the word (Greek: ἀλλάσσω; English: *allássō*) meaning "to change" or to "make different" (Rom 5:11;11:15; 2 Cor 5:18–19). Most Bible versions in English translate the various forms of this word as "reconciling" or "reconciliation" (see NIV, ESV, KJV, TLB, MSG, NASB, NCB, NKJV, NLT, RSV, NRSV, et al.).

At times, another word (Greek: ἱλαστήριον; English: *hilasērion*), associated with the mercy seat covering the ark of the covenant, is translated as the place of atonement, as Table 2 demonstrates. Speaking of Jesus, John wrote, "He is the propitiation (Greek: ἱλασμόσ; English: *hilasmos*) for our sins, and not for ours only but also for the sins of the whole world" (1 John 2:2). In 1 John 4:9–10 the apostle continued, "In this the love of God was made manifest among us, that God sent his only Son into the world, so that we might live through him. In this is love, not that we have loved God but that he loved us and sent his Son to be the propitiation (*hilasmos*) for our sin."

Table 1: The Meaning of or *hilastērion* [ἱλαστήριον]

Bible Version	*Translation*
Good News Translation	"The place where sins are forgiven"
Jubilee Bible 2000	"The seat of reconciliation"
New International Readers Version	"The place where sin was paid for"
New Living Translation	"He himself is the sacrifice that atones for our sins
New International Version	"He is the atoning sacrifice for our sins"
Christian Standard Bible	"the atoning sacrifice"
Contemporary English Version	"the sacrifice that takes away our sins"
English Standard Version	"the propitiation for our sins"
The Message	"a sacrifice for our sins"
The Revised Standard Version	"the expiation for our sins"
Wycliffe Bible Translation	"the forgiveness for our sins"
New King James Version	"He Himself is the propitiation for our sins"
Worldwide English New Testament	"He himself is the sacrifice God offered to pay for the wrong we have done."

Often, the word choice by modern English translations of the New Testament helps us understand the meaning of a word. This is certainly true of the concept of atonement. In Table 2, note the recurring concepts, including reconciliation, expiation, forgiveness, sin paid for, propitiation, atonement, sacrifice, and others. Theologically, the word *hilastērion* reflects the Lord's cleansing of humanity's sin by his shed blood at Golgotha's killing field. This cleansing, forgiving, and reconciling payment had to be made before God could forgive sin and the sinner.

The atonement paid by Jesus Christ was always a part of God's redemptive plan. It was also the subject of many prophetic statements. The entirety of Psalm 22 and Isaiah 53 prophesy that Jesus would suffer and die to reconcile us to God. Jesus himself said, "O foolish ones, and slow of heart to believe all that the prophets have spoken! Was it not necessary that the Christ should suffer these things and enter into his glory"? (Luke 24:25–26).

Elsewhere, Jesus said, "I have come into the world to give sight to those who are spiritually blind and to show those who think they see that they are blind" (John 9:39 TLB).

The twentieth-century Anglican clergyman and scholar John Bertram (J.B.) Phillips captured the idea of the atonement thoroughly when he translated Romans 5:9–11 as follows:

> Moreover, if he did that for us while we were sinners, now that we are justified by the shedding of his blood, what reason have we to fear the wrath of God? If, while we were his enemies, Christ reconciled us to God by dying for us, surely now that we are reconciled we may be perfectly certain of our salvation through his living in us. Nor, I am sure, is this a matter of bare salvation—we may hold our heads high in the light of God's love because of the reconciliation which Christ has made.

While the atonement Jesus made for us has an impact that extends backward to eternity past and forward to eternity future, the act of atonement itself is confined to the hours when Jesus was on the cross at Golgotha (John 19:30; Col 1:19–20).

"Atonement" is something of an all-encompassing word.[3] It's like motherhood. Being a mother entails much more than child care. It's being a wife. It encompasses keeping a good home. It means mentoring children. It's being a homemaker. Sometimes it means working outside the home as well. A mother is the resident family doctor, the Home Ec teacher, and the weary chef. Being a mother is a "many-splendored thing." That's the way atonement is. N.T. Wright notes:

> All doctrines, you see, are portable stories. We fold the stories up, like clothes for a trip, and we pack them into a suitcase so we can carry them easily into and out of discussions. But the point of carrying a suitcase isn't because I like having a suitcase in my hotel room. The point of having a suitcase is so that I can carry clothes, books, and personal items all together. The word 'atonement' is a suitcase into which the longer biblical story is folded up."[4]

In a sense, the word "atonement" encompasses all the other accomplishments of Christ's death on the cross. However, we must begin with its specific reference to Jesus' work at Golgotha. How did Jesus' death on the cross make atonement real, actual, and personal for you and me?

Clearly, not every Christian tradition interprets this word in the same way. Thus, a brief description of how the atonement has been interpreted is essential for our understanding of what Jesus accomplished during those six hours that ended in his death at Golgotha.

Table 3 presents several theories about the meaning of the atonement that have developed over the centuries. Unfortunately, the theories represented in this chart are either inadequate or flat-out wrong.[5]

Table 2: Inadequate or Incomplete Theories of the Atonement

The Theory	*The Proponent*	*The Explanation*
Recapitulation	Irenaeus	Jesus' death reversed the course of human life by repeating in himself all of life's experiences as sinners.
Ransom to Satan	Origen	Jesus' death was a ransom paid to Satan to purchase our freedom from the devil and hell.
Commercial	Anselm	Jesus' death was a commercial transaction restoring God's honor that was violated by sin and the sinner.
Moral Influence	Peter Abelard	Jesus' death was not a ransom but rather a revelation of God's love. This awakens a response in the sinner's heart that delivers us from the penalty of our sin.
Unnecessary	Thomas Aquinas	Jesus' atoning death was unnecessary; Jesus' life was the saving work, not his death.
Example	Faustus Socinus	Jesus' death did not pay the penalty for our sin; the pure mercy of God did.
Arbitrary	Duns Scotus	Jesus' death was not necessary for our atonement because God could have chosen other methods.
Government	Hugo Grotius	Jesus' death was merely symbolic. It did not pay the penalty for our sin, but was only a symbol of atonement.
Mystical	Edward Irving	Jesus' death purified human nature when he assumed a corrupt human nature and purified it through suffering.

Having examined briefly some of the inaccurate or incomplete theories espoused in the past, let's focus on three theories that are quite prominent today. The first two offer either an inadequate explanation for Jesus' sacrifice at Calvary or are simply incorrect, failing to understand the true meaning of Christ's death.

MORAL INFLUENCE ATONEMENT

Those who hold the moral influence theory of the atonement focus less on Jesus' shedding of blood and death and more specifically on the moral aspect of the cross. The moral influence theory—sometimes called the example theory—was first presented and then propagated by Peter Abelard, a medieval French philosopher and theologian (1079–1142 AD). Given his legendary affair with writer, abbess, and teacher Héloïse d'Argenteuil, it's ironic that Abelard would advance anything related to morality. It should be noted that Abelard's views were challenged by Bernard of Clairvaux and condemned at the Second Council of Lateran (1139 AD). Eventually, he was excommunicated from the Roman Catholic Church. So, what is wrong with this theory?

One-sided perception of God

This theory focuses on changing man's perception of God into a loving, kind, yet never judgmental, supreme being. According to the moral influence theory, Jesus died not to atone for our sins but as a demonstration of God's love for us, a love that, through his example, can change the hearts and minds of sinners. Those who hold this view see the crucifixion as a tragic martyrdom, designed to teach us moral lessons. The moral influence theory emphasizes Jesus' words rather than his death.[6] This view marginalizes God's wrath, his holiness, and his need for justice. It sees only his love, which presents a distorted view of the essence of God.

Liberal Protestants sometimes gravitate to this view. Both the moral influence view and the substitutionary view are held among Roman Catholics. Still, Catholics must balance their view of the atonement with their perceived duty to perform "acts of reparation to Jesus Christ," which are "some sort of compensation to be rendered for the injury" that caused the sufferings of Jesus.[7] More recently, Pope John Paul II referred to these "acts of reparation" as "the unceasing effort to stand beside the endless crosses on which the Son of God continues to be crucified" (Vatican Archives). This sounds like the tired falsehood that we must somehow "work" our way to heaven.

The crucifixion: a one-time event

On the contrary, Protestants, especially Evangelicals, understand the crucifixion to be a one-time, one-of-a-kind event in which Jesus died to atone for our sin. Evangelicals do not understand Christ's atonement as solely a demonstration of God's love, although it is that. The Protestant and Evangelical communities see the crucifixion as a place of reconciliation between God and humankind. They do not believe Jesus is continually being crucified on "endless crosses." Their belief is based on Hebrews 7:27, "He [Jesus] has no need, like those high priests, to offer sacrifices daily, first for his own sins and then for those of the people, since he did this once for all when he offered up himself" (see also Heb 9:12, 26; 10:10). Very few Evangelicals or Protestants hold to the moral influence theory of the atonement.

CHRISTUS VICTOR ATONEMENT

Among Eastern Orthodox Christians, there is a standard view of the atonement known as the *Christus Victor* ("Christ the Victor") view. This name was taken from the title of Gustaf Aulén's book of the same name, first published in 1931.[8] Here is the substance of this theory.

The atonement displayed the victory of God

In the *Christus Victor* view, the atonement was part of the divine conflict between God and Satan. It focused on Christ's victory at Calvary over the hostile powers that held humanity in subjection. Aulén argued that the atonement was a drama, the plot of the Passion Week story being God the Father triumphing over the enemies in his Son's death. This theory makes the atonement more of a dramatic story than a theological event. Gustav Aulén wrote, "The work of Christ is first and foremost a victory over the powers which hold mankind in bondage: sin, death, and the devil."[9]

The *Christus Victor* view is also attractive to so-called "Paleo-orthodox Evangelicals"[10] because of its connection to the early Church Fathers. Some Anabaptists, Mennonites, and other peace-advocating denominations also hold it. However, in his book *The Nonviolent Atonement*, Mennonite theologian J. Denny Weaver traces the further development of the *Christus Victor* theory into the liberation theology movement in South America, as well as into the feminist and black theologies of liberation.[11]

Theologian Marcus Borg says, "This [the *Christus Victor*] view, the domination system, understood as something much larger than the Roman governor and the Temple aristocracy, is responsible for the death of Jesus . . . The domination system killed Jesus and thereby disclosed its moral bankruptcy and ultimate defeat."[12]

The Christus Victor view also believes the crucifixion of Jesus of Nazareth was much bigger than a struggle between the Jews and the Romans. It was a struggle between God and Satan in which Christ was victorious over his long-time archenemy. While this is true, this was not the primary purpose for Jesus' death at Calvary.

For the average person, the *Christus Victor* view of the atonement simply means that Jesus Christ won at Calvary. He defeated Satan by his death on the cross (see Chapter 11). This, of course, is true, but it was the result, not the purpose, of the atonement. Jesus' death at Calvary was not just a cosmic contest; it was the plan and program of God for cleansing sinful humans, settling our sin debt (Rom 6:23), and removing the shame of sin. Among Protestants and Evangelicals, this view is not widely held.

SUBSTITUTIONARY ATONEMENT

According to the substitutionary atonement view, Jesus' death is the centerpiece of God's plan for our salvation. This view holds that Jesus voluntarily gave up his life for ours, took on our sin, and paid the price for it on our behalf. Romans 5:6–8 declares, "For while we were still weak, at the right time Christ died for the ungodly. For one will scarcely die for a righteous person—though perhaps for a good person one would dare even to die—but God shows his love for us in that while we were still sinners, Christ died for us." Jesus died in our place. He was our substitute to receive the wrath of God for our sin. That's the essence of the substitutionary atonement view.

> "In social life, substitution is a universal phenomenon. Even the structure of vocation, the division of labor, has a substitutionary character. One who has a vocation performs this function for those whom he serves."—Wolfhart Pannenberg

One has died for all

Paul explained it this way. "For the love of Christ controls us, because we have concluded this: that one has died for all, therefore all have died; and he died for all, that those who live might no longer live for themselves but for him who for their sake died and was raised" (2 Cor 5:14–15).

"The miracle of the gospel is that this link between our sin and our death has been broken. Christ died for our sins. Substitution is at the heart of the gospel. Christ died so that we don't need to die. Christ bore our sins so that we don't need to bear them."[13]

As our sinless sacrifice, Jesus' death entirely satisfied our need to appease the wrath of God and, at the same time, secured salvation for those who believe. "For Christ also suffered once for sins, the righteous for the unrighteous, that he might bring us to God, being put to death in the flesh but made alive in the spirit" (1 Pet 3:18). The substitutional atonement view, in my thinking, keeps what Scripture says at the forefront.

Paul's testimony seals the deal.

"For I delivered to you as of first importance what I also received: that Christ died for our sins in accordance with the Scriptures, that he was buried, that he was raised on the third day in accordance with the Scriptures" (1 Cor 15:3–4).

By now, you have discerned that I do not hold to any of the views of the atonement except the last one. Jesus died in my place, as my substitute. That's what the Bible says, and I believe it. For followers of Jesus, that's the bottom line. To deny or downplay the substitutionary aspect of the atonement is to marginalize the cross and empty Jesus' crucifixion of its essential purpose.[14]

Some object to the substitutionary atonement view, and we must not brush aside their objections. Examine them with me.

OBJECTIONS TO SUBSTITUTIONARY ATONEMENT

Keith Mathison, professor of systematic theology at Reformation Bible College in Sanford, Florida, describes the problem.

> It should come as little surprise to learn that the doctrine of the substitutionary atonement of Christ has come under renewed criticism in recent decades. The Reformers dealt with such criticisms and attacks from the Socinians. Our more recent forefathers in the faith dealt with such criticisms and attacks from rationalists and liberals. Today, we hear such criticisms and attacks from a wide variety of sources. We are surrounded by so much anti-Christian rhetoric, however, that it is hardly a shock to hear the doctrine of substitutionary atonement referred to

> derisively as "cosmic child abuse" by a popular contemporary Christian author."[15]

There are many, especially more liberal theologians, who object to the substitutionary view of Christ's atonement. This induces them to migrate to one of the less scriptural views of the atonement. Here, we examine only three objections to the substitutionary atonement view, as they are the most popular and plausible currently raised.

The time objection

Some see six hours on the cross as too little time to atone for all the sin of all the world, of all time. They say Jesus spent too few hours on the cross to pay for all the sinners in hell. But those who object fail to understand that when we are dealing in the spiritual world and not the physical one, as we are with the concept of atonement, length of time, length of distance, quantity, etc., are irrelevant. These kinds of parameters or limitations are meaningless to the God who is eternal.

In his book, *Why the Cross?*, H. E. Guillebaud writes prolifically and convincingly of the validity of Christ dying as our substitute. Guillebaud remarks: "The sacrifice of the Son of God is not measured by the duration in time of his sufferings, but by their quality, and above all by the quality of him who suffered. The very idea of balancing those sufferings in quantity against the doom of lost mankind is entirely alien to the Bible."[16] Lewis Sperry Chafer adds, "The value of the sacrifice is not discovered in the intensity of the Saviour's anguish but in his dignity and infinite worth."[17] Said differently, the validity of Jesus' sacrifice on the cross is not determined by the degree of his suffering but by the deity of his person.

The objection to substitutionary atonement based on the duration of Jesus' suffering on the cross is an inadequate reason to cast aside this view. This criticism only addresses the issue of time. It prioritizes quantity over quality. The Triune God spent an eternity planning the Calvary event. The time needed to implement that eternal plan is of no consequence.

The transfer of guilt objection

While this objection appears to have more substance than the previous one, it suffers from a foundational misunderstanding. Those who object that it is unjust to transfer guilt from a guilty person to an innocent person have not understood that sin and guilt are not the same things.

Sin is the evil that produces guilt. Sin creates all kinds of malicious effects on our lives, and that separates us from a holy God. When Jesus took our place on Calvary's Cross, our sin—all of it, throughout all of our lives—was transferred judicially to the Lord Jesus. He bore the curse of that sin, as well as the guilt that was the consequence of sin. The essential issue in the atonement is our reconciliation with God as the result of the penalty for our sin having been fully satisfied by Christ's shed blood and ultimate death.

"We implore you on behalf of Christ, be reconciled to God. For our sake he made him to be sin who knew no sin, so that in him we might become the righteousness of God" (2 Cor 5:20–21). There is no mention of guilt here because the transfer of our guilt to Jesus on the cross was not the purpose of his being nailed there. The purpose was so the Sinless One, the Righteous One, could carry our sin and unrighteousness on his back, pay the tragic penalty of death for that unrighteousness, and remove both sin's curse and its consequences from our permanent record.

This objection also fails to grasp how, in God's eternal plan (Ps 139:16; Eph 1:4, 11; 1 Pet 1:20), Jesus chose to be our representative and substitute. There can be no validity to the objection that the transfer of guilt from the guilty to the innocent is because this was a transfer of sin, not guilt. Guilt is the by-product of sin. What Jesus became on the cross was not guilt; it was sin—our sin. Besides, we must never view Calvary as a stand-alone event. While it was the centerpiece, it was but one element of God's eternal purpose. Remember, on the third day, Jesus would rise from the dead. That's a pretty big deal, too.

The "divine child abuse" objection

Although this is a popular and widespread objection, it is the silliest and most fictitious one of all. Because God the Father allowed the sin of the entire world to be placed on Jesus' shoulders, some accuse him of "divine child abuse."

But first, let's eliminate one modifier in this objection, and that's the word "child." God the Father and God the Son are equal partners in the Holy Trinity, along with God the Holy Spirit. The distinction between Father and Son here is functional, not relational. Jesus did not generate from his Father; he glorified the Father. Read John 17.

"Divine child abuse" cannot be an objection to penal substitutionary atonement. Jesus was a man in the prime of his life when he died on the cross, and not a helpless little child. So, we must at least shorten this objection to "divine abuse."

Was Jesus' death a tyrannical form of divine abuse? Not according to the Scriptures. This objection fails to understand the pain and suffering Jesus sustained at the hands of Caiaphas, Pilate, and their goons. Nor does it apprehend the shame Jesus endured on the cross. And it certainly does not comprehend the seriousness of that moment when God looked away from the sin his Son was atoning on the cross. None of this was done to hurt or abuse anyone. Yes, Jesus endured it all, just as the Prophet Isaiah foretold in Isaiah 53. But this was the action of God's love, not his vengeance. "This is how much God loved the world: He gave his Son, his one and only Son." And this is why: "So that no one need be destroyed; by believing in him, anyone can have a whole and lasting life. God didn't go to all the trouble of sending his Son merely to point an accusing finger, telling the world how bad it was. He came to help, to put the world right again" (John 3:16,17 MSG). The cross was the indispensable centerpiece of God's redemptive plan, not an act of uncontrolled, abusive behavior. For all to see, the cross put on display the ugly disobedience of humankind and the uncanny obedience of God the Son.

Read again Jesus' words to Nicodemus, who visited the Savior one night after dark:

> For God loved the world so much that he gave his only Son, so that everyone who believes in him may not die but have eternal life. For God did not send his Son into the world to be its judge, but to be its savior. (John 3:16,17 GNT).

Rather than "divine child abuse," the cross was a case of "divine substitution." Jesus took our place and paid the penalty for our sin, demonstrating just how much the Father loves us. To think of God the Father as some demonic abuser flies in the face of all we know about God, and that idea must be scuttled as a critique of substitutionary atonement. Calvary graphically illustrates the divine justice of God, tempered by the divine mercy of God, portrayed by the divine love of God.

The "Western Idea" objection

Some people have objected to the penal substitutionary death of Jesus at Golgotha, saying that the idea of justice represented in the cross event is not that of the Middle East but of Western culture. Western justice demands that a debt be paid. Western justice is retributive justice, but justice in the Bible was more restorative than retributive.

This objection is not only theologically inconsistent but also philosophically illogical. It is theologically inconsistent because in Scripture, it is legitimate to think of "justice" and "righteousness" relating to "God making all things right." That would be the restorative sense. God's righteousness is the basis for his salvation (Ps 31:1; 36:10; 71:2; Isa 45:8; 46:13; 51:4–8).

However, since God is holy and just, for him "to put the world right again," he is duty-bound to eliminate all the wrong in this world. Remember this. God's holiness is the standard of what is right or wrong, not the shifting scruples of society. It is God, not your friends, who is "righteous in all his ways" (Ps 145:17). It is God who loves justice, not your employer or associates. "Righteousness and justice are the foundation of your throne; steadfast love and faithfulness go before you (Ps 89:14). It is God who will do what is right, not you. "Shall not the Judge of all the earth do what is just? (Gen 18:25).

Therefore, as the righteous Judge, God must hold us accountable for our actions, reward us when we do what is right, and punish us when we do what is wrong or sinful (Exod 34:6–7; Pss 9:5–6, 15–20; 94:7–9; Prov 24:12; Rom 1:18—3:20). God's justice is restorative only because God *is* just and he punishes evil and sin.

This objection is philosophically illogical, as it reverses the truth of history. The question is not, "Has Western culture demonstrated an understanding of Christ's atonement, or has the theology of Christ's atonement informed Western culture? The truth is that Scripture has affected Western ideas of justice and what is right. Before Western culture became secularized, it was built on the truth of God's Word. History has shown that Western culture originated in biblical ideas of justice and ultimately deteriorated into secularism and humanism as society began to reject those ideas. Biblical concepts of justice were replaced with humanistic, socialistic, and often fascist ideas of justice.

It is a tribute to God's justice that the Holy Trinity does not allow sin to go unpunished. It is a testament to God's grace that the Holy Trinity offers salvation to the unjust (Rom 5:6–8). Those who understand Scripture the way God intended it to be understood, the plain and simple truth of Scripture, must praise God for the death of Jesus that generated the atonement. We must never kneel to secular ideas that undermine the Heavenly Father's love or Jesus' obedience at Calvary.

THE BOTTOM LINE OF ATONEMENT

I understand the substitutionary view, and in particular, the penal substitution view, to be the biblical view of the atonement. When Jesus died at

Calvary, he did not simply stand in solidarity with sinners; he stood in their place. His death was a substitution, not a show of unity. In addition, Jesus' death was not just an example of morality at its best. It was not a contrast between the morality of God and the immorality of Satan. It was a planned, one-time, life-saving event in which Jesus took our place, died for our sin, and on the third day rose for our justification.

Righteousness is imputed from faith

Because of Jesus' death on Calvary's Cross, our faith, which is imputed as righteousness, "will be counted to us who believe in him who raised from the dead Jesus our Lord, who was delivered up for our trespasses and raised for our justification" (Rom 4:24–25). That simply means that when we trust Jesus to have died for us, to have appeased God's wrath toward us, and to have paid the penalty for our sin, God credits our eternal account with righteousness. This can only happen when Christ's righteousness is credited to us in place of our sin. That's atonement in a nutshell.

> "When man justifies the wicked, it is a miscarriage of justice that God hates, but when God justifies the ungodly, it is a miracle of grace for us to adore."—J. I. Packer

In the middle of the last century, the influential pastor of Riverside Church in New York City, Harry Emerson Fosdick, famously stated that the traditional view of the cross and the doctrine of the atonement rendered Christianity a "slaughterhouse religion."[18] He also suggested the idea that Jesus suffered as a substitutionary sacrifice in our stead was a "pre-civilized barbarity." It appears Fosdick failed to understand the atonement even a little.

When I was a boy in grammar school, I remember teachers over and over again threatening one of my classmates with "the mother of all threats." If a student did something bad, the teacher would yell, "That's going on your permanent record. Mark it down. It's going on your permanent record!" That was enough to scare anybody. The permanent record was kept in the principal's office, in a file labeled with your name. The last thing you needed was a black mark on your permanent record.

That's what Christ's atonement did for us. Heaven has a permanent record, too. It contains all the damning things we have done in our lives. But at Calvary, Jesus died to incapacitate our permanent record. The blood of

Jesus Christ that washes us clean also washes our permanent record clean. It wipes away all the damning black marks from our permanent record and gives us a clean record instead. That's how our amazing God did the impossible—he made us fit to live with him forever.

A victory for the Holy Trinity

Regardless of what people see in the Passion narratives, the victory of Christ on the cross was, first and foremost, a victory for the Godhead.[19] It was a victory, not so much over their enemies (although that is true), but over the challenge for God to balance being just in his treatment of sinners and their sin, while at the same time demonstrating his unfailing love toward those same sinners, you and me. Although that sounds like an impossible task, that's precisely what Christ did at the cross, and what makes the atonement one of the significant accomplishments of Jesus' death. "It was God's matchless, everlasting love that moved him to provide us with a means, commensurate with both his holiness and our helplessness, to put away our sin and guilt."[20]

Wading into a subject like atonement can be a challenge. It is quite involved and easily misunderstood. There is, however, much more to understand about it. The crucifixion of Jesus of Nazareth was all about our atonement. The word "atonement" may be something of a "catch-all" term for the totality of God's salvation, but first and foremost, it was to catch all who were falling toward the pit of hell that God intended to save. Let's rejoice in God's wisdom, his planning, his power, and his love. He is the God who atones for our sins and thus deserves our continual praise. Accomplishments don't get much bigger than this!

Christ has for sin atonement made,
What a wonderful Saviour!
We are redeemed! The price is paid!
What a wonderful Saviour!

I praise Him for the cleansing blood,
What a wonderful Saviour!
That reconciled my soul to God;
What a wonderful Saviour!

He cleansed my heart from all its sin,
What a wonderful Saviour!
And now He reigns and rules therein;
What a wonderful Saviour!

—E. A. Hoffman (1839–1929)

Chapter 2

Jesus Became a Curse to Remove the Curse from Us

Adam's disobedience at Eden's center tree was nullified by Jesus' obedience on Calvary's center tree (Rom 5:18–19). Jesus did not die as an unfortunate itinerant teacher from Galilee. He died to pay the penalty for our sin and to remove the curse that was infused within us.

The Curse or the Blessing
The Cause of the Curse
The Curse Upon the Serpent
The Curse Upon Satan
The Curse Upon the Woman
The Curse Upon the Planet
The Curse Upon the Man
The Curse Upon our Earth Removed
The Cruse Upon Humanity Removed
The Curse of Guilt and Shame Removed

Perhaps you're familiar with the Hope Diamond. This famous jewel is unusually large with a calming blue hue. It is estimated to be worth more than $250 million. But it is believed to have been cursed since the seventeenth century and to bring great misfortune and misery to its wearer.

In 1922, Howard Carter, a British archaeologist and Egyptologist, found the largely intact tomb of King Tutankhamen (a.k.a. King Tut). But there was a legendary curse of bad luck, illness, and even death on anyone who violated the boy king's final resting place. Disasters struck several people involved with the grave's discovery, leading many to think that Carter unleashed the curse of King Tutankhamun's tomb.

Whenever we speak theologically of "the curse," we are not talking about anything in folklore. We are speaking of something very real. Also, in the biblical sense, a "curse" is not like swearing today. When you fire off a curse word, you are expressing frustration at someone or something. That's not the idea here at all. To better understand, let's examine the dominant word used in the original languages that is translated as "curse" or similar. There are some surprises.

But first, a word of warning. This chapter is heavy. It deals with a difficult, unpleasant subject that is therefore often passed over. Since it will be challenging for us, get on your high boots, your Himalayan hiking gear, and let's begin the steep climb. Ask the Holy Spirit to be your spiritual Sherpa as you proceed.

THE CURSE OR THE BLESSING

In the Bible, the word (Hebrew: בָּרַךְ; English*: bârak*), which Hebrew writers used for "cursing," is found in 1 Kings 21:10. "And set two worthless men opposite him, and let them bring a charge against him, saying, 'You have cursed God and the king.' Then take him out and stone him to death." The word is *bârak.*

Oddly enough, the very same word (English*: bârak*) is more often than not translated as "blessing," as in Psalm 5:12, "For you bless (*bârak*) the righteous, O LORD; you cover him with favor as with a shield." Such words are called contronyms, such as rent, bolt, seed, or left. We must allow the context to decide whether a person is the only one left or the only one who has left the meeting.

To understand the prevalence of "bless" as the translation for the Hebrew word, using the King James Version as a universally standard translation, consider these facts.

The Hebrew bârak (בָּרַךְ) is translated as Table 1 indicates:

Table 1: The English Translation of Bârak (בָּרַךְ) in the King James Version

Translation	*Scripture*
"kneeled down"	Gen 24:11; 2 Chron 6:13
"congratulate"	1 Chron 18:10
"thanked"	2 Sam 14:22
"praise"	Judg 5:2; Ps 72:15
"salute, saluted"	1 Sam 13:10; 25:14; 2 Kgs 4:29:2 Kgs 10:15
"curse"	Job 1:5, 11; 2:5, 9
"bless, blessed, blessing"	The remaining 274 times Bârak (בָּרַךְ) is found

Of the 289 times the word *bârak* occurs in the Hebrew Old Testament, only fifteen times is it not translated as "bless" in one form or another in the KJV. In fact, it is translated as "curse" only four times. The ratios may differ in other translations, but only slightly.

There's insight to be gained here. The God of the Bible is not negative, not vengeful, nor a God who enjoys cursing people when they persist in their sin. He would much rather "bless" (*bârak*) than "curse" (*bârak*), as the grammatical record shows.

Did Mrs. Job get a bum rap?

So, where are these four times the word is translated as "curse," and what was cursed? The Hebrew *bârak* is translated "curse" in the first chapter of Job, verses 5 and 11, and in the second chapter, verses 5 and 9. This would completely escape our attention if it were not for that last verse. Job 2:9 is where Job's wife says, "Curse (*bârak*) God and die." She has been painted forever as the impatient wife, tired of the troubles Job brought her. Good-intentioned preachers have railed at her for being so callous and "unspiritual." But was this really the case?

Remember, this word primarily means "bless," almost all the time. Has Mrs. Job gotten a bad rap over the years? Is it possible she was advising her husband to "Bless God and die"? This is the same word Job used when he said, "The LORD gave, and the LORD has taken away; blessed (*bârak*) be the name of the LORD."

Represented here are some prominent verses in which *bârak* is translated as "bless" or "blessing." The word is translated as "curse" only 0.01 percent of the time. Perhaps that should tell us something about Mrs. Job and how we view her.

Table 2: Examples of bârak *Translated as "Blessing"*

Genesis 12:1–3	Exodus 18:10	Leviticus 9:23	Numbers 22:12
Deuteronomy 7:12–14	Joshua 14:13	Judges 18:24	Ruth 2:20
1 Samuel 25:32, 33	2 Samuel 22:47	1 Kings 8:56	2 Kings 10:15
1 Chronicles 4:10	2 Chronicles 31:10	Ezra 7:27	Nehemiah 8:6
Job 42:12	Psalm 103:1, 2	Proverbs 22:9	Isaiah 51:2
Jeremiah 17:7	Ezekiel 3:12	Haggai 2:19	Zechariah 11:5

The blessing of Abraham

A fine example of how *bârak* is used as a blessing is the call of Abraham. Notice how frequently the word *bârak* is found in three short verses.

> Now the Lord said to Abram, 'Go from your country and your kindred and your father's house to the land that I will show you. And I will make of you a great nation, and I will bless (*bârak*) you and make your name great so that you will be a blessing (Hebrew: בְּרָכָה; English: *beràkâh*). I will bless (*bârak*) those who bless (*bârak*) you, and him who dishonors you I will curse (*'ârar*), and in you all the families of the earth shall be blessed (*bârak*)" (Gen 12:1–3).

In these verses, *bârak* is used for "bless" but another word is used for "curse." It is the word *'ârar* that is always translated "curse." The use of *'ârar* for "curse" allows a more apparent distinction between "blessing" and "cursing."

The verb *bârak* was also chosen for the blessings the Israelites pronounced from Mount Gerizim upon entering the Promised Land (Deut 28). The verb for the cursings they pronounced was the normal *'ârar* (Deut 27).

Table 3 compares the words in both the Old and New Testaments that are translated in English as "curse," "vilification," "contempt," and related terms.

Table 3: Biblical Words for "Curse"

Original Word	*English Translation*	*Meaning*	*Part of Speech*	*Scripture*
קָלַל	*Qâlal*	contempt, despising	noun	1 Sam 17:43; 2 Sam 6:5, 7; Neh 13:2; Job 3:1
קְלָלָה	*q*^e *âlâh*	vilification, curse	noun	Jer 24:9; 44:12
בָּרַךְ	*Bârak*	blessing, curse	noun	Job :5,11;2:5,9; Ps 62:4
רַך	*'âra*	vilification, curse	noun	2 Kgs 9:34; Jer 20:14
καταναθεματίζω	*Katanathematízō*	Curse	verb	Matt 26:74
καταράομαι	*Kataráomai*	Curse	verb	Mark 11:2; Luke 6:28; Rom 12:14; Jas 3:9
ἐπικατάρατος	*Epikatáratos*	Accursed	adjective	Gal 3:10, 13
βλασφημέω	*Blasphēméō*	defame, revile	verb	Rev 16:9, 11, 21
ἀναθεματίζω	*Anathematízō*	speak evil of	verb	Mark 14:71
ἀρά	*Ará*	doom, curse	verb	Rom 12:14

There are more than sufficient Hebrew and Greek words to describe the concept of a curse in the Bible. There are also plenty of words that describe God's curse upon this world. That leads us to drill down into the cause of the curse.

THE CAUSE OF THE CURSE

God cursed a sinful world. Why would he do that? Is the God of heaven a vindictive God? Is he a childish God whose creation ticked him off so he gave vent to his wrath by cursing the whole world? Let's see.

God placed Adam and Eve in the most perfect environment. They had plenty to eat from both the ground and the fruit of the trees. It was a veritable smorgasbord that our first parents just picked and ate. There were no germs, no bacteria, and no nasty things to pick out of their meals. The Food and Drug Administration was not needed. Better than claims of organic, no preservatives, or non-GMO, everything was pure, certified 100 percent by God himself.

Adam and Eve lived in a vegetarian paradise. What could go wrong?

A single prohibition

There was, however, one restriction that God placed on Adam and Eve. Genesis 2:15–17 says, "The LORD God took the man and put him in the garden of Eden to work it and keep it. And the LORD God commanded the man, saying, 'You may surely eat of every tree of the garden, but of the tree of the knowledge of good and evil you shall not eat, for in the day that you eat of it you shall surely die.'"

One prohibition. That was it—just one. Eat of every tree of the garden except that one, the tree of the knowledge of good and evil. However, if you eat of that tree, it will bring God's curse upon humankind, and you will die as a result.

However, our first parents, Adam and Eve, disobeyed God and ate from the one forbidden tree. The cause of death in our world can be traced to the disobedience to that one prohibition. One sin, one act of disobedience, would make all of Adam and Eve's descendants sinners and ultimately lead to our deaths.

The Apostle Paul could not be clearer about that, as demonstrated in the fifth chapter of Romans. "Sin came into the world through one man, and death through sin, and so death spread to all men because all sinned" (v. 12). "Many died through one man's trespass" (v. 15). "Judgment following one trespass brought condemnation" (v. 16). "Because of one man's trespass, death reigned through that one man" (v. 17). "One trespass led to condemnation for all men" (v. 18). "By the one man's disobedience the many were made sinners" (v. 19). Get the picture? Six times, Paul traces death and sin back to that one sin, the first sin of Adam, disobeying the direct will of God.

Inspired by God the Holy Spirit, the apostle lays the cause of the curse upon this world, not on God, but on Adam and his sin, influenced by Satan. All the misery, all the violence, all the wars, all child and spousal abuse, you name it, it is the result of Satan's deception and Adam's original sin.

The entrance of sin into humanity

Here is what God says initiated the chain of sin that led to death.

> Now the serpent was more crafty than any other beast of the field that the Lord God had made. He said to the woman, "Did God actually say, 'You shall not eat of any tree in the garden'?"

> And the woman said to the serpent, "We may eat of the fruit of the trees in the garden, but God said, 'You shall not eat of the fruit of the tree that is in the midst of the garden, neither shall you touch it, lest you die.'" But the serpent said to the woman, "You will not surely die. For God knows that when you eat of it your eyes will be opened, and you will be like God, knowing good and evil." So when the woman saw that the tree was good for food, and that it was a delight to the eyes, and that the tree was to be desired to make one wise, she took of its fruit and ate, and she also gave some to her husband who was with her, and he ate"(Gen 3:1–6).

Notice the distinguishable verb trail in verse 6. "The woman saw," [she] "desired," "she took," and "she also gave." The four common steps to sin (see also Achan, Josh 7:21–26, and David, 2 Sam 11:2–6, 24) are followed by us all the time.

A universal rule

It is now a universal principle: "The one who sins is the one who will die" (Ezek 18:4, 20 NIV). The universal principle is that because of Adam's sin and God's subsequent curse on him, because of that sin, today if we sin, and we all do, we will die, and we all will.

In the first chapter, we investigated the atonement—the price Jesus paid to avenge God's wrath, secure our redemption, and demonstrate God's love for us. I wanted you to see that God already had a plan for our redemption in place before we got to this chapter, focusing on the curse that brought sin to the world, death to us, and a need for God's atonement.

Death in our world is the result of the curse. The curse is the result of sin. And sin is the result of disobedience to God when Adam and Eve fell into Satan's trap. So ultimately, Satan caused deceitfulness, temptation, sin, the curse, and now death. Do not blame God. It was all of Satan.

So far, we have only referenced the negative consequences of sin, as enumerated in Romans 5. Read the end of that chapter to see what God did about those bad results. You'll see how good God is.

Having read the historical account of the cause of God's curse on sin and sinners, we now must explore each portion of the curse for content and results. You will want to notice how wide and deep the curse upon humanity and our environment became. We'll address each curse in the approximate order in which they occur in the Genesis text.

THE CURSE UPON THE SERPENT

The LORD God first spoke to the snake, which Satan used as a Trojan Horse to enter the idyllic Garden of Eden.[21] His threefold curse made the snake: (1) the most cursed of God's animal creations; (2) caused it to crawl on its belly rather than stand erect like most other animals; and (3) because it had to crawl on its belly, the curse made the snake eat filthy, tasteless, and germ-filled dust. Snakes eat rodents, amphibians, eggs, birds, lizards, etc. But because of the curse, snakes eat their prey with a huge side salad of dust, dirt, germs, and animal droppings.

Snakes and humans generally do not mix

People have a special relationship with snakes, and it's not a good one. The latest available Gallup poll found that 51 percent of Americans fear snakes. Compare that to only 36 percent who fear heights.[22] Another interesting finding from this poll is a gender gap in our fears. The poll showed that 38 percent of men feared snakes, while a whopping 62 percent of women did. It appears that the effects of Eve's encounter with Satan in the form of a snake still linger in humanity. Clearly, the snake has become the most cursed among God's animal creations.

Belly crawlers and snake charmers

The second aspect of God's curse on the serpent is that it must crawl on its belly rather than stand erect or move with the aid of legs like most animals. Herpetologists are zoologists who specialize in the study of reptiles and amphibians. The word herpetology comes from the Greek word *herpeton*, meaning "creeping animal." While herpetologists have a bond with their snakes, they are in the minority.

Perhaps you have seen a snake charmer raise a snake out of a basket with his flute and wondered how that snake could rise so erectly. Those who practice this ancient ritual can be found in abundance at the Jemaa El Fnaa, the central square of Marrakesh, Morocco. Once on a visit there, I gave the snake charmer a couple of dollars so I could lie on the ground in front of him and take plenty of pictures from ground level of the snake emerging from the basket. When I sat up and was still taking pictures, another snake charmer placed a King Cobra around my neck. He thought it was hilarious; me not so much.

Although we cannot say for sure, some assume snakes would have been upright creatures like cattle or wild animals (Gen 3:1, 14) had it not been for Satan using the serpent to gain clandestine entry into the Garden of Eden. A snake slithering through the weeds may be scary, but it slithers as a result of the curse. Imagine a snake with the devil living inside of it.

The dust of the ground

Finally, because of God's curse on the snake, it couldn't help but ingest the filthy, tasteless dust of the ground. Snakes have an organ called the Jacobson's organ located on the roof of their mouths that acts as a chemical receptor. This organ helps the snake smell and, as a snake's forked tongue darts out to sense its surroundings, it licks the air and picks up dust particles. The snake then inserts the tips of its forked tongue into two openings in Jacobson's organ to identify and analyze the dust particles. In this way, the snake really does eat dust.

Some believe this verse to be a metaphor. Later in history, "eating dust" was used to describe people of low social standing or those facing a difficult life situation. This would relate to what the preceding verses said about the serpent being the lowest form, the most cursed of all God's animal life.

When reading about the serpent's curse in Genesis 3, people often skip over it or inadequately consider it. But this curse was real, just like God's curses on the planet, the woman, and the man are real.

THE CURSE UPON SATAN

Next, the LORD God turned his attention to Satan himself. His curse was explained as, "I will put enmity between you and the woman, and between your offspring and her offspring; he shall bruise your head, and you shall bruise his heel" (Gen 3:15).

This is also a threefold curse. (1) There would be enmity, hatred, and conflict between Satan and the woman, Eve. The (2) curse would extend beyond Satan and Eve to their posterity [Satan's offspring are all the wicked angels and wicked humans, and the offspring of the woman are Jesus Christ and subsequently all true believers]. The fact that the curse extends to many generations beyond the devil and Eve proves that Satan's war with God will be a very long one. Furthermore, (3) while Satan would be successful in bruising the heel of his great enemy, that great enemy of the devil [Jesus] would bruise Satan's head (Gen 3:15). Ponder each phase of this curse with me.

The hatred between Eve and the serpent

First, Satan's curse would entail enmity, hatred, and conflict between Satan and Eve personally. While we do not know much about the personal hatred and conflict between Satan and the original "first lady," it is clear that such animosity existed. There are hints that, through the early chapters of Genesis, Eve clung to God in her everyday life to avoid further confrontation with Satan.

God drove Adam and Eve out of the garden and prohibited them from ever entering it again (Gen 3:23–24). But when Eve gave birth to Seth, she again acknowledged the work of God in her life, saying, "God has appointed for me another offspring instead of Abel, for Cain killed him" (Gen 4:25). Here, Eve, now as one estranged from God, witnessed an appointment by God. The name *Seth* sounds like the Hebrew for "he appointed" when it is spoken. While the Genesis record makes no mention of specific conflicts between Satan and Eve, the few references to Eve in the Bible suggest that she clung to the promise of victory in Genesis 3:15. This implies that hatred and conflict between Satan and Eve did exist.

Satan's air force

The second element of God's curse on Satan is that it would extend far beyond Satan and Eve to their posterity. Satan's progeny are the evil angels that were deceived by him and drawn out of heaven, rebelling against the Almighty. They became Satan's celestial soldiers, evil angels, and unseen spirits operating in the air all around us. As Paul told the Ephesian believers, "For we do not wrestle against flesh and blood, but against the rulers, against the authorities, against the cosmic powers over this present darkness, against the spiritual forces of evil in the heavenly places" (Eph 6:12). Evil angels are the real "sons of Satan."

But Satan's progeny also consists of every person who joins Satan's long war with God. Every man, every woman, every teenager, and every child who rejects the God of the Bible, and usually the Bible as well, has joined the forces of Satan. The sad reality, I believe, is that most men and women in Satan's army aren't even aware they enlisted. They rejected Jesus as God's only Savior but did not realize that choice would secure their eternal destiny in the Lake of Fire (Rev 19:20; 20:10, 14, 15).

Today, we think in terms of East versus West, black versus white, Republican versus Democrat, rich versus poor, and so many other humanly-created categories. However, God doesn't view humanity in any of these ways. He sees only two kinds of people—saved and lost. In his first epistle, the Apostle John could not make the real separation between people any clearer. "Whoever has the Son has life; whoever does not have the Son of God does not have life" (1 John 5:12). There it is, cut and dried. If we have the Son Jesus, if we have trusted him to save us from the curse of our sin, we have life, curse-free, joyful, and eternal. However, consider the alternative. If we have rejected Jesus as Savior, we have lost eternal life with God. We must experience the alternative—eternal life with Satan in hell. So, what do you think? Have you trusted him or not? Have you repented of your rebellion against God in your life and confessed your sin to him? Have you freely received God's salvation through his Son or not? How do you honestly answer those questions?

Don't allow these questions to pass without serious consideration? They are far too important!

Satan and our daily walk

While the choice to fight with Satan against God has eternal consequences, it also impacts our daily lives. This is also true for those who choose to be soldiers in God's army. The Bible contains numerous verses that outline how a Christ-follower should live after salvation. At times, Jesus spoke of this (Luke 16: John 8:12; 11:9; 12:35) and at times the book of Acts recorded it (Acts 9:31; 21:24). It was the writing apostles, however, and especially Paul, who most often addressed the topic of walking in the ways of the Lord.

The apostle begged the believers in Ephesus, "I therefore, a prisoner for the Lord, urge you to walk in a manner worthy of the calling to which you have been called" (Eph 4:1). This idea of walking in a manner worthy of a follower of Jesus is a frequent theme in Paul's letters (see also Col 1:10; 2 Thess 2:12).

Table 4: Biblical Commands to Walk Worthy of Jesus Christ

The Commandment for the Christian	*Scripture*
"Walk in the footsteps of the faith."	Romans 4:12
"Walk in newness of life."	Romans 6:4
"Walk according to the Spirit."	Romans 8:1,4
"Walk properly as in the daytime."	Romans 13:13
"We walk by faith, not by sight."	2 Corinthians 5:7
"Walk by the Spirit."	Galatians 5:16
"Walk by the rule that brings peace and mercy."	Galatians 6:16
"Walk in good works."	Ephesians 2:10
"Walk in a manner worthy of the calling."	Ephesians 4:1
"Walk in love."	Ephesians 5:1–2
"Walk as children of light."	Ephesians 5:8
"Walk worthy of [Paul's] example."	Philippians 3:17
"Walk in a manner worthy of the Lord."	Colossians 1:10
"If you have received Christ Jesus as Lord, so walk in him."	Colossians 2:6
"Walk in wisdom."	Colossians 4:5
"Walk in a manner worthy of God."	1 Thessalonians 2:12
"You ought to walk and to please God."	1 Thessalonians 4:1
"Walk properly."	1 Thessalonians 4:12
"Walk in the light."	1 John 1:7
"Walking in the truth."	2 John 1:4
"Walk according to his commandments."	2 John 1:6
"Walking in the truth."	3 John 1:3, 4
"Walk with me in white, for they are worthy."	Rev 3:4

Every day is an authentic struggle to walk in a way worthy of our calling as followers of Christ. Satan and his minions are aligned against us in a massive army. Their assignment is to destroy our faith through doubt, foolish discussions, some university professor, personal sin, or any way they can. Most in Satan's army do not know they are cursed. They do not comprehend the severity and finality of the judgment they face. That's why Satan's army grows every day. They have no idea what awaits them.

The third element of the curse against Satan is that the old snake will successfully bruise the heel of his great enemy, Jesus Christ (Gen 3:15). This aspect of his curse interests us the most, because the bruising of Jesus' heel was the essence of the Calvary event. Satan inspired the Jews to plot the killing of the Savior (Matt 26:3–4; Mark 14:1; Luke 22:1–2; John 5:18; 7:1, 25; 8:37, 40; 11:53). Satan put the questions in Annas' mind as he interrogated Jesus. Satan prompted Caiaphas and the Sanhedrin to hold an unjust trial to find Jesus guilty. Pilate and the Roman soldiers cared little for Jesus, so the soldiers beat him within an inch of his life, and the Roman killing squad finished the task. Jesus was dead. Satan had bruised the heel of the offspring of the woman. Nevertheless, Satan knew the war wasn't over.

The end of the story is this: "The devil who had deceived them was thrown into the lake of fire and sulfur where the beast and the false prophet were, and they will be tormented day and night forever and ever" (Rev. 19:10; see 19:20 and 20:14). It seems to me that "forever and ever" is a very long time.[23]

Let's move on to the next portion of God's curse on sin.

THE CURSE UPON THE WOMAN

Although the Bible doesn't say much about Eve, we know she bore children with Adam. "Now Adam knew Eve his wife, and she conceived and bore Cain, saying, 'I have gotten a man with the help of the LORD.' And again, she bore his brother Abel" (Gen 4:1–2). After sin flared in Cain's heart and he killed his brother, "Adam knew his wife again, and she bore a son and called his name Seth." (v. 25). And there were more children, siblings, male and female, to propagate the race. Eve became the mother of all humanity. All of us, regardless of ethnicity, language, tribe, dialect, or whatever, can trace our DNA back to this one woman and her husband.

The infrequent references to Eve

Most translators and interpreters of Scripture hold that the name Eve is derived from the Hebrew verb חיה (*haya*), meaning "to live" or "have life." Thus, it is through the woman, Eve, that all humanity has life. It seems strange, then, that of the sixteen references to Eve in the Bible, only four mention her by name, two in the Old Testament and two in the New.

Genesis 3:20, "The man called his wife's name Eve, because she was the mother of all living." This mention of Eve is to identify her as the mother of the human race. Notice that when she was first called Eve, there were no "living human beings." That Eve was the mother of "all" means every person descended from Adam and Eve.

In 2 Corinthians 11:3, the apostle notes, "I am afraid that as the serpent deceived Eve by his cunning, your thoughts will be led astray from a sincere and pure devotion to Christ." Eve was the first person in a very long line to sin. Her sin was to distrust God, to disobey God, and to disavow any responsibility for her sin. She influenced her husband to join her in her disobedience.

Paul clarifies in 1 Timothy 2:13–14: "For Adam was formed first, then Eve; and Adam was not deceived, but the woman was deceived and became a transgressor." Here, the apostle identifies that while Satan did not deceive Adam in the form of a snake, Eve was deceived, and she became the first transgressor against the will of God. Paul was not placing all the blame on Eve, but was indicating the order in which sin infiltrated human society. Eve sinned first, then Adam, but it is Adam's sin that Paul treats so thoroughly in Romans. This epistle helps explain why it was Adam's sin, not Eve's, that was so significant in the fall of the human race.

The Protoevangelium of Genesis 3:15

The curse upon the woman was the beginning of our human struggle with sin, sorrow, and shame. However, within this curse lies what theologians often call the *Protoevangelium*. This is a compound of two Greek words: *protos*, meaning "first," and *evangelion*, meaning "good news" or "gospel." Thus, the *Protoevangelium* is commonly referred to as the first announcement of the good news of God's salvation.

Genesis 3:15 is the earliest promise of God's redemption of his own. It is the promise that, while there would be a day when Satan would bruise the heel of the woman's offspring, there would also be a day when the offspring of the woman would bruise the head of Satan and his offspring.

It is important to note that the word "offspring" (Hebrew: זֶרַע; English: *zera'*) ["seed" in KJV] is like the word "deer" in English, a countable noun that can refer to one or many. You can spot a single deer in the woods or a herd of deer. The same word can refer to one or more. So, how do we determine to whom the word *zera'* refers? Are there any clues?

Jesus: the bruiser of Satan's head

There are clues. One of the most profound is when Genesis 3:15 shifts from the noun "offspring," which can be singular or plural, to the pronoun "he," which must be singular. "He shall bruise your head, and you shall bruise his heel." "His" is a third-person, singular pronoun.

Paul cleared up any mystery when he clarified Genesis 3:15 to the Galatian believers. "Now the promises were made to Abraham and to his offspring. It does not say, 'And to offsprings,' referring to many, but referring to one, 'And to your offspring,' who is Christ" (Gal 3:16). Jesus Christ is that single descendant of Eve who will ultimately defeat Satan in his long war with God.

The promise of Satan bruising Jesus' heel transpired one Friday afternoon in Jerusalem at a place called Calvary. The second promise, about the offspring of the woman [Jesus] bruising the head of Satan, will occur millennia later. A bruise to the heel is usually not fatal, but a hard-enough bruise to the head is always fatal. That's why the diagnosis of victims in movies and on TV always seems to be "blunt force trauma." A blow to the heel hurts; a blow to the head kills.

However, there is much more to this curse, which focuses strictly on Eve, the woman. First, there would be enmity between Satan and Eve. The confirmation of that enmity is explained in the next verse. "To the woman he said, 'I will surely multiply your pain in childbearing; in pain, you shall bring forth children. Your desire shall be contrary to your husband, but he shall rule over you'" (Gen 3:16).

It is difficult to explain this curse without appearing to be misogynistic. However, the truth of Holy Scripture must always prevail over a society so ready to cancel it. This is a curse upon Eve because she was the first to succumb to Satan's duplicity and deceitfulness. Again, this curse is threefold. (1) The woman will have dramatically increased pain in childbirth. (2) The woman's desire would conflict with her husband's desire. However, (3) even though the woman desires something contrary to her husband's desires, she must acquiesce to her husband.

Let's unpack the threefold curse on the woman due to her sin.

The curse of multiplied birth pains

To the woman, the God of all creation said, "I will surely multiply your pain in childbearing; in pain you shall bring forth children." All my children were born in the days when fathers were not allowed in the birthing room with their wives. The father's pain came as he paced nervously in a room filled with putrid smoke from fathers lighting up cigars at the news of their child's birth. As a consistent finding, labor pain is ranked high on the pain scale when compared to other painful life experiences.[24]

The mothers of the world cannot imagine what childbirth would have been like had it not been for the first woman's sin and the curse that sin brought upon Eve and her offspring. Ladies, don't blame that pain on your husband. Don't blame it on God. Blame it on Satan and sin, the real culprits for your pain in childbirth.

The curse of a woman's desire

The second layer of the curse upon the woman was that her desires, ideas, and longings would be strong, but often at odds with those of her husband. We have no idea of the marital spats Adam and Eve may have had after being kicked out of the garden, but this curse ensured they had some. Men and women are different. We want different things. We want to vacation at different places. We understand "date night" to mean different things. The fact that there is no meeting of the minds and flare-ups still occur today is the direct result of the curse.

Christians are people too, fallen people, sinful people, and those who follow Jesus as Savior and Lord are no more exempt from "intense fellowship" than any others. Billy and Ruth Graham's oldest child, Gigi, told me personally that someone once asked Ruth Graham if she ever considered divorcing Billy. With tongue in cheek, Ruth said, "Divorce no. Murder, yes."

This curse does not imply that women are the contrarian half of the marriage relationship. Not at all. The woman was created from the side of the man and is equal to him. When two equals encounter different opinions or desires, it can get intense.

However, this layer of the curse upon the woman is tied to the next.

The curse of a woman's acquiescence

This principle is violated every day in modern society, including in Christian homes. When was the last time you heard anyone say this out loud? Since the first stirrings of the Women's Liberation Movement, few have even dared to speak of this portion of the curse upon women. I wish I could soften this somehow, but there it is. Right there in Genesis 3:16. "Your desire shall be contrary to your husband, but he shall rule over you."

Two things must be established here. First, this command was not cultural. Many times, when people want to remove God's condemnation of their behavior, they claim that what the Bible says fits the time of the Old or New Testament, but things are different today. They sure are, but God's Word is not different.

It's little wonder that cancel culture has done its best to terminate the Bible. It doesn't fit with today's societal desires or norms. Liberal politicians and educators say the Bible was for another time, that it isn't relevant today. The concept of "He shall rule over you" is not appropriate in today's society. And yet, Psalm 119:89 declares, "Forever, O LORD, your word is firmly fixed in the heavens." The Prophet Isaiah proclaimed, "The grass withers, the flower fades, but the word of our God will stand forever" (Isa 40:8). Jesus himself said, "Scripture cannot be broken" (John 10:35; see also Num 23:19; Josh 21:45; Ps 138:2; Isa 55:11; Matt 5:18; Heb 4:12;1 Pet 1:25; and many more). You can deny the truth of God, but you cannot hide from the consequences of your denial.

The acquiescence of a wife to her husband when they legitimately disagree is not a principle rooted in the culture of Abraham, David, Nehemiah, or Jesus. This command was issued in Genesis 3. There was no developed culture in Genesis 3. There were no people to have a culture in Genesis 3. There was just Adam and Eve in Genesis 3, and God had already established the rules of engagement for a happy marriage. Unhappy marriages often stem from neglecting God's plan.

The second important point that needs to be made is that Genesis 3:16 does not negate the primary equality between the male and the female as explained in Genesis 1:27, "So God created man in his own image, in the image of God he created him; male and female he created them." God intentionally created two different kinds of human beings—males and females—equal in his sight.

Nevertheless, we must never confuse equality with functionality. Because the woman was created equal to the man, the plan was for them to work together to build a life as equal partners. Building a society with peaceful homes is always better done by two than by one.

However, God knew that no family could have two heads. Partners can be equal, but someone has to take the lead. Thus, part of the curse upon the woman was to establish the family order by designing that Adam, "shall rule over you" (Gen 3:16). No one has to like it, but no one can deny that's what the Bible says.

This is the concept of *primus inter pares*, "first among equals." It refers to a person who holds a position of authority but is still considered equal to their peers. The term originated in ancient Rome, where it described the role of the consul. The husband is not just a tie breaker. He is God's designated authority as one who retains equality with the wife but does not exceed it. Paul clarified this further in a letter to the Christ-followers in Ephesus. He said, "Wives, submit to your own husbands, as to the Lord. For the husband is the head of the wife even as Christ is the head of the church, his body, and is himself its Savior. Now as the church submits to Christ, so also wives should submit in everything to their husbands" (Eph 5:22–24).

So that husbands would not use these verses to lord their God-given authority over their wives, Paul continued, "Husbands, love your wives, as Christ loved the church and gave himself up for her, that he might sanctify her, having cleansed her by the washing of water with the word" (Eph 5:25–26).

The marriage relationship is somewhat akin to a symbiotic one, in which each partner contributes to the other's well-being. But in our society, thinking about the needs of yourself has superseded thinking about the needs of your spouse-equal, and the result has bred selfish, ego-centric aliens from God's perfect plan in marriage.

Some of our best and brightest astronauts, architects, and astronomers today are women. Gender is a level playing field for intelligence and ability, even if it hasn't always been for opportunity. But to ridicule those whose chosen career is to be a homemaker is to disrespect the God-given structure for a happy home and to attack the very basis of a continuous and enduring society.

Before we explore God's curse on Eve's husband, we must examine how the caretakers of God's planet brought a curse on the very planet they were charged to protect.

THE CURSE UPON THE PLANET

First, it was the curse upon the snake. Then, the curse on Satan. After that, the curse upon the woman. And now, Adam and his environment are cursed. We'll first investigate the environmental curse on our planet, as it is mentioned next in the biblical text.

Genesis 3:17, 18 informs us, "And to Adam he said, 'Because you have listened to the voice of your wife and have eaten of the tree of which I commanded you, "You shall not eat of it," cursed is the ground because of you; in pain you shall eat of it all the days of your life; thorns and thistles it shall bring forth for you; and you shall eat the plants of the field.'"

Here's what this curse meant to Adam and now means to us.

The whole earth is no longer a friend to humanity

This curse is on the "ground" (Hebrew: אֲדָמָה; English: *'ădâmâh*), the very ground out of which Adam was formed. The whole Earth, which God created and prepared for humankind even before he created Adam and Eve, the whole Earth and everything in it, the whole Earth over which man had both possession and dominion, the whole Earth that Adam and Eve and their descendants were supposed to enjoy in comfort, pleasure, and ease, this whole Earth was no longer the friend of Adam and his family.

The Earth, which was itself our greatest blessing this side of heaven, because of Adam's sin, is now cursed and has become his greatest earthly challenge. The beauty and lusciousness of Eden have now been traded for the sandy mounds of the Middle East. Gone is the green of the garden. Gone is the gentle work of tilling and preserving it. Now, tilling and preserving the Earth will be back-breaking and challenging.

Sterile and unproductive land outside of Eden

The language of Genesis 3:17 does not imply that, as a result of the fall, our physical planet underwent a severe and debilitating change. The land outside of Eden did not look like the vestigial remains of the Ice Age or the violent post-apocalyptic world depicted in the Denzel Washington movie *The Book of Eli*. On the contrary, this verse simply announces that, because of Adam's transgression, he would find the land beyond Eden sterile and unproductive. The Bible describes Eden's sublime setting, but does not directly address the less sublime ground outside it.

The "blue beauty," as the Earth is sometimes called, was given to us as a habitable planet that others in our solar system are not. Still, ask any farmer how easy it is to provide a healthy crop year after year. How easy is it to get a yield that will cover the year's gigantic expenses? This is the result of the divine curse on the ground that is the consequence of the first man's sin. Without that sin, there would be no place for the Sierra Club or the Nature Conservancy. We would still be living in that idyllic Edenic environment.

THE CURSE UPON THE MAN

Interspersed in the curse upon the planet are elements of God's curse on man and subsequently all humankind. Here is the text that reveals the curse upon Adam.

Genesis 3:17–19, "And to Adam he said, 'Because you have listened to the voice of your wife and have eaten of the tree of which I commanded you, 'You shall not eat of it,' cursed is the ground because of you; in pain you shall eat of it all the days of your life; thorns and thistles it shall bring forth for you; and you shall eat the plants of the field. By the sweat of your face you shall eat bread, till you return to the ground, for out of it you were taken; for you are dust, and to dust you shall return.'"[25]

By now, Adam knows he has lost everything except Eve, and she is in the same deplorable environment he is. Together, they have lost the whole enchilada—the whole Earth—and their unique relationship with the Almighty. That's the consequence of disobedience to the Holy God. You lose everything.

Notice the five elements of the curse upon the man.

- *"In pain you shall eat of it all the days of your life."* No longer could Adam pick a mango from the tree or pull up a carrot. Now those delicacies came at a price, and the price was pain in working the land. Notice, too, that Adam ate those wild weeds and herbs of the field with pain. He didn't eat with discomfort or difficulty. Adam had all thirty-two teeth. He could chew fine, but he would always eat with pain. Pain is a problem. It's part of the curse. Pain is like a bad roommate, always around but never helpful.

  Sometimes pain presents itself as a dull thud. At other times, it's like squeezing the juice from a lemon into a paper cut. My pain, and yours too, is part of the price we pay for being such skillful sinners. Nevertheless, when the Lord comes in power and great glory, "God will wipe away every tear from their eyes; there shall be no more death, nor sorrow, nor crying. There shall be *no more pain*, for the former things have passed away" (Rev 21:4 NIV). Hallelujah!!

- *Thorns and thistles it shall bring forth for you."* The second element of the curse upon the man was that, instead of luscious fruits and vegetables in abundance, the ground outside Eden would constantly produce thorns and thistles. Leave a field uncultivated for several years, and the good Earth will produce nothing but a bad yield. Over seventy species of brambles, thistles, briers, and other thorny, prickly plants grow wild in Israel. Thorns, thistles, weeds, and more appeared to produce spontaneously, but if Adam wanted anything else, he would have to work for it. In pain, Adam had to till the ground for food, but that same ground would give weeds, brambles, and thistles with no effort. It's still that way today.

- *"You shall eat the plants of the field."* In his commentary on Genesis 3:18, John Calvin believed the intimation of this clause was that henceforth man was, "to be deprived of his former delicacies to such an extent as to be compelled to use, in addition, the herbs which had been designed only for brute animals."[26] The diet of Adam and Eve in the garden was never enjoyed outside of Eden. Instead, they ate what "plants of the field" they could coax to grow. They could eat, but not as before. It was like giving up dining at The Ritz and eating at some dimly-lit diner with cockroaches running up the wall. You still could be fed, but the experience would be far different.

- *"By the sweat of your face you shall eat bread."* The ground outside of the garden would be very different from the highly enriched and well-watered ground within Eden. Adam would soon discover that his days of instant shopping were over. No longer would he just pick an orange and enjoy it. The ground beyond the garden›s gates would present Adam with a new reality. He had to work for everything he ate; what he ate didn't present itself to Adam and Eve easily. He had to work the ground, plant the seed, and wait for the harvest. "See how the farmer waits for the precious fruit of the earth, being patient about it, until it receives the early and the late rains" (Jas 5:7). Adam was learning to be a farmer, and he was learning to be patient. And through it all, his aching body was drenched in sweat.
- *"Till you return to the ground."* Every element of the curse upon the man thus far has only produced difficulty. However, this final element ultimately leads to death. Because he participated in Eve's disobedience and his subsequent disobedience, both Adam and Eve were condemned to die one day. This is why you and I will one day die as well. The reason is our sin and the curse that has been placed upon us as disobedient sinners. "For the wages of sin is death," said Paul in Romans 6:23. "The soul who sins shall die," records Ezekiel 18:4, 20. Genesis 3:18 says the same thing. "For you are dust, and to dust you shall return." Sin is the reason we all return to the ground after living above it. The intermediate result is pain. The ultimate result is death. The Bible tells us that, and our life experience confirms it. The only difference is that the Bible answers the why question. The Holy God placed a curse on the unholy responses of Adam and Eve and all their descendants. No disobedience, no curse. No curse, no death. It's just as simple as that.

The devastating impact on the Earth

What does such a wide-ranging curse entail? Everything you can think of. Sin's curse accounts for all the disease, depredation, decay, deterioration, devastation, and death evident in our world. Everything that is decaying, everything that is evil, everything that is dying, is the result of the curse God placed on the environment in which we sinful humans live.

Theologian Floyd Barackman wrote:

> With the moral fall of Earth's noblest creature, God imposed a curse upon the ground and lower forms of life (Rom 8:20–22). This made man's work toilsome and his life hazardous. Both plants and animals developed defense mechanisms. Undomesticated animals became ferocious toward other animals and humans. The blight of disease and death settled upon all forms of animal and plant life. Insects became destructive, and many forms of vegetation became inedible and hurtful.[27]

Nothing on Earth was left untouched by the curse that resulted from sin. Likewise, nothing on Earth will be left untouched when God removes his curse from the Earth because of Jesus' sacrifice at Calvary. That's next up, and it's time for some good news. What we have been exploring is heavy, to be sure, but if we don't understand the curse upon sin, we can never truly appreciate the cleansing that occurred at Calvary.

The curse is bad news for everything and everybody. But, is there any way the curse can be removed? Can the world be cleaned up? Can humanity live out from under the curse? Is there any way to have the curse lifted? Can our future look a lot brighter? That's where God's grace enters the picture and dominates the curse.

Although the curse was deep and wide, in Christ's work on Calvary's Cross, it encompassed the cancelling of three specific curses. They are:

- the curse upon the world at large;
- the curse specifically upon humankind for our sin against God; and
- the curse upon anyone hanging on a tree [cross].

These three curses are inextricably linked together, as you will see while we address each in turn. At Calvary's Cross, God provided the remedy for the curses, all the curses. In some ways, Jesus' death on the cross reversed the curse; in others, he removed it. Let's see how.

THE CURSE UPON OUR EARTH REMOVED

Thus far, the curse upon humanity has been all bad news. However, the gospel is "good news," and we now seek a brighter future through it. Man's sin was devastating, but God's response was also devastating.

The first curse removed by Jesus' death on the cross was the curse upon our world—that is, our planet, with its plants, animals, marine life, and so on (Gen 3:17–18). When God cursed the ground, it meant everything related to the earth (Rom 8:20–21). Paul wrote, "For we know that the whole creation has been groaning together in the pains of childbirth until now. And not only the creation, but we ourselves, who have the firstfruits of the Spirit, groan inwardly as we wait eagerly for adoption as sons, the redemption of our bodies" (Rom 8:22–23).

The Drought of the Good Earth

The Earth, God's specific creation for humankind, today groans because of our sin. Seismologists listen to the Earth's groan every day. And now we sinful humans are destroying our planet, and all the Earth can do is groan.

The reason we're making so little headway on saving the planet is because we're focusing on the tree's branches when we should be concentrating on its roots. The branches include climate change, clean energy, clean water, and many other things. However, if you cut those off, new branches will grow to replace them, as the tree's roots are still strong. You have not addressed the root cause of the problem. Our rebellion against God is what brought the curse upon our planet, and it doesn't matter how many windmills we build or charging stations we install; until we come to grips with our sin, we will have little success in saving our planet.

Humankind has a spiritual problem, more than an energy problem. That's what the Bible addresses, but our politicians do not. They cannot. They don't know how.

A glimpse of our future without the curse

Just as God imposed this curse, he has also promised to remove it from the Earth in his coming Kingdom. He will accomplish this symbolically through the cleansing the Earth receives as a result of Jesus' atonement on the cross (Rom 8:19–22; Isa 11:6–9; 35:1–10; Hos 2:18; Amos 9:13), but one day he will physically remove the curse from the Earth entirely.

Everything mentioned above about the planet's curse will one day be null and void. These curses are real, but at the cross, Jesus did everything God required to lift the curse on the Earth. One day, God has promised, all the curses will be removed, and we will live in an environment even better than the Garden of Eden.

In the Revelation of Jesus Christ, we gain a glimpse of what life without the curse will be like. John writes:

> Then I saw a new heaven and a new earth, for the first heaven and the first earth had passed away, and the sea was no more. And I saw the holy city, new Jerusalem, coming down out of heaven from God, prepared as a bride adorned for her husband. And I heard a loud voice from the throne saying, "Behold, the dwelling place of God is with man. He will dwell with them, and they will be his people, and God himself will be with them as their God. He will wipe away every tear from their eyes, and death shall be no more, neither shall there be mourning, nor crying, nor pain anymore, for the former things have passed away. And the city has no need of sun or moon to shine on it, for the glory of God gives it light, and its lamp is the Lamb. And its gates will never be shut by day—and there will be no night there (Rev 21:1–4, 23–25).

The most wonderful aspect of this promise is not our new environment but that "the dwelling place of God is with man. He will dwell with them, and they will be his people, and God himself will be with them as their God." Better than silver and gold, better than free food, better than breathable air is the fact that we will dwell personally and intimately with God himself.

No more let sins and sorrows grow
nor thorns infest the ground:
He comes to make his blessings flow
far as the curse is found.

—Isaac Watts (1674–1748)

THE CURSE UPON HUMANITY REMOVED

The second important curse removed by Jesus' death was the curse upon all humankind. "By the sweat of your face you shall eat bread, till you return to the ground, for out of it you were taken; for you are dust, and to dust you shall return" (Gen 3:19).

Think of the many far-reaching effects of Adam's sin. Not only must we work hard to put food on the table and a roof over our heads, but in the end, we all die anyway. The formula has always been the same: Obedience brings life; disobedience brings death. Disobedience in the Garden of Eden, according to Genesis 3, brought death to Adam (Gen 5:5) and to Eve (whose death is not mentioned in the Bible), and eventually to all of their descendants (Ezek 18:4, 20; Rom 6:23).

> Nothing is certain except for death and taxes."—Daniel Defoe, Benjamin Franklin, et al.

Just before he died, Moses said to Israel, "I call heaven and earth to witness against you today, that I have set before you, life and death, blessing and curse. Therefore choose life, that you and your offspring may live" (Deut 30:19). The curse upon humankind brings death, but the removal of that curse brings life. This is why Moses told his people to choose life. Paul said it most succinctly: "For the wages of sin is death, but the free gift of God is eternal life in Christ Jesus our Lord" (Rom 6:23). Death comes as the result of sin; life comes as a result of the Savior.

Choose life and the removal of the curse

Remember this promise from God that everyone can grasp. "He will wipe away every tear from their eyes, and death shall be no more, neither shall there be mourning, nor crying, nor pain anymore, for the former things have passed away" (Rev 21:4).

Think about this.

- The loving Father will gently and tenderly wipe the tears from our eyes, tears that have resulted from all the evil that Adam's original sin brought upon humanity.
- When God lives in our presence, there will be no more mourning. All that has caused us to mourn—the death of our children, the loss of our

house in a flood, anything and everything—will be removed because at Calvary, Jesus' death removed the curse upon humanity.

- In God's heaven, there will be no room for crying. All the tears we bring with us, plus the tears we may shed at the Judgment Seat of Christ because of some bungled service to God or bungled opportunities we failed to take, all those tears will be a thing of the past.
- And here's an especially meaningful promise. The pain that Jesus endured at Caiaphas' palace, the pain he received at Pilate's Praetorium, the pain he sustained at the hands of the Roman soldiers, and the pain of being nailed to a cross, hanging there for six hours and finally dying on that cross, that pain and our pain is now in the rearview mirror because his death removed the curse upon us.[28]

Death is the ultimate curse

Jesus' death on the cross made it possible for God to offer us eternal life rather than the eternal death that comes as a result of the curse. It is the death curse resulting from our sin that we are most frequently talking about when we say Jesus' atonement removed the curse from us.

Donald Macleod adds:

> This is a matter on which the Christian canon is unambiguous. Death is the curse pronounced on sin. It follows from this that the question of whether Christ's sufferings were penal immediately becomes a factual, not a theological, one. Did he receive the wages of sin? The answer has to be a categorical 'Yes!'[29]

By removing the curse that resulted from human disobedience (Gen 3:6), our loving, heavenly Father opened the way for us to be saved by his grace from the punishment our sin deserved. "But where sin abounded, grace abounded much more" (Rom 5:20, NKJV), or as J. B. Phillips translates it, "Though sin is shown to be wide and deep, thank God his grace is wider and deeper still!" He's just that kind of God.

But there's more good news.

THE CURSE OF GUILT AND SHAME REMOVED

The third curse removed by Jesus' substitutionary atonement is the curse placed on anyone who is hung on a tree, a pole, a cross, or anything designed to exacerbate their guilt and shame in death. We have alluded to

Deuteronomy 21:22–23 often in this series of books on Roman crucifixion and the death of Jesus. These verses say, "And if a man has committed a crime punishable by death and he is put to death, and you hang him on a tree, his body shall not remain all night on the tree, but you shall bury him the same day, for a hanged man is cursed by God." These are the key Old Testament verses linked to Roman crucifixion and Jesus' sacrifice at Calvary.

Christ redeemed us from the curse

That the New Testament Church understood the removal of the curse to have a direct relationship to Jesus' crucifixion is evident from the words of the Apostle Paul: "Christ redeemed us from the curse of the law by becoming a curse for us—for it is written, 'Cursed is everyone who is hanged on a tree'" (Gal 3:13).

> "Just as Christian came up to the cross, his burden loosed from off his shoulders, fell from off his back, and began to tumble down the hill, and so it continued to do till it came to the mouth of the sepulchre. There it fell in, and I saw it no more!"—John Bunyan

Eusebius of Caesarea (263–339 AD), the famous church historian and Constantine's representative theologian at the Council of Nicaea, wrote:

> Not only did the Lamb of God endure sufferings and punishments for us, but he suffered torments and tortures he did not deserve. It is we who deserved them because of our sins. He became for us the cause of our sins' being forgiven, for he accepted in our place the death, the blows, and the disgrace we deserved. He transferred them to himself and took upon himself the curse that was rightly ours, thus becoming a curse for us. What was he, except the substitute for our life?[30]

By the third century, a theology of the cross and Christ's substitutionary death were being formed. Rising from the pages of Holy Writ, this understanding of what Jesus accomplished on the cross is the one that has stood the test of time.

Christ's death eliminated the curse

Because of the precious blood of Christ, spilled for our benefit at Calvary, the writers of the Bible can confidently and boldly record Jesus' promises of eternal life. John was meticulous in telling us that we can have eternal life through believing in the Savior's death as an atonement for our sins. When we trust Christ as Savior, the curse is gone forever, and the promise of eternal life is here forever.

Joy to the world, the Lord is come!
Let Earth receive her King!
Let ev'ry heart prepare Him room,
and heav'n and nature sing,
and heav'n and nature sing,
and heav'n, and heav'n and nature sing.

—Isaac Watts (1674–1748)

When we say that Jesus' death removed the curse of sin, we mean he eliminated the curse (Gen 2:15–17; 3:6). With the curse removed, Jesus' death opened a window for us to receive his forgiveness.

Jesus' death at Calvary satisfied all of God's requirements to remove the curse from our world and us. Adam's disobedience at Eden's center tree was nullified by Jesus' obedience on Calvary's center tree (Rom 5:18–19). Jesus did not die as an unfortunate itinerant teacher from Galilee. He died to pay the penalty for our sin and to remove the curse that was infused within us. He was not merely caught up in the commotion of the Passover weekend. He did not die as an example for you and me to follow. His death was not to show us how a righteous person dies. Jesus died to pay the penalty for our sin and to remove the curse that was infused within us.

> The shedding of that spotless blood—blood utterly untainted by the stain of sin—was absolutely essential to effect a redemption that could pass legal muster in the court of heaven. But a sacrificial death that would once and for all time annihilate the curse spawned by rebellion had to be an obedient death on the tree. There had to be thorns at that tree because thorns were a God-declared outcome of that curse's unfolding (Gen 3:17–18). It had to be a naked and shameful death because the very first indicator that Adam and Eve had fallen under the potent power of sin was

> their shame-filled realization of their own nakedness. There was no other possible death for that "Seed" promised to Eve.[31]

One day, long ago, our first parents disobeyed God and ate of the tree in the middle of the garden. That brought a curse on them, on us, and everything around us. One day, long ago, our Savior obeyed God and gave His life on the middle cross of Jerusalem's killing field to remove the curse from us and everything around us. That's salvation, and one of the most significant accomplishments of Christ's death is not the most enchanting or exciting, but it is undoubtedly one of the most necessary and vital. Accomplishments don't get much bigger than this!

"Let the redeemed of the LORD say so, whom he has redeemed from trouble" (Ps 107:2). "I will give to the LORD the thanks due to his righteousness, and I will sing praise to the name of the LORD, the Most High" (Ps 7:17).

I will sing of my Redeemer,
And His wondrous love to me;
On the cruel cross He suffered,
From the curse to set me free.

I will tell the wondrous story,
How my lost estate to save,
In His boundless love and mercy,
He the ransom freely gave.

Sing, oh sing, of my Redeemer,
With His blood, He purchased me.
On the cross, He sealed my pardon,
Paid the debt, and made me free.

—P. P. Bliss (1838–1876)

Chapter 3

Jesus Assumed the Weight of Our Sin

John the Baptist, Paul the Apostle, and John the Apostle, three heavyweights of the New Testament, all testify that the world may have many religions, but it still has only one Savior—Jesus.

The Weight of the World's Sin
Jesus Carried the Weight of All Past Sin
Examples of Despots Whose Sin Jesus Bore on the Cross
Jesus Paid it All, All to Him I Owe

The human mind is incapable of fully appreciating what it means that Jesus bore the weight of the world's sin. Jesus took upon himself and within himself the full load of my sin and your sin, plus the full weight of all humanity's sin. Not just one of our sins, but all of them, every one. None is tucked away so secretly in a dark corner of your life that the light of the gospel cannot shine upon it. Jesus died for that sin.

When we say Jesus died for the sins of the world, we are speaking about planet Earth. According to NASA, Earth's mass is 5.9722×1024 kilograms, or around 13.1 septillion (13,100,000,000,000,000,000,000) pounds. But when we say Jesus died for the sins of the world, we are not talking about the weight of the Earth. We are talking about the weight of sin. On the cross that Friday, Jesus shouldered the weight of sin for everyone living in Africa, Asia, Australia, Europe, North America, South America, and even Antarctica. He bore the sin of everyone in the Northern Hemisphere and everyone in the

Southern Hemisphere, everyone from the East and everyone from the West. Every sin of every person. But not just every person living today, every person who has ever lived in every era of history, and every sin of every person who ever will live in eons to come. All of it, every sin, was loaded onto Jesus by God the Father while the Son was being crucified. This is ne'er impossible to grasp, so let's explore further what dying for the sin of the whole world means. It's a bit mind-blowing.

THE WEIGHT OF THE WORLD'S SIN

What is the world like that we live in? Is life like a ride in a theme park? Is our world the most idyllic place since the Garden of Eden? Or is it tinged with a few shady people living in dark corners? Actually, neither of these describes the twenty-first-century world. We live in a world where a woman stops at a red light and is carjacked. We live in a world where a little girl is killed in her bedroom by a stray bullet from rival gangs shooting it out in the street. We live in a world where a teenage driver runs down a man on a bicycle, killing the man while laughing about it. We live in a world where each scenario I just presented is real and has recently been in the news. We live in a violent, chaotic world where evil doesn't occasionally raise its ugly head; today, evil constantly holds its head high.

On December 16, 2014, gunmen affiliated with the terrorist organization Tehrik-i-Taliban barged into the Army Public School in Pakistan's Peshawar city and opened fire on students and staff of the school. The result was the death of 141 people, including 132 schoolchildren between the ages of eight and eighteen. That's the world we live in.

The militant group Al-Shabaab carried out one of the deadliest terrorist attacks in Kenya when terrorists stormed into the Garissa University College in Garissa on April 2, 2015. The terrorists took over 700 students hostage, freeing the Muslims and killing 148 of those who identified themselves as Christians. That's the world we live in.

A three-day-long siege at the Beslan School starting on September 1, 2004, was initiated by armed Islamic Groups. This involved the imprisonment of 1,100 people, including 777 children, as hostages. On the third day, Russian forces stormed the school building with the use of incendiary rockets, tanks, and other heavy weapons, killing 330 hostages, including 186 children. That's the world we live in.

On the morning of October 7, 2023, heavily armed Hamas terrorists breached the fences separating Israel and Gaza and entered southern Israel. At least 1,400 people were slaughtered, most of them civilians, including children, according to Israeli officials. The subsequent war to root out Hamas in Gaza took thousands of Palestinian lives. That's the world we live in.

Russians were attending a Friday night concert on March 23, 2024, at the Crocus City Hall when ISIS terrorists attacked the event. When the shooting stopped, 180 people were injured, and 139 lay dead. This has not been the first such attack in Moscow. That's the world we live in.

As a young boy, my father would take us to the Butler County Fair every year. Butler County was the next county over from Beaver County, Pennsylvania, where I grew up. On July 13, 2024, at that same fairgrounds, an assassin shot out the top of President Donald J. Trump's right ear, narrowly missing the president's head. Had the bullet been an inch more to the right, the President would have been mortally wounded. That's the world we live in.

Sad to say, these are not anecdotal incidents. These are actual daily occurrences. This is what our world has become. Life is no longer considered precious. God is no longer respected. We have never been closer to the well-deserved and inevitable judgment of God.

The weight of the world's sin is heavy. It is unimaginable. It is why Jesus went to Calvary and died on the cross. Over 63,000,000 abortions have occurred in the U.S. since the Roe v. Wade decision in 1973. Today, an average of over 600,000 babies a year are killed in America alone. That's the equivalent of killing the entire city of Memphis, Tennessee, Baltimore, Maryland, or Milwaukee, Wisconsin, every year. These lives are taken by the "choice" of the mother and her doctor. We are no better than the Canaanites, the Amalekites, or the Ammonites of biblical days. That's the world we live in.

Man's inhumanity to man

Only a fool would deny there is something instinctively and inherently wrong with human beings. We are not all good at heart. We are sick people, sinful people, and violent people. Of course, there is a fantastic amount of humanitarianism in the world, thank God, and it predominantly comes from the Christian religion. Wells are dug in remote villages. Doctors risk their lives to treat those desperately in need of medical attention in dangerous places. Houses are built for veterans who have lost their limbs during a war. Food banks feed people experiencing poverty. Orphanages are built to care for the parentless. There's a lot of good in the world.

Nevertheless, this does not discount the fact that people can be ruthless and cruel. They can savagely kill an old couple living alone just to steal their meager belongings. They can bully online those they see as weak or socially unacceptable. They can abuse a child to feed their sick sexual desires. The list goes on, but we need not say more. Our experiences in everyday life confirm the fact that men and women are sinful. But our experience is corroborated by the Bible. King David was correct when he said:

> The fool says in his heart, 'There is no God.' They are corrupt, they do abominable deeds; there is none who does good. The LORD looks down from heaven on the children of man, to see if there are any who understand, who seek after God. They have all turned aside; together they have become corrupt; there is none who does good, not even one" (Ps 14:1–3).

The Apostle John was also right when he wrote, "The whole world lies in the power of the evil one" (1 John 5:19). But it was the Apostle Paul who gave what amounts to the most succinct, yet most complete legal indictment describing God's view of humankind, even "good" men and women.

Paul's indictment against humanity

Romans is Paul's most theological letter. It's his reasoned case demonstrating the need for our salvation. The problem, as Paul states, is that God is righteous, and we are unrighteous. Unless that disparity is resolved, we can never live with a holy God in his eternal home, heaven. Think of "Pigpen" knocking on Lucy's door and wanting to come in, or the dog leaving muddy tracks on your beautiful kitchen floor. Clean and unclean just don't mix.

The purpose of the epistle to the Romans is to prove three truths that Paul views as essential to our salvation. First, all humanity has sinned against God and must pay a steep penalty for that sin (Rom 3:23; 6:23a). Second, the only way to have our sin debt paid is not through our works but through faith in Jesus' work at Calvary (Rom 6:23 b). And, third, we live our new life in Christ the same way we obtained it—through faith (Rom 1:17; 5:1–2; 12:1–2; 16:26).

According to the dictionary, an indictment is "a formal written statement framed by a prosecuting authority and found by a jury charging a person with an offense." When more than one offense is included in an indictment, the offenses are listed as separate counts.

In Romans 3:11–18, the rabbi-turned-preacher laid out God's case against sinful humanity. He indicted humankind with no fewer than fourteen counts. This is the most definitive biblical accounting of the sinfulness of men and women since the days of Adam and Eve.

Any reasonable person would have to admit that this list is impressive. It's also depressing because it truly reflects who we really are.

Table 1: The Fourteen-Count Indictment Against Humanity in Romans 3

Paul's Indictment Against Humanity	*Verse*	*Supporting Scriptures*
"None is righteous, no, not one."	v. 11	Gen 6:5; Pss 52:3; 143:2
"No one understands."	v. 11	Pss 14:2; 49:20; 82:5; Jer 5:22
"No one seeks for God."	v. 11	Isa 9:13; 31:1; Hos 7:10; Zeph 1:6
"All have turned aside."	v. 12	Isa 59:8; Pss 14:3; 53:4
"They have become worthless."	v. 12	2 Sam 23:6; Jer 2:5; Nah 1:11
"No one does good, not even one."	v. 12	Pss 14:1, 3; 53:1, 3; Eccl 7:20
"Their throat is an open grave."	v. 13	Ps 5:9; Prov 20:17; Nah 1:14
"They use their tongues to deceive."	v. 13	Pss 5:6; 120:3; Prov 12:5; 14:25
"Venom of asps is under their lips."	v. 14	Deut 32:33; Ps 14:3
"Their mouth is full of curses."	v. 14	Pss 10:7; 59:12–13; 109:18
"Their feet are swift to shed blood."	v. 15	Prov 1:16; Isa 59:7
"Their paths are ruin and misery."	v. 16	Pss 73:18; 146:9; Isa 59:7–8
"The way of peace they have not known."	v. 17	Pss 28:3; 35:20; 120:6; Isa 59:8
"There is no fear of God."	v. 18	Job 4:6; 15:4; Pss 36:1; 55:19

Sin is a reality we must admit

Before we can examine the weight of the world's sin, we must be willing to admit that the world's sin is real and that it is hefty. The Apostle Paul and others have well established this. Men and women have rejected God and all he has provided for us, including his mercy, grace, peace, and love. Our foolishness could not have been greater. However, we can be thankful that "Where sin multiplied, grace multiplied even more" (Rom 5:20 CSB).

Heavy though the world's sin is, there is only one person capable of bearing it, atoning for it, paying the penalty for it. Only Jesus, the Son of God, was capable of holding up under the weight of the sin of the world.

How are we to understand how much weight from sin was borne by Jesus at Calvary? Let's see.

JESUS CARRIED THE WEIGHT OF ALL SIN, PAST, PRESENT, AND FUTURE

In Greek mythology, Atlas was a leader of the Titanes (Titans) in their war against Zeus. After their defeat, he was condemned to carry the heavens upon his shoulders. This is why he is often depicted as bearing a globe. In reality, that depiction should have been reserved for Jesus of Nazareth as he carried the weight of the world's sin on his shoulders.

In this chapter, we examine the extent of the sin for which Jesus was crucified. To understand this correctly and completely, we must define the word "extent." William Greenough Thayer Shedd, better known as W. G. T. Shedd, was an American Calvinist and one of the most notable systematic theologians of the American Presbyterian Church, as evidenced in his comprehensive work, *Dogmatic Theology* (3 vols., 1888–1894). Dr. Shedd provides an excellent analysis of the word "extent" relative to Christ's atonement.[32]

Shedd notes that the word "extent" is used with two meanings. Passively, it means "value," for instance, the extent of one's holdings, such as property or a financial portfolio. Actively, it refers to "the act of extending." According to this distinction, when speaking of Christ's atonement at Calvary, passively it relates to its value, which is sufficient to satisfy God's righteous demands against the entire world's sin, and actively it refers to the application of that value to those who by faith trust Christ as their Savior. We must investigate further.

Jesus died for the sin of the world

I see this as a useful distinction. In the passive sense, the atonement is unlimited and available to all, but in the active sense, it is limited to the elect, to people of faith. Here, we examine only the extent of Christ's atonement passively and note that Jesus died for the sin of all humanity. Convincing Scriptures that God has a heart to provide salvation for everyone follow.

- John 3:16–18, "For God so loved the world, that he gave his only Son, that whoever believes in him should not perish but have eternal life. For God did not send his Son into the world to condemn the world, but in order that the world might be saved through him. Whoever believes in him is not condemned, but whoever does not believe is condemned already, because he has not believed in the name of the only Son of God."

- 1 Corinthians 2:14–15, "For the love of Christ controls us, because we have concluded this: that one has died for all, therefore all have died, and he died for all."
- 1 Timothy 2:3–6, "This is good, and it is pleasing in the sight of God our Savior, who desires all people to be saved and to come to the knowledge of the truth. For there is one God, and there is one mediator between God and men, the man Christ Jesus, who gave himself as a ransom for all."
- 1 John 2:2, "He [Jesus] is the propitiation for our sins, and not for ours only but also for the sins of the whole world."

These verses all indicate that the death of the Savior on the cross was sufficient to cover the sins of all humanity, over all the ages of time—every sin, every person, every millennium.

Jesus is the Savior of the world

As a result, the Bible says that Jesus is the Savior of the whole world. Again, notice the biblical evidence.

- John 1:29, "The next day he [John the Baptist] saw Jesus coming toward him, and said, 'Behold, the Lamb of God, who takes away the sin of the world!"
- 1 Timothy 4:10, "For to this end we toil and strive because we have our hope set on the living God, who is the Savior of all people, especially of those who believe." [passive and active atonement].
- 1 John 4:14, "We have seen and testify that the Father has sent his Son to be the Savior of the world."

John the Baptist, Paul the Apostle, and John the Apostle, three heavyweights of the New Testament, all testify that the world may have many religions, but it has only one Savior—Jesus.

Jesus blood must be applied to be effective

While it is true that Jesus carried the weight of the world's sin at the cross, it is also true that the atonement he made is provisional. It must be applied, not just understood. The lamb was slain. The blood was gathered. But until the Jews applied it to their door, it was of no value to them. Jesus' blood flowed freely at Golgotha, but unless it is applied to our lives, it is of no value to us.

This truth was foreshadowed by that fateful Passover night in Egypt. "Then they shall take some of the blood and put it on the two doorposts and the lintel of the houses. For I will pass through the land of Egypt that night, and I will strike all the firstborn. I will execute judgments: I am the LORD. The blood shall be a sign for you. And when I see the blood, I will pass over you" (Exod 12:7–13).

As I understand the atonement, no one is excluded from the payment Jesus made on the cross for sin, but not all are redeemed by that payment either. Only those who actively believe with the kind of faith that saves find Jesus' blood of value to them. Jesus' blood is sufficient for all, but efficient only for those who trust him as Savior.

Jesus died for all sin, of all time

Mentioned above is that Jesus not only carried the sin of all men and women living today, but the sin of everyone who lived in the past as well. By his atoning work, the blood of the Lord Jesus covered the sin of all the pre-cross Old Testament saints. So, the sin of Adam and Eve was borne by Jesus at the cross, just as was the sin of Peter and James, the sin of young and old, male and female, from the distant past to the distant future. All sin, of all people, throughout all time, was borne by Jesus at Calvary. He carried the weight of every sin, by everyone, throughout every generation.

While the sin of pre-cross saints was temporarily covered by the blood of animal sacrifices (Gen 3:21; Lev 17:11), the blood of animals could never fully atone for their sin (Heb 10:4). It was not until the perfect sacrifice, the ultimate sacrifice, the sacrifice of the innocent Son of God, that their sin was dealt with in a final and permanent way.

He took my sins and my sorrows,
He made them His very own;
He bore the burden to Calvary,
And suffered and died alone.

—CHARLES H. GABRIEL (1856–1932)

Hebrews 10:11–14 reminds us:

> And every priest stands daily at his service, offering repeatedly the same sacrifices, which can never take away sins. But when Christ had offered for all time a single sacrifice for sins, he sat down at the right hand of God, waiting from that time until his enemies should be made a footstool for his feet. For by a single offering, he has perfected for all time those who are being sanctified.

Every person, every sin, from every era of time—past, present, and future—every man, every woman, every race, every language, everyone who has ever lived or will live, Jesus took their sin upon himself at Golgotha. He not only took every sin, but also took all the sins. Every sin, not just the big ones or little ones, but every sin from the whole world was placed on Jesus that Friday in Jerusalem.

Exploring more deeply the weight of the sin that Jesus carried at Calvary

It's difficult for us to wrap our minds around the extent of the weight placed on Jesus on that fateful day at Calvary's Cross. So, let's think about a hypothetical example and dig deeper into what that means. Take John Doe. John is a 60-year-old sinner. Let's say the average person sins a dozen times a day. That's undoubtedly an extremely low number, but we'll go with it for John. If John sinned twelve times a day (bitterness, jealousy, cheating, stealing, adultery, etc.), it means that during his lifetime, John would have sinned 262,800 times. Jesus would have borne all 262,800 of John's sins at Calvary and paid the penalty for each of them.

Nevertheless, the current 2026 world population is believed to be 8,300,678,396. When you add you and me, plus everybody else alive today, to John's equation, the number of global daily sins against the holy God is 99,608,140,752. That's a gigantic number. An incomprehensible number.

However, and you need to follow this carefully, if there have been about 117 billion people that ever lived (95 billion of them living before 1900, having an average life expectancy of 30 years, 5 billion living from 1900–1950, with an average life expectancy of 45 years, and 8.3 billion living now, with a global average life expectancy of 73 years), then with an average of 12 sins a day, Jesus would carryroughly 25.19 quadrillion (that 25.19,000,000,000,000,000) sins while dying on the cross. Although we are not dealing with the physical weight of sin here, if we were and if each sin weighed a measly ounce, the total weight would be just over 995,000,000,000,000 pounds, or 497,500,000,000 tons. That's the equivalent of over 165,000,000 Great Pyramids of Egypt or more than 10,000,000 Great Walls of China.

The average weight of a casket is 175 pounds, which means that if Jesus died today and were buried in a casket, the physical weight of the sins Jesus bore at Calvary would equal 20,475,000,000,000 caskets. That's enough for everybody to be buried 691 times, each with a different casket.

If every sin cost just a penny, the world's sin would cost almost $1,170,000,000,000,000 USD. The global GDP last year was $117,165,000,000 USD. And yet, while the cost for our sin was high, the benefits of Christ's death are free to us. Now, that's amazing grace!

Now you're beginning to get the picture. The number of every sin, of all people in the world, throughout all the years of history and those yet to come, is indescribably large and unquestionable, unfathomable, and incomprehensible. And yet, Jesus bore every one of them that Friday on Calvary's Cross.

Stop. Read no further. Think for a moment.

Allow time for your mind to absorb the meaning of this. Concentrate on the fact that during those hours at Calvary, at the very hour when Passover lambs were being sacrificed, Jesus was being sacrificed to atone for the sin of the entire world. He was shouldering every sin, from the first by Adam and Eve until you and me now, and beyond into the future. All the sin of all time is laser-focused on the Savior at a single moment in time.

If you think I am over-emphasizing this, I am. I do it purposefully. We often acknowledge that Jesus died for the sin of the world and move on. But I'd like you to take a minute and contemplate this. All sin. From all people. Throughout all time. That's one of the things that made the Calvary event so difficult. I believe Jesus experienced more emotional and spiritual pain than he did physical pain on that Sabbath Friday. The crushing weight of the world's sin must have been dreadful.

I stand amazed in the presence
Of Jesus the Nazarene,
And wonder how He could love me,
A sinner condemned, unclean.

He took my sins and my sorrows,
He made them His very own;
He bore the burden to Calv'ry,
And suffered, and died alone.

When with the ransomed in glory
His face I at last shall see,
'Twill be my joy through the ages
To sing of His love for me.

—Charles H. Gabriel (1856–1932)

In the fifth chapter of Paul's letter to the Romans, he wrote, "Christ died for the ungodly. For one will scarcely die for a righteous person—though perhaps for a good person one would dare even to die—but God shows his love for us in that while we were still sinners, Christ died for us" (Rom 5:6–8).

Put that on the sticky side of your mind. "Christ died for the ungodly." Christ did not just die for the sin of Peter and John. He died for the sin of Caiaphas and Pilate as well. The blood of Christ covers the most despicable people on the planet. Child molesters, rapists, anarchists, those who scam the elderly, child traffickers, and worse, all are those for whom Christ's blood was shed, as well as pastors, Christian mothers, those who care for the elderly, run food shelters, or provide medical aid to those living in poverty. His blood covered the sin of the saintly old grandmother in a rocking chair with her Bible in her lap, but it also covered the vilest, most wicked people driving around in the middle of the night, looking for trouble.

Here are some ungodly people for whom Christ died. Don't let these names slide by you too quickly.

EXAMPLES OF DESPOTS WHOSE SIN JESUS BORE ON THE CROSS

Let your mind wander through the pages of history and consider the depths of sin for which Jesus paid the penalty when he died on the cross. The Bible says people are complete sinners, even though some do good in the world. Here are some examples of the most evil people who needed the blood of Jesus.

Nero, the cruel Roman emperor

Nero was Rome's fifth emperor from 54 to 68 AD. He burned entire cities and murdered thousands of people, including his aunt, stepsister, stepbrother, ex-wife, mother, and wife. Over time, Nero systematically murdered every member of his family. He poisoned, beheaded, burned, boiled, crucified, and impaled people at will. He raped too many women to count. The sins of this cruel, crazed emperor were many, but where Nero's sin abounded, God's grace abounded more (Rom 5:20).

The Mongolian general, Genghis Khan

Genghis Khan, the ruthless, vengeful, bloodthirsty general and ruler of the Mongolian Empire from 1206 to 1227 AD, killed numerous soldiers, civilians, and children by pouring molten metal into their eyes and ears. In one massacre alone, Genghis Khan killed 700,000 people. That's more than the combined population of these thirteen U.S. State Capitals: Carson City, NV, Jefferson City, MO, Augusta, ME, Pierre, SD, Juneau, AK, Concord, NH, Annapolis, MD, Olympia, WA, Charleston, WV, Cheyenne, WY, Bismarck, ND, Santa Fe, NM, and Lansing, MI. Although Genghis Khan's army killed somewhere between 20,000,000 and 60,000,000 people, where the sin of this exterminator abounded, God's grace abounded more (Rom 5:20).

Tamerlane, the decapitating despot

Tamerlane was the fourteenth-century conqueror of Western, Central, and South Asia. In India, he killed 200,000 civilians and soldiers who had already surrendered. Tamerlane was responsible for decapitating 20,000 citizens in Aleppo, Syria, 70,000 in Isfahan, Iran, 70,000 in Tikrit, Iraq, and 90,000 in Baghdad. Tamerlane killed 15,000,000 to 20,000,000 people, but even his sins could be covered by the death of Christ Jesus at Calvary, for where Tamerlane's sin abounded, God's grace abounded more (Rom 5:20).
As you can see from Table 2, the Bible describes us as sinful people with a wide variety of expressions. You cannot read what the Bible says about you and escape the conclusion that you are a sinner in need of a Savior. Fortunately for you and me, Romans 5:20 is entirely true. We should be grateful.

Table 2: Twenty-five New Testament Descriptions of Sin

The authors of the New Testament used various words and expressions to describe the sinful condition of humankind. Here is a sampling of those expressions.	
Humankind Descriptor	*Scriptures*
"Blinded"	John 12:40; 2 Cors 4:4; 1 John 2:11
"Corrupt"	Matt7:17–18; 1 Tim 6:5
"Dead in sin"	John 5:24; Rom 8:6; Col 2:13; 1 John 3:14
"Hard-hearted"	Eph 4:18
"Deceived"	Titus 3:3
"Defiled"	Titus 1:15; 2 Pet 2:20; Rev 22:11
"Disobedient"	Matt 7:23; Eph 2:3; Titus 3:3
"Carnal"	Rom 8:6, 13
"Spiritually stillborn"	Eph 2:1–2
"Deprived of the truth"	Rom 1:18, 25; 1 Tim 6:5
"Darkened"	Matt 6:23; John 3:19; Rom 1:21; 1 John 1:6–7
"The Enemy of God"	Jas 4:4
"Foolish"	Matt 7:26; Eph 5:15; Titus 3:3
"Self-sufficient"	Rev 3:17
"Malicious"	Titus 3:3
"Unrighteous"	1 Cor 6:9; Rev 22:11
"Enslaved to sin"	John 8:34; Rom 6:16–17, 20; Titus 3:3
"Self-lover"	2 Tim 3:2
"Proud"	Rom 1:30; 1 Tim 6:4; Jas 4:6; 2 Tim 3:4
"Hypocritical"	Matt 6:2, 5, 16; 23:13, 28
"Evil"	Matthew 6:22; 12:33–34; John 3:20
"Alienated from God"	Ephe 4:18
"Guided by the devil"	John 8:44; Eph 2:3
"Gone astray"	1 Pet 2:25
"Full of hate"	Titus 3:3

Here are more people covered by the blood of the Savior.

Adolf Hitler, evil personified

Adolf Hitler was the epitome of evil. Born in Austria, he rose to power as the leader of the Nazi Party and became Chancellor of Germany in 1933. World

War II was the result of the Nazi army's invasion of Poland in 1939. Hitler was responsible for the Holocaust, the torture and murder of six million Jewish people. Can anyone pay the unfathomable debt Hitler owes to have his sin forgiven? Only one—a Jew, the Lamb of God, only Jesus, for where Hitler's sin abounded, God's grace abounded even more (Rom 5:20).

The Cambodian Devil, Pol Pot

Pol Pot, leader of the revolutionary group Khmer Rouge in Cambodia, was educated at Cambodia's elite schools. While in Paris, he joined the French Communist Party and, upon returning to Cambodia, got involved in a Marxist-Leninist organization. This led to guerrilla warfare against the government. When Pol Pot rose to power, he forcibly relocated Cambodians to the countryside to work on collective farms. Pol Pot systematically killed between 1,500,000 and 2,000,000 Cambodians, approximately a quarter of the country's population. Can anybody do anything to atone for sin of the Cambodian Devil? Jesus can, for where Pol's sin abounded, God's grace abounded more (Rom 5:20).

> "Unless we see ourselves as deserving of the verdict that Pilate gave to Jesus, unless we see ourselves as worthy of hell, we will never understand the cross."—Erwin Lutzer

Vladimir Putin, a modern-day monster

Vladimir Putin amassed 150,000 Russian soldiers on the border with Ukraine. Although he repeatedly denied plans to attack Ukraine, on the morning of February 24, 2022, Russian missiles rained down on key Ukrainian cities, and Russian troops invaded the country. However, Putin miscalculated the will of the Ukrainian people and the skill of their army. Russian troops fought poorly. As young Russian soldiers died by the thousands, Putin conscripted ordinary people to fight in his war. At times, as many as 1,000 Russian soldiers were killed every day. The madman continued the war, killing hundreds of thousands of Ukrainians and his own Russian people, but where Putin's sin abounded, God's grace abounded more (Rom 5:20).

My Guy Paul, the playground bully

His name was Paul. You may not have heard of him, but Paul was a bully at North Star School in the 1950s. I should know; that was my elementary school. Paul was always picking fights on the playground. The only thing dirtier than his fighting technique was the constant stream of profanity spewing from his mouth. I don't know what happened to Paul. He hurt a lot of young boys on that playground. I hope life turned out better for him than elementary school did. His sin may not rank alongside those of Genghis Khan or Adolf Hitler, but it was sin nonetheless. Jesus died on the cross to make atonement, to provide a divine covering for our sin, great and small, for where the bully Paul's sin abounded, God's grace abounded more (Rom 5:20).

At that one precise moment, at that one single place in the universe, a place called Calvary, God the Father gathered up all the sins of humanity, past, present, and future, the sins of every man, woman, and child who has ever lived or ever will live, and laser-focused them all on Jesus. He died to pay for each one for where your sin and my sin abounded, God's grace abounded more (Rom 5:20).

JESUS PAID IT ALL, ALL TO HIM I OWE

Songwriter Phillip P. Bliss, who went by the initials P.P., was born in a log cabin in Hollywood. No, not that one. In Hollywood, Clearfield County, twenty-five miles north of Dubois, tucked away in the rugged hills of central Pennsylvania. He lived most of his life in Rome. No, not that one either. Rome, also tucked away in the rugged hills of Pennsylvania, was thirty-five miles southwest of Binghamton, NY. I love P.P. Bliss's simple lyrics, especially . . .

> Jesus paid it all,
> all to him I owe;
> sin had left a crimson stain,
> he washed it white as snow."

Very simple and to the point: Jesus' death atoned for our sin. When we stop and take the time to think about what happened that day at Calvary, our only response can be what Paul expressed in 2 Corinthians 9:15: "Thanks be to God for his inexpressible gift!"

On that special day, that Good Friday, the day of Preparation for the Sabbath and the Passover, on that day, Jesus carried the weight of our sin on his shoulders to the Roman killing field in Jerusalem. It was an eight-minute walk from the spot where Abraham went to sacrifice his son, Isaac, saying, "God will provide for himself the lamb for a burnt offering" (Gen 22:8).

God did provide a lamb himself, the Lamb of God, Jesus Christ, his one and only Son. The location where this happened is called 'The Place of the Skull." In Hebrew, it was Golgotha. In Latin, it was Calvary. But in heaven, it was "The Place of Obedience." It's where God the Father and God the Holy Spirit affirmed, because of the obedience of God the Son, that Satan's long war with God was over. Jesus not only carried our debt, our guilt, and our shame to the cross, but he took our place there and paid the penalty for all those things. Why? Because God does things right. God plans, God predestines, and God performs. Hanging on Calvary's Cross, Jesus carried the weight of the world's sin, and that was a significant accomplishment in the plan of God for our salvation. Accomplishments don't get much bigger than this!

I hear the Savior say,
Thy strength indeed is small;
Child of weakness, watch and pray,
Find in Me thine all in all.

And when before the throne
I stand in Him complete,
Jesus died my soul to save,
My lips shall still repeat

Jesus paid it all,
All to Him I owe;
Sin had left a crimson stain,
He washed it white as snow.

—Phillip P. Bliss (1838–1876)

Chapter 4

Jesus Endured Divine Wrath Against Our Sin

We must beware that we do not water down the words "God is Love" into "God is loving." Is God loving? Of course, but that's not enough. Does God love us? He does, but again, that's not enough. These three words, 'God is love,' do not refer to how God acts. They refer to who God is.

The anger of the gods is a popular theme in ancient literature. Homer's *Iliad*, the first and greatest Greek epic poem, begins with the theme of rage and murderous anger.

> Sing, Goddess, sing of the rage of Achilles, son of Peleus—that murderous anger (Greek: μένις; English: *mēnis*) which condemned Achaeans to countless agonies and threw many warrior souls deep into Hades, leaving their dead bodies carrion food for dogs and birds—all in fulfillment of the will of Zeus.[33]

In epic literature, the word *mēnis,* meaning "anger," is frequently seen from Homer's time (c. 750 BC) forward. The word designates wrath, both human and divine. It was vengeful wrath, petulant wrath, often appeased only by sacrifice. However, the wrath of the God of the Old and New Testaments is much different from that of the Greek epics.

Before we can appreciate what Jesus did at Calvary that appeased divine wrath, we must first understand the concept of God's wrath and why it is necessary. So, let's investigate.

THE RICH VOCABULARY OF WRATH

It may strike some as surprising that in the Hebrew text of the Old Testament, nouns for God's wrath appear some 375 times. Little wonder, then, that there are so many Hebrew words that in English refer to wrath, particularly God's wrath. Most people have given little thought to the wrath of God. In fact, in any discussion of justice, more is usually said about the love of God than the wrath of God. Still, God's wrath is a prominent feature in his relationship with sinful men and women.

The richness of the vocabulary is seen in the diversity of words that convey the meaning of "wrath."

- The most common word (Hebrew: אַף; English: *aph*) means "to snort" and is related to the nostrils of a horse vibrating and snorting when the animal is angry. Psalm 18:7,8 says, "Then the earth reeled and rocked; the foundations also of the mountains trembled and quaked, because he was *angry* (*chêmâh*). Smoke went up from his nostrils (*aph*), and devouring fire from his mouth; glowing coals flamed forth from him."
- Deuteronomy 29:23NKJV declares that when God overthrew Sodom, Gomorrah, Admah, and Zeboiim, "The whole land *is* brimstone, salt, and burning (Hebrew: שְׂרֵפָה; English: s^{e}*rêphâh*; it is not sown, nor does it bear, nor does any grass grow there, like the overthrow of Sodom and Gomorrah, Admah, and Zeboiim, which the Lord overthrew in His anger anger (*aph*) and his wrath (Hebrew: חֵמָה; English: *chêmâh*)." The word *chêmâh* refers to divine wrath at least eighty-five times. Its meaning is related to a root word that means "to be hot" or "to be ardent."
- Another Hebrew noun (קֶצֶף; English: *qetseph*) is usually related to a divine form of indignation, as in Isaiah 34:2, "The LORD is *enraged* against all the nations, and furious against all their host; he has devoted them to destruction"(see also Deut 29:28; 2 Chron32:26; Ps 38:1; Isa 60:10; Jer 10:10; Zech 1:15).

- This Hebrew word (Hebrew: חָרָה; English: *chârâh*) means "to burn" and in its noun form is translated as "anger" or "burning anger" (Judg 14:19). When YHWH (Jehovah or Yahweh) took note that his chosen people were a grumbling, ungrateful bunch, he said to Moses, "Let me alone, that my wrath (*aph*) may burn hot (*chârâh*) against them and I may consume them, in order that I may make a great nation of you" (Exod 32:10).
- In the Maschil of Asaph, the account of Egypt's continuing stubbornness in the face of God's unrelenting plagues is described. Perhaps Psalm 78:49 best illustrates the rich variety of Hebrew words in a single verse. "He [God] let loose on them his burning *anger* (Hebrew: אַף; English: *aph*), wrath (Hebrew: עֶבְרָה; English: *'ebrâh*), indignation (Hebrew: זַעַם; English: *za 'am*), and distress (Hebrew: צָרָה; English: *tsârâh*), a company of destroying angels."

  Then the psalmist sets apart three Hebrew words related to God's wrath.

- The word *'ebrâh* means a hot outburst of rage. Thirty times in the Old Testament, this noun *'ebrâh* is used as an expression of wrath, and five times the verb *'êber* connotes "to be angered." In most instances, the noun and verb imply divine wrath. For example, Isaiah 9:19 states, "Through the *wrath* (*'ebrâh*) of the LORD of hosts the land is scorched, and the people are like fuel for the fire" (see also Gen 49:5–7; Job 40:11; Ps 78:49; Isa 13:9; Lam 2:2; Ezek 21:31).
- The word *za 'am* likens God's holy indignation toward sin to someone who is frothing at the mouth in a rage.
- And while *tsârâh* is not directly used for God's anger or wrath, it does speak of his bringing affliction, adversity, and anguish upon the disobedient through divine anger.
- Finally, the verb (Hebrew: קָצַף; English: *qetseph*) and its related noun involve indignation as well as wrath and anger. The noun form reflects God's indignation, which is emotionally explosive and often destructive. "For the LORD is *enraged* against all the nations, and furious against all their host; he has devoted them to destruction" (Isa 34:2).

> "God's wrath is 'the holy revulsion of God's being against that which is the contradiction of his holiness'; it issues in 'a positive outgoing of the divine displeasure.'"—John Murray

You don't need to read Hebrew to note that the vocabulary of wrath is significant. Not many other concepts in the Bible are captured in such rich terminology. These eight Hebrew words demonstrate that the wrath of God is more prevalent than most realize and more intense than any of us can imagine. Don't miss this. God's wrath is mentioned twice as many times as God's love in the Bible. Yet, we know so little of this counterbalance to the love of God.

Why so many words for "wrath"?

What is the point of these many words meaning wrath? Why are they so numerous, and what are their distinctives? Good questions. God's wrath is multifaceted. It cannot be described entirely even by two or more words. For example, each of the following words differentiates either the intensity of God's wrath or the purpose for it.

The verb *chârâh* means to "burn" and appears to be more intense than the verb *qasap.* Its counterpart noun, *charon,* means "anger" or "burning anger." "Therefore the Lord was *angry* (Hebrew: אַף; English: *aph*) with Amaziah and sent to him a prophet, who said to him, 'Why have you sought the gods of a people who did not deliver their own people from your hand?'" (2 Chron 25:15).

The verb form of the noun *zaam* could mean either "curse" or "be angry." The noun, related to the concept of "blazing fire," is found twenty-one times related to God, and almost always appears as a term for the blazing wrath of YHWH. It is frequently translated as "indignation" (see Ps 78:49).

The word *rogez* usually means "disturbance" and less frequently "anger." Seven passages relate *rogez* to God's revelation of power. For example, in giving a command to destroy the fortresses of the obscene Canaanites, Isaiah 23:11 asserts that it was in his anger that God "shook the kingdoms."

Thirty times in the Old Testament, the noun *ebra* denotes "anger," "wrath," or an "expression of wrath," and five times the similar verb *abar* means "be angered." In most instances, the noun and verb refer to divine wrath. Isaiah 9:19 states, "Through the wrath of the LORD of hosts the land is burned up, and the people shall be as fuel for the fire; no man shall spare his brother." Both words are often combined with other words referring to anger.

With such rich and diverse Old Testament vocabulary describing God's wrath against sin and sinful people, perhaps we have never fully comprehended before how important wrath is to the character of God. We must be certain we know what it is. Let's look more closely.

Scottish theologian Donald Macleod defines God's anger as, "the deliberate, measured, judicious response of God to our collective revolt against his rule, and to the systemic injustice which marks human society."[34] You may not have ever conceived of God's wrath in this way before, but Macleod is spot on.

> There is a consistency about the wrath of God in the Old Testament. It is no capricious passion, but the stern reaction of the divine nature towards evil. It is aroused only and inevitably by sin. This may be thought of in general terms (Job 21:20; Jer 21:12; Ezek. 24:13), or it may be categorized more precisely as the shedding of blood (Ezek 16:38; 24:8).[35]

YHWH is not a whiny, jealous God who is angry at everybody and everything. He is a holy God who is furious at sin and the debilitating consequences of sin for the sinner. God's wrath is juxtaposed with our rebellion against his authority, and the damning effects that rebellion has brought upon us.

The New Testament words meaning "wrath"

Unlike the rich and varied vocabulary in the Old Testament, the New Testament word for "anger" or "wrath" (Greek: ὀργή; English: *orgḗ*) is found only thirty-six times, with a third of those in Paul's letter to the Romans. There, Paul describes God's salvation of those who deserve His wrath.

The New Testament writers use another word eighteen times for "wrath" or "anger" (Greek: θυμός; English: *thymós*). "Now the works of the flesh are evident: sexual immorality, impurity, sensuality, idolatry, sorcery, enmity, strife, jealousy, fits of anger (*thymós*), rivalries, dissensions, divisions, envy, drunkenness, orgies, and things like these. I warn you, as I warned you before, that those who do such things will not inherit the kingdom of God" (Gal 5:19–21). If you are known by the company you keep, anger keeps some pretty bad company.

In Ephesians 4:26, a third word (Greek: παροργισμῷ; English: *parorgismō*) for wrath is used. This is not a common word; it is used only in this form in the New Testament. This leaves *orgḗ* as the preferred New Testament word for "anger" and "wrath." In the Gospels, *orgḗ* is used ten times, whereas *thymós* is used only once.

With this in mind, remember that God's anger is always triggered by sin. God is not an angry God, *per se*. The Old Testament writers are clear that "the LORD, the LORD, [is] a God merciful and gracious (Ps 103:8; 116:4), slow to anger (Ps 145:8; Joel 2:13; Nah 1:3), and abounding in steadfast love (Exod 34:6–7; Num 14:8; Ps 17:7; 25:6), and faithfulness" (Deut 7:9; Ps 35:10; 36:92:1,2; Rom 3:3); "Give ear, O LORD, to my prayer; listen to my plea for grace" (Ps 86:6; see Jer 31:2; Zech 12:10). The attributes of God are always positive, but some are seen as more godlike than others. That doesn't negate the fact that YHWH is multi-faceted, good God.

THE PATIENCE OF GOD WITH OUR SIN

The Bible presents a fair and balanced view of God. He is neither a tyrant nor a patsy. He is not unforgiving nor unfair. He is not easily angered, but is extremely patient with us.

In the face of his need to be angry at sin and the sinner because of our sin, the Bible overwhelmingly indicates that God is not anger, but "God is love" (1 John 4:7–16). When God's anger is aroused, it is always after long periods of patience toward us, as Table 1 indicates.

Table 1: The Biblical Record that God is "Slow to Anger"

Scripture	*Record of God being "Slow to Anger"*
Exod 34:6	"The LORD, the LORD, a God merciful and gracious, *slow to anger*, and abounding in steadfast love and faithfulness.
Num 14:18	'The LORD is *slow to anger* and abounding in steadfast love, forgiving iniquity and transgression, but he will by no means clear the guilty.
Neh 9:17	"But you are a God ready to forgive, gracious and merciful, *slow to anger* and abounding in steadfast love."
Ps 86:15	"But you, O Lord, are a God merciful and gracious, *slow to anger* and abounding in steadfast love and faithfulness.
Ps 103:8	"The LORD is merciful and gracious, *slow to anger* and abounding in steadfast love."
Ps 145:8	"The LORD is gracious and merciful, *slow to anger* and abounding in steadfast love."
Joel 2:13	"Return to the LORD your God, for he is gracious and merciful, *slow to anger*, and abounding in steadfast love, and he relents over disaster.
Jonah 4:2	"I knew that you are a gracious God and merciful, *slow to anger* and abounding in steadfast love, and relenting from disaster."
Nah 1:3	"The LORD is *slow to anger* and great in power, and the LORD will by no means clear the guilty."

God's patience with us, his slowness to become angry with us, is because of his love for us. We must beware that we do not water down the words

"God is Love" into "God is loving." Is God loving? Of course, but that's not enough. Does God love us? He does, but again, that's not enough. These three words, "God is love," do not refer to how God acts. They refer to who God is.

> *God is love*] This is the third of S. John's great statements respecting the Nature of God: 'God is Spirit' (John 4:24); 'God is light' (1 John 1:5), and 'God is love'. See on 1 John 1:5. Here, as in the other cases, the predicate has no article, and expresses not a quality which He *possesses*, but one which embraces all that He *is*.[36]

God doesn't simply show Himself as loving; He doesn't just appear to be a loving God; he is love and he is God. Love is an indispensable quality of his character. So, while God may be obliged to display his wrath on sin, God is not, in essence, wrath. However, when he shows his love for us, it's because his fundamental nature is love. This love, however, does not negate wrath as it is also fundamental to his nature.

God's demonstration of his love

To say "God is love" is easy, but to understand it demands a demonstration. We know God only by what he shows us. We do not understand God in the abstract; we know him in the hard concrete of everyday life. So, what is the correspondence between God's love and his wrath?

> "Never was more meaning crowded into a few words than in this short sentence—*God is love.*"—Albert Barnes

Immediately following John's statement "God is love" are these words from the apostle: "In this the love of God was made manifest among us, that God sent his only Son into the world, so that we might live through him" (1 John 4:10).

God is not just love in essence; he is love in evidence. God showed his love to us. He validated it by sending his only Son into this world to die for us so we may live through him. The cross is the primary manifestation of God's love for us. The death of Jesus was not just an act of cruelty by the Romans. It was also an act of love by God himself. God's wrath was appeased by Christ's death, infused with his love. His love and his wrath are not simply balanced in God's nature. It is his love that appeases God's wrath. His love removes the "heat" of God's wrath. It satisfies and assuages the divine wrath.

HOW THEOLOGIANS SEE GOD'S WRATH

Theologians view God's wrath in very different ways. Some seek to explain away his wrath by separating it from his character. They understand divine wrath as an impersonal expression. C. H. Dodd, for example, understood the term the wrath of God "not to describe the attitude of God to man, but to describe an inevitable process of cause and effect in a moral universe."[37] A. T. Hanson said, "The wrath was not an emotion or attitude of God; it was simply a word for what happened to those who broke God's moral laws. It was, in fact, the 'principle of retribution in a moral universe.'"[38]

Dodd and Hanson's understandings are wholly wrong. You cannot say that God's anger is simply a moral reaction to sin. His wrath is not reactionary. Wrath is the quality of God's holiness against which the law of sin is broken. The Apostle Paul argued that the wrath of God was revealed (Rom 1:18), not a reaction to sin. God's wrath is not selective; it is "revealed from heaven against all ungodliness and unrighteousness of men, who by their unrighteousness suppress the truth" (v. 18).

Because God's wrath is directed against all sinful people, the Bible correctly says we are all, by our very nature, "children of wrath" (Eph 2:3). God's wrath comes upon "the sons of disobedience" [meaning every son and daughter of Adam] (Eph 5:6; Col 3:6). Also, God's wrath does not end with this age, for Paul speaks of "the wrath to come" (1 Thess 1:10).

P. T. Forsyth suggested that "To water down Paul's teaching on the wrath of God to a mere emotion and not an essential part of his character has serious consequences for our understanding of who God is." Forsyth stressed that this watered-down version of God "empties of meaning the wrath of God," and "reduces the holy law of his nature to a by-law he can suspend, or a habit he can break."[39]

Leon Morris adds, "Clearly Paul thought of God as implacably opposed to sin in every shape and form, and as exerting himself in opposition to it. To gloss over this is to manufacture a god who is not the God of the Bible."[40]

No one likes to speak of wrath, especially God's wrath. In church, we sing of God's love, but rarely of God's wrath. Nevertheless, these are equally rooted in the essence of who God is.

WHY DID GOD'S WRATH NEED TO BE APPEASED?

In their book, *The Last Week: A Day-by-Day Account of Jesus's Final Week in Jerusalem,* Marcus Borg and John Dominic Crossan ask, "Did Good Friday have to happen? As divine necessity? No. As human inevitability? Virtually. Good Friday is the result of the collision between the passion of Jesus and the domination systems of his time."[41]

This is a human explanation of a divine event. What these authors are claiming is that Jesus' death at Calvary was a terrible human tragedy, entirely avoidable, with no theological or salvational impact. Those who trust the reliability of the New Testament find this position untenable and unsupportable. I also think it is considerably naïve.

An Artist's Conception of
The Wrath of God in Art

If divine wrath against sin and the sinner is as much a part of God's character as divine holiness is, then his wrath cannot merely be swept under the cosmic rug. It must be appeased somehow, or we will all feel the devastating and damning effects of that wrath, and deservedly so. The Gospel narratives, as well as Apostles Paul and Peter, teach that appeasement of God's wrath came when Jesus endured this divine wrath on the cross while paying the penalty for our sin. A holy God has every right to be angry when he has provided so abundantly for his children and, in return, we have behaved so badly toward him and each other. While God's love motivated him to find a way to deliver sinners from sin's ruin, his holiness determined he must accomplish this deliverance himself by penal satisfaction (John 3:16; Rom 3:25–26). God would appease his wrath himself.

HOW GOD BALANCED JUSTICE WITH MERCY

Here is the million-dollar question: "How could an infinitely holy God deal with our sin in an infinitely just way, and still satisfy his infinite holiness?" Only one way—the God way. Motivated by his infinite love for us, God the Father sent God the Son to the cross to be the "propitiation for our sins, and not for ours only but also for the sins of the whole world" (1 John 2:2; 4:10).

"The propitiation for our sins." This concept is entirely foreign to our thinking, so let's spend some time getting a handle on it.

> "Love and justice coexist in God. If there were no divine wrath against sin, then God's love would be deficient of moral content and the cross would become an irrational exhibition of cruelty and injustice."—Samuele Bacchiocchi

What does propitiation mean?

The meaning of "propitiation" (Greek: ἱλαστήριον; English: *hilastērion*) is to make amends, to appease the wrath of an offended party, or to atone for a wrong.[42] God always acts in concert with his character and nature; he cannot deny himself (2 Tim 3:13). God could not merely set us free from the penalty of our sin; he had to deal with that sin completely and terminally. This he did at the cross when Jesus endured the full weight of God's wrath against our sin and the human rebellion that precipitated that wrath on us.

Propitiating the wrath of God and regaining God's favor after we so grievously sinned against him required more than the ethical teachings of Jesus the Nazarene. It required the death of a perfect sacrifice. "When Paul tells us that God sent forth Jesus to be a propitiation 'by his blood,' his point is that what quenched God's wrath and redeemed us from death was not Jesus' life or teaching, nor his moral perfection nor his fidelity to the Father, as such, but the shedding of his blood in death."[43]

The Apostle Paul's explanation of Jesus enduring our sin and its consequences is found in Romans 3:21–26.

> But now the righteousness of God has been manifested apart from the law, for all have sinned and fall short of the glory of God, and are justified by his grace as a gift, through the redemption that is in Christ Jesus, whom God put forward as a propitiation by his blood, to be received by faith. This was to show God's righteousness, so that he might be just and the justifier of the one who has faith in Jesus.

Expressions like "manifested apart from the law" and "justified by his grace as a gift" clearly show that Paul understood how the wrath of God toward us was not appeased from within us. It was God the Son who appeased divine wrath—Jesus and no one else, at the cross and nowhere else.

Is Christianity a "Slaughterhouse Religion"?

But why this plan? Why the cross? Why the blood? Doesn't this resonate with the criticism that Christianity is a "bloody religion"? Twentieth-century liberal theologian and pastor of the Riverside Church in New York City, Harry Emerson Fosdick (1878–1969), believed that the doctrine of the atonement, where "Jesus suffered as a substitute for us" because of our sins, is a "pre-civilized barbarity."[44]

I once heard an interview with Brian McLaren, the twenty-first-century leader of the short-lived emerging church movement, in which he questioned the idea that a loving God would send his Son to die for us. McLaren said, "The cross is almost a distraction and false advertising for God."[45] One definition of advertising is, "A form of communication used to persuade an audience to take some action." In one sense, that does define the gospel, but McLaren says that the cross represents false advertising, i.e., a false gospel. Dangerous words, indeed.

So why did God choose to send his son to the cross and stain that cross with his blood? That question needs some perspective.

Blood sacrifices in antiquity

Pagan gods were thirsty for blood sacrifices. People in antiquity, as well as isolated peoples today, believed that appeasing their gods required sacrificing an animal, and sometimes a human. The Celts practiced human sacrifice as part of their religious rituals, largely to appease their gods Teutates, Esus, and Taranis. Human ritual killing to gain the gods' favor was also practiced by the Carthaginians, Incas, Etruscans, Hawaiians, Chinese, Aztecs, and Mesopotamians, among many others, worldwide.

The God of Israel also demanded sacrifice. There was a vast difference, however, between YHWH and the pagan gods. YHWH forbade human sacrifice. "You shall not worship the LORD your God in that way, for every abominable thing that the LORD hates they have done for their gods, for they even burn their sons and their daughters in the fire to their gods" (Deut 12:31).

The God of Israel viewed the practices of the people of Canaan as an abomination. He forbade the Israelites from practicing the barbaric practices of the pagans. "There shall not be found among you anyone who burns his son or his daughter as an offering" (Deut 18:10). Thus, while the God of Israel required blood sacrifices, only animal blood was to be shed.

But why? Why require a blood sacrifice at all? What was the meaning of such a sacrifice? These sacrifices appear useless until we see them in their larger context. The context gives a broader picture of the sacrifice of lambs, bulls, or goats. The big picture defines the purpose of Old Testament sacrifices in relation to the one sacrifice that effectively appeases God's wrath. The larger context focused on a place called Calvary. The Old Testament animal sacrifices foreshadowed Jesus' sacrifice on the cross. They were a type; Christ was the antitype.

The reason God required a blood sacrifice is that "the life of every creature is its blood: its blood is its life" (Lev 17:14), and "without the shedding of blood there is no forgiveness of sins" (Heb 9:22). The shedding of blood equates to the shedding of life.

The first instance of this principle occurred in the Garden of Eden. The garden had the perfect ecosystem, temperature, and living environment. Everything was peaceful and idyllic. One day, however, the stillness of the serene air was pierced with the shrill shrieks of an animal whose life was taken by God for the benefit of the first man and woman. "And the LORD God made for Adam and for his wife garments of skins and clothed them" (Gen 3:21). Those skins did not magically appear; an animal died so Adam and Eve's sin and shame could be temporarily covered.

That's the meaning of the word "atonement." It's a covering of our sin and shame. God required animal sacrifices to provide a temporary covering for sin. But they also foreshadowed the ultimate sacrifice, the perfect sacrifice, the complete sacrifice of Jesus Christ on Calvary's Cross (Lev 4:35, 5:10) where God permanently covered our sin.

The inadequacy of animal sacrifices

Sacrifice meant death. In the blood, there was life. To shed blood meant exchanging life for death. This makes blood sacrifice the ultimate form of sacrifice, whether it is animal or human. There were no Mulligans with a blood sacrifice. No do-overs when you take life as a sacrifice.

God established the grand sacrificial system of the Jews to appease his justified and well-deserved wrath. But since the sacrifice of animals' blood was not a "perfect" sacrifice, not as precious as the sacrifice of human blood, for the sin of humankind to be covered and the wrath of God to be appeased, there was no sacrifice available throughout Old Testament history that was perfect, sinless, or human, able to meet the divine requirement to appease divine wrath against sin.

The writer of Hebrews was very clear about this. "For it is impossible for the blood of bulls and goats to take away sins" (Heb 10:4). "For if the blood of goats and bulls, and the sprinkling of defiled persons with the ashes of a heifer, sanctify for the purification of the flesh, how much more will the blood of Christ, who through the eternal Spirit offered himself without blemish to God, purify our conscience from dead works to serve the living God" (Heb 9:13–14). Hebrews 10:5 informs us that this is why Jesus Christ came into the world—to provide what bulls and goats could not—a perfect, effective, complete, acceptable, and enduring sacrifice to appease God's wrath permanently and to provide us with a Savior from our sin.

What could appease divine wrath?

The wrath of God could only be appeased by a sacrifice acceptable to him and sufficient to dissuade him from unleashing his warranted wrath on us because we sinned against him. The only sufficient sacrifice for the perfect God would be a perfect sacrifice. However, where would such a sacrifice be found? Surely not among the descendants of Adam. We are all cursed by sin just as Adam was. Only God possessed the perfection capable of appeasing his wrath.

So, in answer to the question, "Where on Earth could we find a perfect sacrifice?" the answer is "Nowhere. You won't find one." That's why God the Son came to Earth. That's why God himself had to become that sacrifice. That's why Jesus was born of a virgin, lived a sinless life, and offered himself as the perfect sacrifice for our sin. Jesus came, not to heal, feed, or help—those were the by-products of his life—but he came to Earth to give his life to cover your sin and mine.

Jesus said, "I am the good shepherd. The good shepherd lays down his life for the sheep." He said, "I lay down my life for the sheep." Jesus said, "I lay down my life that I may take it up again. No one takes it from me, but I lay it down of my own accord" (John 10:11, 15, 17). In his epistle, John affirmed, "He [Jesus] laid down his life for us" (1 John 3:16). That's the purpose of Jesus' incarnation, his crucifixion, and his resurrection. To offer himself as the only sacrifice acceptable to a holy God.

Jesus is perfect, and God could use only the perfect sacrifice. Jesus was it. He was the only option. There was no Plan B. Jesus alone could appease the wrath of God.

"For even the Son of Man came not to be served but to serve, and to give his life as a ransom for many" (Mark 10:45). At Calvary, Jesus bled and died. At Calvary, the Father's wrath was appeased. At Calvary, atonement was made. At Calvary, everything changed.

Jesus' sacrificial and salvational death on the cross appeased God's wrath by satisfying the demands of divine holiness and justice against us and our sin (1 John 2:2; 4:10; Rom 3:25–26).

God is a God of perfect symmetry. He is not a one-sided deity like many Greek and Roman gods. He is just, but he is fair. He is angry but he is love. He hates sin, but loves the sinner. His wrath is justified, yet he balances it with his mercy. He knows blood needs to be shed, but instead of the blood of those who deserve to die, he sent his Son to die in our place. Accomplishments don't get much bigger than this!

Read the amazing truth in what the hymn-writer Robert Lowrey penned:

What can wash away my sin?
Nothing but the blood of Jesus
What can make me whole again?
Nothing but the blood of Jesus

For my pardon this I see
Nothing but the blood of Jesus
For my cleansing this my plea
Nothing but the blood of Jesus.

Nothing can for sin atone
Nothing but the blood of Jesus
Naught of good that I have done
Nothing but the blood of Jesus

Oh precious is the flow
That makes me white as snow
No other fount I know
Nothing but the blood of Jesus.

—Robert Lowrey (1826–1899)

Chapter 5

Jesus Exchanged Our Sin for His Righteousness

There was a simple but very profound exchange at Golgotha. God credited Jesus with our sinfulness so that he could credit us with Christ's righteousness. We unmistakably got the better of that deal.

Important Exchanges in History
Paul's Methodical Case for Humankind's Universal Sin
The Meaning of the Greek Word *Logizomai*
We Were There When They Crucified My Lord?

According to the dictionary, the word "exchange" means "the act of giving one thing in return for another," with a secondary definition of "the act or process of substituting one thing for another." In the case of Calvary, both of these definitions are appropriate.

We engage in exchanges all the time. You order something online. When it arrives, you note that it is the wrong size or the wrong color. You look for the company's exchange policy, follow it, and in no time at all, you have the size and color you desire.

Almost every transaction involving money is nothing but an exchange of things thought to be of equal value. Once, I traded in two older cars for a pre-owned Ford F-150 pickup. It was an even exchange because they were of equal value. You receive a Caramel Macchiato latte in exchange for a $5 bill.

You perceive this to be a commodities exchange of equal value (although with the latte, I never understood why).

While in college, you enroll in a program that enables you to live in Italy for a semester while your Italian counterpart studies in the U.S. In doing this, both of you are referred to as "exchange students."

We are well-versed in the exchange process. One thing swapped for another. Some exchanges, however, are much more earth-shaking than others.

IMPORTANT EXCHANGES IN HISTORY

During the Six-Day War in 1967 between the State of Israel and its surrounding Arab neighbors, fifteen Israeli Defense Forces (IDF) soldiers were captured by Arab armed forces. Eleven of these were captured in Egypt, one in Syria, two in Iraq, and one in Lebanon. Prisoner-of-war exchanges began immediately after the conclusion of the hostilities on June 15, 1967, and ended seven months later on January 23, 1968.

Israeli Soldiers During the Six-Day War

In their POW exchanges with Syria, Israel returned 572 POWs for one Israeli pilot, the bodies of two other Israeli pilots, and one civilian who had been kidnapped and died in captivity. That's a ratio of 572 POWs to 1 live person and three dead bodies.[46] That was a significant exchange.

In the more recent war in Gaza, on a critical day for the Middle East, Hamas released the 20 living Israeli hostages it still held, and Israel released nearly 2,000 Palestinian prisoners under a breakthrough Gaza ceasefire deal. This, too, was a significant exchange.

Other significant exchanges

There have been other significant exchanges in history, two of which involved the United States. The Louisiana Purchase from France in 1803 added thirteen states in exchange for just $15 million—less than three cents per acre. This marked a significant exchange for the U.S.

In 1867, the United States purchased Alaska for $7.2 million, equivalent to approximately two cents per acre. The state encompasses 586,412 square miles or more than 375 million acres. Even at a cost of just $100 per acre, that would equate to more than $37 billion today. Another terrific exchange.

It was called "The Columbian Exchange." Christopher Columbus introduced horses, precious metals, European plants and animals (and sadly, disease), and culture to the New World. In exchange, he carried back to the Old World sugar, tobacco, chocolate, and potatoes. It was one of the most significant exchanges in the history of the West.

History's most significant exchange

Nevertheless, no exchange in history reaches the level of importance as the exchange on a dark Friday at a place called Calvary. There, Jesus exchanged places with you and me when he was crucified in our stead. This was the greatest exchange in history. It was the most glorious, most eternally significant exchange ever made.

"For our sake he [God the Father] made him [God the Son] to be sin who knew no sin, so that in him [God the Son] we might become the righteousness of God" (2 Cor 5:21).

Some other contemporary translations of this verse help illuminate Paul's meaning.

The Contemporary English Version of 2 Corinthians 5:21 reads: "Christ never sinned! But God treated him as a sinner so that Christ could make us acceptable to God."

The Message says, "God put the wrong on him who never did anything wrong, so we could be put right with God."

The Good News Translation, however, misses the point entirely when it says, "Christ was without sin, but for our sake God made him share our sin in order that in union with him we might share the righteousness of God." This translation is misleading at best. Jesus did not share our sin; He took it all upon Himself. At Calvary, we shed our sin, and he suffered for it.

> "He took the punishment we deserved. He took [the] violence and crucifixion of man and used it as the means to salvation. He triumphed over death through death. The ugly regretful moments of our lives are exchanged for His righteousness. This is the beauty of our God."—Brett McBride

The Apostle Paul was the primary theologian of the New Testament Church. God chose him for this role and specially prepared him as a rabbi before coming to faith in Christ (Acts 9).

Like Moses, the framer of Old Testament law, who authored approximately 24 percent of the Old Testament, Paul, the framer of New Testament grace, also authored approximately 24 percent of the New Testament. Paul was a letter writer, and his theological teachings were communicated through the letters he wrote to individuals and churches. His most theological letter was his epistle to the Romans.

Paul's Methodical Case For Humankind's Universal Sin

In his letter to the Roman believers, Paul meticulously built the case for the universality of human sin and our need for a Savior. He also maintained that the cure for human sin was faith in the atoning work of Jesus Christ at Calvary's Cross. See Chapter 3.

After demonstrating the depth of our depravity in the first three chapters, Paul begins in Romans 4 to show how to remove the penalty of sin. He used Father Abraham as an example of a man who had faith in God, and God credited righteousness to Abraham's eternal account because of that faith. Here's what the apostle wrote:

> What then shall we say was gained by Abraham, our forefather according to the flesh? For if works justified Abraham, he has something to boast about, but not before God. For what does the Scripture say? "Abraham believed God, and it was counted to him as righteousness." Now to the one who works, his wages are not counted as a gift but as his due. And to the one who does

> not work but believes in him who justifies the ungodly, his faith is counted as righteousness (Rom 4:1–5).

Like a prosecuting attorney, Paul has now meticulously laid out God's case against us (Rom 3) because of our disobedience and disregard for his will and his law. However, the apostle also outlined God's solution to the pollution of sin in our lives. The key is believing. Jesus died to save us. He did everything that was needed for us. The proper response to what he has done for us is to be broken because we sinned against God, to repent of our sin, to confess our sin to him, trusting him to save us. We accept that at Calvary, Jesus did all that the Father required to atone for our sin. Thus, Paul's methodical case for humankind's universal sin has a happy ending, if we only believe.

THE MEANING OF THE GREEK WORD LOGIZOMAI

The keyword for understanding Romans 4 is "counted" (Greek: λογίζομαι; English: *logízomai*). Paul used the word logizomai no less than fourteen times in Chapter 4 (vss. 3–6, 8–11, 22–24).The word *logízomai* was well known to the writers of the New Testament; it occurs forty-nine times in their writings.[47]

Logizomai is an accounting term. It means to account for, to credit, or reckon something as accurate or true. Paul used it three times in just three verses. By it, Paul meant to take something from one place and account for it in another place. It denotes transferring something from one person's account to another's.

In this case, God credited Abraham's faith as true righteousness. This process is called imputation. God takes one thing and imputes or "chalks it up" as something else. Abraham did not actually become righteous, but God treated him as if he were righteous because one day he would be.[48]

We all understand the concept of *logizomai,* even if we are not familiar with the word. For example, suppose you permitted your children to use your credit card. Suppose they went to the mall and bought some clothes using that card. At the end of the month, you would get a letter containing a statement of all the charges on your card. Their purchases accounted for the largest number on that statement. Now, think of this. Your kids did the shopping, but you did the paying. That's *logízomai.* It means someone did something, but it was credited to another person's account. They shopped, but it was chalked up to you.

Abraham: an example of logízomai

In Romans 4, where the word *logízomai* occurs so frequently, Paul demonstrates that it was not because of Abraham's character, his ancestry, or his good works that he was included in the family of God. It was because of his faith. The apostle poses these questions to his Jewish friends:

> What then shall we say was gained by Abraham, our forefather according to the flesh? For if Abraham was justified by works, he has something to boast about, but not before God. For what does the Scripture say? "Abraham believed God, and it was counted (Greek: ἐλογίσθη; English: e*logisthē*) to him as righteousness."

Abraham believed in God's promises, and his faith was credited to his account as righteousness. Paul then applied the same principle to our salvation. "And to the one who does not work but believes in him who justifies the ungodly, his faith is counted (Greek: λογίζεται; English: *logizetai*) as righteousness" (v. 5). Our salvation, which frees us from the penalty of our sin, does not come from saying the rosary, being baptized, or giving to charity. Just being good or going to church won't cut it. Those are things we *do*, and what we *do* will never save us. Our salvation is simply believing that what Jesus *did* at Calvary was all God required to pay the penalty for our sin. God takes our faith and logs it in the bank of heaven as righteousness. You cannot beat an exchange like that.

David: an example of logízomai

Next, the apostle offers David as an example of faith credited with righteousness. "Just as David also speaks of the blessing of the one to whom God counts (Greek: λογίζεται; English: *logizetai*) righteousness apart from works: 'Blessed are those whose lawless deeds are forgiven, and whose sins are covered; blessed is the man against whom the Lord will not count (Greek: λογίσηται; English: *logisētai*) his sin'" (vv. 6–8).

Paul concludes chapter 4 by making an application from the examples of Abraham and David. He says of Abraham: "He grew strong in his faith as he gave glory to God, fully convinced that God was able to do what he had promised. That is why his faith was "counted (Greek: ἐλογίσθη; English: e*logisthē*) to him as righteousness." However, the words "it was counted to him" were not written for his sake alone, but for ours also. It will be counted (Greek: λογίζεσθαι; English: *logizesthai*) to us who believe in him who raised from the dead Jesus our Lord, who was delivered up for our trespasses and raised for our justification (vv. 20–25).

Abraham's life was not about shepherding, becoming rich, or having a nice life in Ur of the Chaldees or Haran, Syria. His life was about trusting God's promise when he left Ur, not knowing where God would lead him. Abraham had never been to the Promised Land before. This was a whole new journey for him, a journey of faith.

King David Playing The Harp by Gerard van Honthorst (1622).

How logízomai works

This same process of attributing what occurs in one person's life to another is precisely what happened at Calvary. Our sin was placed on Jesus, and he bore the penalty for it even though he was completely innocent. We did the sinning; he did the paying. We did the sinning; he did the suffering. We did the sinning; he did the dying. That's *logízomai.*

The verse we examined above, 2 Corinthians 5:21, speaks of this process of imputation. Here, Paul wrote that God imputed the righteousness of

Christ to our account, just as at Golgotha, He imputed our sin to Christ's account. In the clause, "For our sake he made him to be sin who knew no sin," the words "to be" are not in the original. They have been added for clarity. What the apostle said was, "For our sake, he made him sin who knew no sin."

This means Christ carried all the sin of humankind to atone for us, but never became a sinner like us in the process. It was our sin, not his, for which he made atonement. As a result of the shed blood of Jesus and our faith in his sacrifice for us, we do not yet actually become righteous (look around you; look within you), but God treats us as if we were. That's excellent news.

Logízomai for Luther and Calvin

Among the many theologians who have written about this process of imputation, two men stand out head and shoulders above the others. One was a German theologian, the other was Swiss. As the German Reformer, Martin Luther observed:

> This is the mystery which is rich in divine grace to sinners: wherein by a wonderful exchange our sins are no longer ours but Christ's and the righteousness of Christ not Christ's but ours. He had emptied himself of his righteousness that he might clothe us with it and fill us with it. And he has taken our evils upon himself that he might deliver us from them. In the same manner as he grieved and suffered in our sins, and was confounded, in the same manner we rejoice and glory in his righteousness."[49]

So too, the Swiss Reformer John Calvin remarked:

> This is the wondrous exchange *(mirifica commutatio)* made by his boundless goodness. Having become with us the Son of Man, he has made us with himself sons of God. By his own descent to the earth, he has prepared our ascent to heaven. Having received our mortality, he has bestowed on us his immortality. Having undertaken our weakness, he has made us strong in his strength. Having submitted to our poverty, he has transferred his riches to us. Having taken upon himself the burden of unrighteousness with which we were oppressed, he has clothed us with his righteousness."[50]

If these words do not fill your heart with joy exceeding and abundant, you had better check your temperature to see if you are still alive. Theology at times tends to be deep and unexciting, but this truth expounded and explained should put a shot in your arm.

It is important to remember, however, that in this great exchange at Golgotha, Christ did not actually become a sinner, but God treated him as if he were. So adamant was Paul that his readers not mistakenly believe that Jesus became a sinner, he immediately added the clause, "who knew no sin," to describe the perpetual righteousness of Jesus Christ. Jesus shouldered our sin to be our blood sacrifice for it, but it never gained entrance into his essence as the perfect Son of God.

> "He became what we are, so we could become who he is."
> —J. Vernon McGee

There was a very profound exchange at Golgotha. We should understand *logízomai* as describing the greatest exchange in history. God credited Jesus with our sinfulness so he could credit us with Christ's righteousness. We unmistakably got the better of that deal.

WE WERE THERE WHEN THEY CRUCIFIED MY LORD?

The old spiritual asks, "Were you there when they crucified my Lord?" The answer is yes. Our holy God was judging us at Golgotha. The difference is that Jesus took our judgment and stood in our place, condemned. Our judgment became his judgment.

However, God was not just trading Jesus for us. He was placing the burden of our sin on the only person who could atone for it. The sacrifice for sin had to be perfect, without spot or blemish (Num 19:2; 28:3, 9, 11; 29:17, 26; cf. Heb 9:14; 1 Pet 1:19). None of us could meet such a high standard, but Jesus could. He is the only sinless person who has ever lived. He was not just the perfect sacrifice for our sin; he was the only legitimate one. "You were ransomed from the futile ways inherited from your forefathers, not with perishable things such as silver or gold, but with the precious blood of Christ, like that of a lamb without blemish or spot" (1 Pet 1:18–19).

Jesus did not die because of the trumped-up charges of the Sanhedrin. He did not die because Pontius Pilate abandoned him to a hateful mob. He did not die because he was a sinner. He died because he was not a sinner. He died because, as the only perfect sacrifice, God foreordained he would. He died, not for himself, but for us!

We may not physically have been in attendance in Jerusalem the day the world turned dark, but our sins were there. Our past was represented there. Our future was represented there as well, because our destiny was represented there. Answer the question for yourself.

Were you there when they crucified my Lord?
Were you there when they crucified my Lord?
O sometimes it causes me to tremble! tremble! tremble!
Were you there when they crucified my Lord?

Were you there when they nailed him to the cross?
Were you there when they pierced him in the side?
Were you there when the sun refused to shine?
Were you there when they laid him in the tomb?

Were you there when the stone was rolled away?
Were you there when he rose up from the grave?
Were you there when they crucified my Lord?
Were you there when they crucified my Lord?
O sometimes it causes me to tremble! tremble! tremble!
Were you there when they crucified my Lord?

—African American Spiritual

Our salvation was accomplished entirely by God

Salvation is not a 50/50 proposition. It was not as if Jesus did his part, and now we must do our part. We have no part in providing our salvation. Everything was done for us by God's Son. All we must do is respond in faith to what Jesus did.

Perhaps the best-known series of verses in the Bible explains this quite clearly. "And as Moses lifted up the serpent in the wilderness, so must the Son of Man be lifted up, that whoever believes in him may have eternal life. For God so loved the world, that he gave his only Son, that whoever believes in him should not perish but have eternal life."

That was verses 14–16 of John 3. They represent God's positive action toward us as sinners. They tell us what God did. But verse 17 continues and represents God's negative action. They tell us what God did not do.

"For God did not send his Son into the world to condemn the world, but in order that the world might be saved through him." Jesus did not die to condemn us; he died to save us. God's purpose at Calvary was not negative but positive.

Finally, verse 18 of John 3 explains the consequences of not believing Jesus' death was necessary to save us from the penalty of our sin. "Whoever believes in him is not condemned, but whoever does not believe is condemned already, because he has not believed in the name of the only Son of God."

> Question #14 asks, "What is sin?" and then gives this answer. "Sin is any want of conformity to, or transgression of, the law of God."—The Westminster Shorter Catechism

What must we do to be guilty of sin?

You may remember that some years ago there was a gospel tract with a red cover that featured the question, "What Must I Do To Go To Hell"? When you opened the tract, the inside was blank. No words at all. Nothing. While this was a rather unusual way to present the gospel, theologically, it was spot on. What do we need to do to be guilty of our sin? Nothing. Nothing at all, because we are already guilty. What must we do to be condemned because of our sin? Again, nothing. "Whoever believes in him [Jesus] is not condemned, but whoever does not believe is condemned already, because he has not believed in the name of the only Son of God" (John 3:18). What can we do to be saved from the penalty of our sin? Believe. That's what the Bible says. "Believe on the Lord Jesus, and you will be saved" (Acts 16:31 NKJV).

Look around you. Watch the evening news. Read the events of the day on your news app. Every time you check out the news, you will see nothing but death and destruction. People are smashing store windows and looting them. Jewelry stores are being hit daily by flash mobs who swarm and steal, robbing the owners blind. People, especially women, are not safe walking the streets, even in small towns like mine. Runners are being kidnapped, raped, and slaughtered so often that we have become numb to the news of another one. No one needs to be convinced of universal sin anymore. The evidence is too obvious, too graphic, and too available to us.

Our world has become so disobedient to God and oblivious to divine truth that we cannot even define good and evil anymore. We should not be surprised. As the prince of the Hebrew prophets sang to the LORD, he also pronounced, "Woe to those who call evil good and good evil, who put darkness for light and light for darkness, who put bitter for sweet and sweet for bitter! Woe to those who are wise in their own eyes, and shrewd in their own sight!" (Isa 5:20–21).

Many politicians and others no longer concern themselves with the truth. They tell their own version of the truth, knowing they are lying the whole time. Our society calls Christians bigots and racists while praising the good of homosexuals, lesbians, and transgender people. People listen to the lyrics of popular songs that are disgusting, if anyone could understand what the singer was saying. They advocate for rape, murder, and the freedom to rape and murder. What has historically been considered good is now viewed as evil. Everything that has traditionally been deemed as bad is now labeled good. A righteous God will not put up with this nonsense forever. Judgment is coming, and it's no laughing matter.

With no apparent effective deterrent to crime in our large cities, and no answer to the growing problems of homelessness, poverty, and disease, no honest person can deny that times are bad and getting worse daily. But here's the kicker. Our twenty-first-century society is so spiritually tone-deaf that it confuses good with evil. It's as if the world has lost its collective mind.

However, that's what Paul saw in his day as well, living under the Roman Eagle. It's why the apostle could say with honesty and clarity, "There is none righteous, no, not one. There is none who seeks after God.There is none who does good, no, not one. Destruction and misery are in their ways; And the way of peace they have not known. There is no fear of God before their eyes" (Rom 3:10–12, 16–18).

The only answer for our sinful condition is God's gift of Jesus' death at Calvary. The only cure is God's *logízomai,* where God the Son died in our stead, and where God the Father exchanged our sin for his Son's righteousness.

We were at the cross that day, but we were not the ones dying on it. We were "spiritual spectators," watching Jesus die for us. When he died, we died. At Calvary, Jesus did everything necessary to secure our salvation, which was another major accomplishment of Christ's death. Accomplishments don't get much bigger than this!

Bearing shame and scoffing rude,
In my place condemned he stood;
Sealed my pardon with his blood;
Hallelujah! What a Savior!

Guilty, vile, and helpless we;
Spotless Lamb of God was He;
"Full atonement!" can it be?
Hallelujah! What a Savior!

—Philip P. Bliss (1838–1876)

Chapter 6

Jesus Redeemed Enslaved Sinners Like Us

The meaning of "atonement" is to cover. When Jesus died for us, he covered our sins with his blood. He ransomed us with the price of his own life.

What is Redemption?
The Hebrew Word *pâdâh* Means "to Redeem"
The Hebrew Word *Gaal* Means "to Deliver"
The Hebrew Word *Kaphar* Means "to Cover"
The Greek Word *Exagorazo* Means "to Atone"
The Greek Word *Lytroo* Means "to Ransom"
Redemption Was an Established Practice
What All This Means to Us

Christians love to sing about their redemption from sin. Fanny Crosby wrote:

> Redeemed, how I love to proclaim it!
> Redeemed by the blood of the Lamb;
> Redeemed through his infinite mercy,
> His child and forever I am.

Songs and hymns about redemption abound. Whether ancient, old, or contemporary, they strike a chord in our hearts. Have you noticed that only Christians sing harmoniously about their God? Hindus chant their mantras.

Buddhist chanting is a key feature of worship in all three major schools of Buddhism. A type of singing is permitted in Islam under certain conditions, but that awful call to prayer you heard at 5:34 am when you visited a Muslim country is anything but harmonious. Is it possible that the harmony of the voice only comes from the harmony of the heart? Can it be that Christians sing harmoniously because we have something to sing about? Ponder this for a moment.

We sing about it, but what do we know about our redemption? What does our redemption provide, now and in the future? And even the most basic question: what does redemption mean? These questions need answers. In this chapter, we'll explore how Jesus redeemed enslaved sinners like you and me and set us free from the bondage of sin. He gave us a song to sing, the song of the redeemed.

I will sing of my Redeemer,
and his wondrous love to me;
On the cruel cross he suffered,
from the curse to set me free."

—James McGranahan (1840–1907)

WHAT IS REDEMPTION?

To redeem means to rescue, deliver, ransom, reclaim, or set free. In biblical terms, it means to deliver by paying a price. In the Old Testament, redemption was applied to property, animals, even people, and nations as a whole. In almost every case, freedom from obligation or bondage was secured by the payment of a ransom. In antiquity, a person acting as a redeemer could buy back property sold under duress (Lev 25:23–32), even if the property was not his.

"In the New Testament, redemption requires the payment of a price, but the plight that requires such a ransom is moral, not material. Humankind is held in the captivity of sin from which only the atoning death of Jesus Christ can liberate."[51]

Three Hebrew root words are most commonly used to convey the biblical concept of redemption. They are *pâdâh* (Hebrew: פָּדָה), *gâ'al* (Hebrew: גָּאַל), and *kâphar* (Hebrew: כָּפַר). The firstborn males of ritually clean animals were sacrificed, while firstborn unclean animals were redeemed (*pâdâh*) (Exod 13:13; 34:20; Num 18:15, 16). Firstborn children were also redeemed, either by the substitution of an animal or by the payment of a predetermined amount of money (Num 18:16).

> "The redemption of firstlings made a memorial sign to Israel of their own redemption."—C. I. Scofield

Perhaps this principle is best seen in Numbers 1815–16.

> Everything that opens the womb of all flesh, whether man or beast, which they offer to the LORD, shall be yours. Nevertheless, the firstborn of man you shall redeem, and the firstborn of unclean animals you shall redeem. And their redemption price (at a month old you shall redeem them) you shall fix at five shekels in silver, according to the shekel of the sanctuary, which is twenty gerahs.

Money was also sometimes paid to deliver a person from death (Exod 21:30; Num 3:46–51; 18:16; Ps 49:7–9). Thus, regardless of what was being redeemed, a ransom price was always part of the process.

Why Redemption is Necessary

When God speaks of redemption in his Word, he is talking about personal redemption from the power and penalty of sin. Sin's power has such a hold on us that even the most righteous among us are enslaved to it. Sin's penalty is the ultimate penalty. Paul wrote to the Romans, "For the wages of sin is death" (Rom 6:23a). The Prophet Ezekiel noted, "The soul who sins shall die" (Ezek 18:4, 20). But it was not always this way. Think back to the accounts of the Garden of Eden. Here's a description from the second chapter of Genesis, verses 7–10:

> Then the LORD God formed the man of dust from the ground and breathed into his nostrils the breath of life, and the man became a living creature. And the LORD God planted a garden in Eden, in the east, and there he put the man whom he had formed. And out of the ground the LORD God made to spring up every tree that is pleasant to the sight and good for food. A river flowed out of Eden to water the garden, and there it divided and became four rivers.

If the Garden of Eden sounds too idyllic, too wonderful, too good to be true, it wasn't. God created the perfect environment for Adam and Eve. There were fruit trees galore, plenty of vegetables, and anything the couple needed to live luxuriously. Anything good for food or pleasant to look at, the garden produced in abundance. Besides this, a four-part river gushed through the garden, providing abundant water for all the trees, plants, and fresh water for Adam and Eve to drink. It was better than paradise. The Garden was God's perfect paradise, given as a gift to the first couple. Yet, what happened in that garden is the reason redemption is necessary.

The tree of the knowledge of good and evil

All Adam and Eve had to do was not eat from the tree of the knowledge of good and evil (Gen 2:9), and they would be at peace with God. That was God's only restriction. Enjoy all the good the garden has to offer, but stay away from that one tree. Why? Why not permit Adam and Eve to enjoy the tree of the knowledge of good and evil as well? Wouldn't that be a good thing?

The Bible doesn't answer this "why question." A reasonable conjecture, however, would be that Adam and Eve were not created perfect; they were created innocent. That means they had a clean slate—no black marks on their record. Having been created by God, Adam and Eve were initially free from sin. They were blameless. However, they were inexperienced. Most Bible scholars understand this special tree as a test of Adam's obedience to God. At this point, Adam could go either way—choose to follow God or disobey God and side with "Satan in a snake." God was testing Adam's moral fortitude. Could Adam hold in check his human desire to indulge in what was inaccessible or forbidden?

Because Adam and Eve were created with moral awareness and self-determination, their allegiance to their Creator had to be tested. What would Adam do? Whatever he did would have lasting consequences for all humankind. Eating from the forbidden tree would not increase Adam's moral acuity, but the prohibition of eating the tree would test the acuity he already possessed. If Adam obeyed God and shunned the forbidden tree, he would achieve experiential knowledge, that is, he would exercise his moral judgment, pass God's test of allegiance, and enjoy a permanent state of holiness.

As everyone knows, this did not happen. By disobeying God's one prohibition in the garden, Adam did achieve experiential knowledge, but it was the knowledge of evil, not the knowledge of good. As a result, he and all his posterity would enter a state of spiritual depravity, moral ruin, and eternal death. The test was designed to assess obedience and moral determination.

To whichever principle Adam yielded himself—good or evil—he would not only surrender to that principle but would be controlled by it.

The principle of evil now directed the lives of Adam and Eve, as it does all their descendants to this day. That's you and me. "The LORD God sent him out from the garden of Eden to work the ground from which he was taken. He drove out the man, and to the east of the garden of Eden he placed the cherubim and a flaming sword that turned every way to guard the way to the tree of life" (Gen 3:23–24). Adam and Eve would never return to the Garden of Eden. Think about that, and don't let it slide by you too quickly!

Indeed, something had to change if humanity was to reconnect its relationship with God, a connection that sin had severed. Unmistakably, something had to change if humans hoped to have a home with God in heaven. Something had to reverse the curse that now controlled Adam and Eve, as well as the rest of us. Our first parents and all their descendants need to be redeemed, retrieved from the condemnation of God, the control of Satan, and the curse of the law.

There has never been a time like what Adam and Eve experienced in the Garden of Eden. Everything around them was magnificent and eye-catching. Every day, moment by moment, they lived in a joyous relationship with God. Nonetheless, that was all gone now because of their moral failure. Would it ever return? Read on.

The future restoration of God's garden

Would it ever return? Yes, it will. Our relationship with God, severed in Eden, will be restored, reattached, reconciled, and reclaimed. In short, it will be redeemed. Our redemption by the blood of the Lamb today means our relationship with God is reestablished.

The Bible envisions a day when God's people will inherit a new heaven and a new earth. These will produce abundant food without the sweat of their brow, without the thorns, and without the pain in our backs working the land. Revelation 22:1–2 describes that day saying, "Then the angel showed me the river of the water of life, bright as crystal, flowing from the throne of God and of the Lamb through the middle of the street of the city; also, on either side of the river, the tree of life with its twelve kinds of fruit, yielding its fruit each month. The leaves of the tree were for the healing of the nations."

Think of it. In God's heavenly future, we will trade:

Darkness for light
Pain for pleasure
Worry for worship
Doubtfulness for certainty
Worldliness for godliness
Waging war for welcome peace
Tears of sorrow for tears of joy
Loneliness for companionship
Eternal death for eternal life
Children of wrath for children of God
Naivety for maturity
Bondage for freedom
Animosity for charity
Malice for kindness
Hell for Heaven
. . . and so much more.

The biblical evidence for redemption is strong, but to understand it, we must grasp the diverse terms used to describe it, along with their unique meanings. Let's explore how modern translation teams have understood the meaning of the word "redemption."

THE HEBREW WORD PÂDÂH MEANS "TO REDEEM"

The English Standard Version (ESV) has been used throughout this book, as well as in the other books in this series on Roman crucifixion and the death of Jesus. The ESV translated Isaiah's hopeful promise for Israel's future as, "And the *ransomed* of the Lord shall return and come to Zion with singing; everlasting joy shall be upon their heads; they shall obtain gladness and joy, and sorrow and sighing shall flee away" (Isa 51:11). The NKJV translators also chose the word "ransomed."

However, the CSB and NASB chose the word "redeemed." "And the *redeemed* of the LORD will return and come to Zion with singing, crowned with unending joy. Joy and gladness will overtake them, and sorrow and sighing will flee."

Other translators chose other words. For example, the NIV translated Isaiah 51:11 as, "Those the LORD has *rescued* will return" (see also the CEV and GNT). The CSB chose to translate this word as "ransomed," as did the NKJV and RSV.

Another example is Psalm 119:134, where David prays, "*Redeem* me from man's oppression, that I may keep your precepts." This is the most common word choice for *pâdâh* (e.g., NIV, NASB 1995, NRSV, HCSB, CSB, et al). It is not, however, the universal word choice for modern translators. The NET and KJV chose, "*Deliver* me from oppressive men, so that I can keep your precepts." The NCB and TLB selected "*Rescue* me," and the NLT chose "*Ransom* me."

Why is this comparison significant? Because the prevailing idea behind *pâdâh* is redemption or deliverance, with a twist toward the meaning of rescue. When Jesus died on Calvary's Cross, he was redeeming us from the debt for our sin and death that was the result of our sin (Rom 6:23). Jesus rescued us from death and hell. All who have come to faith in God's Son as their Savior may sing, "Redeemed by the blood of the Lamb; Redeemed through his infinite mercy, his child, and forever, I am."

Jesus rescued us; he redeemed us from the slave market of sin.

THE HEBREW WORD GÂ'AL MEANS "TO DELIVER"

The second verb *gâ'al*, is a legal term used 104 times for the deliverance of a person or property by a family relative. The *goel*, from *gâ'al*, is the person who performs the duties of "redeemer." Found eighteen times in the Old Testament (thirteen of these in Isaiah), it was the duty of a man's redeemer, usually his next of kin, to buy back the freedom that the man had lost, often through acquiring debt.

An example of such "redemption" is recorded in Leviticus 25:47–49, where an Israelite who had been sold into slavery due to poverty may be redeemed by a kinsman.

The Levitical law says:

> If a stranger or sojourner with you becomes rich, and your brother beside him becomes poor and sells himself to the stranger or sojourner with you or to a member of the stranger's clan, then after he is sold he may be *redeemed*. One of his brothers may *redeem* him, or his uncle or his cousin may *redeem* him, or a close relative from his clan may *redeem* him (Lev 25:47–49).

Property sold under similar conditions could likewise be redeemed, thus keeping it within the clan or family (Lev 25:24–25; Jer 32:6–9).

The prophets often used the word *gâ'al*. Here are some examples.

- Isaiah 54:26, "All flesh shall know that I am the LORD your Savior, and your *Redeemer*, the Mighty One of Jacob."
- Isaiah 54:5, "The Holy One of Israel is your *Redeemer*, the God of the whole earth he is called."
- Isaiah 62:12, "And they shall be called The Holy People, The *Redeemed* of the LORD; and you shall be called Sought Out, A City Not Forsaken."
- Jeremiah 50:34, "And they shall be called The Holy People, The *Redeemed* of the LORD; and you shall be called Sought Out, A City Not Forsaken."
- Lamentations 3:58, Jeremiah, the 'Weeping Prophet' said, "You have taken up my cause, O Lord; you have *redeemed* my life."
- Hosea 13:14, "I shall *ransom* them from the power of Sheol; I shall redeem them from Death. O Death, where are your plagues? O Sheol, where is your sting?"

Of course, the prime example of *gâ'al* redemption in the Old Testament is the story of Ruth (see Ruth 4:1–6).

In the ancient Near East culture, the family was highly valued. Families took care of each other. If one member needed help, the clan stepped in. If a family member was in debt and sold himself into slavery, another family member was required to redeem him. This is what Jesus did for us. The blood he shed on the cross delivered us from an eternity without God and welcomed us back to his family. Simply put, Jesus redeemed us.

THE HEBREW WORD KÂPHAR MEANS "TO COVER"

The meaning of "atonement" is to cover. When Jesus died for us, he covered our sins with his blood. He ransomed us with the price of his own life. This third verb *kâphar* is often used in the sense of covering sin or making atonement for sin. The noun form (Hebrew: כֹּפֶר; English: *kôpher*) signifies the price or ransom that is paid for someone's life (Exod 21:30; 30:11–16).

Although the concept of redemption is central to the New Testament, the use of redemption terminology is quite limited. Perhaps this is because, when reflecting on the death of Jesus Christ at Golgotha, New Testament writers more frequently used the images of atonement, justification, and sacrifice than they did redemption. This is evidenced by the fact that the noun "ransom" (Greek: λύτρον; English: *lytron*) only appears in three texts of the New Testament (Matt 20:28, Mark 10:45, and 1 Tim 2:6).

Mark 10:45 records Jesus' words, "The Son of Man came not to be served but to serve, and to give his life as a *ransom* for many." When the Apostle Paul used the noun "redemption," he generally intended to convey the idea of deliverance (Rom 3:24; 8:23; 1 Cor 1:30; Eph 1:14; 4:30).

However, when speaking of Jesus' death in Ephesians 1:7, Paul had in mind the substitution of Jesus for us, paying the ransom for our sin debt. "In him we have *redemption* (Greek: ἀπολύτρωσιν; English: *apolytrōsin)* through his blood, the forgiveness of our trespasses, according to the riches of his grace."

You can see how one word can have multiple meanings, but each meaning relates to the death of the Savior. When Jesus died for us, he covered our sin with his blood. He ransomed us with the price of his own life. What should our response be, given this knowledge? "You are not your own, for you were bought with a price. So glorify God in your body (1 Cor 6:19–20). That's the only acceptable response for followers of Jesus.

Paul was not alone in using this word to convey the idea of a ransom. The writer of Hebrews used the same word (Greek: ἀπολύτρωσιν; English: *apolytrōsin*). "For this reason Christ is the mediator of a new covenant, that those who are called may receive the promised eternal inheritance—now that he has died as a *ransom* to set them free from the sins committed under the first covenant" (Heb 9:15 NIV).

Jesus atoned for our sin when his blood covered all that we are and all that we do that opposes God, our Creator. He ransomed us. He redeemed us. He atoned for our sin. He did it all for us, and for the glory of the Father.

THE GREEK WORD EXĒGORAZO MEANS "TO ATONE"

In Galatians 3:13 (see 4:5), when Paul said Jesus' death redeemed enslaved sinners, he used the Greek equivalent (Greek: ἐξηγόρασεν; English: *exēgorasen*) of the Hebrew Old Testament words above, meaning "to atone" for sin.

The apostle explained to the Galatians how Jesus took the curse that was upon them (and us too) because they had sinned against a holy God. He wrote, "Christ redeemed (exegorasen) us from the curse of the law by becoming a curse for us—for it is written, 'Cursed is everyone who is hanged on a tree'" (Gal 3:13). Paul used a form of the word *exagorázō* because he wanted to emphasize that Jesus' sacrifice on the cross covered the stain of our sin.

In explaining how Jesus fulfilled all the Law, Paul wrote the Galatians, "When the fullness of time had come, God sent forth his Son, born of woman, born under the law, to *redeem* those who were under the law, so that we might receive adoption as sons" (Gal 4:5). This verse explains that one purpose in Jesus' death was to redeem God's children, the Jews, so we Gentiles could be adopted into God's family as well.

In the early church, which was composed almost entirely of Jews who had placed their faith in the Messiah Yeshua (Jesus), there was a palpable tension between the Jews and those Gentiles who trusted Jesus as well. This tension almost caused a schism in the first-century church had it not been for Paul, Barnabas, James, Peter, and the Jerusalem council as recorded in Acts 15. Paul wanted his kinsmen, the Jews, to understand that the blood of Jesus Christ could cover the sin of the Gentiles as well as the Jews. Christ's blood was sufficient to "cover" (*exagorázō*) the sin of anyone who comes to faith in Jesus as Savior.

THE GREEK WORD LYTRÓŌ MEANS "TO RANSOM"

In Titus 2:14, the infinitive (Greek: λυτρώσηται; English: *lytrōsētai*) signifies the payment of a ransom to recover what has been enslaved. In the twenty-first century, we know all too well what it means to pay a ransom. The FBI defines ransomware as "a type of malicious software—or malware—that prevents you from accessing your computer files, systems, or networks and demands you pay a ransom for their return." The Bureau goes on to say, "The best way to avoid being exposed to ransomware—or any type of malware—is to be a cautious and conscientious device user. Malware distributors have gotten increasingly savvy, and you need to be careful about what you download and click on."

Since Paul didn't have a computer, he had no worries about electronic ransom, especially cryptoransom. However, he told his younger protégé Titus that people of faith are, "waiting for our blessed hope, the appearing of the glory of our great God and Savior Jesus Christ, who gave himself for us to *redeem* us from all lawlessness and to *purify* for himself a people for his own possession who are zealous for good works." This is one of the two purposes recorded for Christ redeeming us, that is, "to *redeem* us from all lawlessness," and "to *purify* for himself a people for his own possession." If you exhibit evidence of the first purpose but not of the second, you have a legitimate reason to question the validity of the first in your life.

In the ransom Jesus paid, both he and we received something in return. We got released from the penalty of our own lawlessness, and Jesus got a people—people of faith in him—who were saved to perform zealous and good works for the Savior. The moment we believe in Jesus as our Savior, we become members of the family—the family of God. We are now in the possession of God the Son with all the rights and privileges appertaining thereto (1 Cor 6:19–20).

As his possession, however, we have been saved for his purpose and not just to escape hell. We should never quote Ephesians 2:8 and 9, which speak of the grace by which we were saved, without quoting verse 10. "For we are his workmanship, created in Christ Jesus for good works, which God prepared beforehand, that we should walk in them." Verse 10 explains God's purpose in our salvation. Good works can never save us, but once redeemed by the blood of the Lamb, the Father expects us to produce good works for him. As the old Southern preacher said, "God didn't save us to sit, soak, and sour." God saved us to serve him, which begs the question, "How are you doing at fulfilling your purpose? Have you found your place of service yet? You'll be miserable until you do, and you'll feel so fulfilled once you do.

Having examined the various ways Greek words describing the concept of redemption can be translated, and having observed that God describes our salvation in multiple ways, let us remember that this principle did not begin with the New Testament. This was a principle of the Jewish people in the Old Testament as well. It's there that we must look to understand the full meaning and implications of the practice of redemption. So, let's go back many years from the cross of Calvary to practices that pointed toward the cross.

REDEMPTION WAS AN ESTABLISHED PRACTICE

The Jews, who made up the first-century church, were well aware of the concept of redemption. It was an established practice in the Jewish religion. So, Paul, Peter, John, James, and the other writers of the New Testament histories or epistles could speak of redemption in Christ Jesus, and every Jew already had a primary understanding of what they meant.

Exodus 34:20, "The firstborn of a donkey you shall redeem with a lamb, or if you will not redeem it, you shall break its neck. All the firstborn of your sons you shall redeem. And none shall appear before me empty-handed."

Redemption was the point of the Passover

The redeeming of the firstborn was instituted as a result of, and in memory of, God's sparing Israel's firstborn on that Passover night when the firstborn of Egypt, both of man and beast, were destroyed. A condensation of the Passover account in Exodus 12 follows:

> The LORD said to Moses and Aaron in the land of Egypt. Tell all the congregation of Israel that on the tenth day of this month, every man shall take a lamb according to their fathers' houses, a lamb for a household. Your lamb shall be without blemish, and you shall keep it until the fourteenth day of this month, when the whole assembly of the congregation of Israel shall kill their lambs at twilight. Then they shall take some of the blood and put it on the two doorposts and the lintel of the houses in which they eat it. They shall eat the flesh that night, roasted on the fire, with your belt fastened, your sandals on your feet, and your staff in your hand. And you shall eat it in haste. It is the LORD's Passover. For I will pass through the land of Egypt that night, and I will strike all the firstborn in the land of Egypt, both man and beast; and on all the gods of Egypt I will execute judgments: I am the LORD. The blood shall be a sign for you, on the houses where you are. And when I see the blood, I will pass over you, and no plague will befall you to destroy you, when I strike the land of Egypt.

The fourteenth day of the first month on the Jewish calendar was to be a memorial day. It was the Passover feast, a celebration commanded by God to be kept forever. Redemption of the firstborn was the essence of that memorial. Exodus 13:12–14 outlines the redemption requirement:

> You shall set apart to the LORD all that first opens the womb. All the firstborn of your animals that are males shall be the LORD's. Every firstborn of a donkey you shall redeem with a lamb, or if you will not redeem it, you shall break its neck. Every firstborn of man among your sons you shall redeem. And when in time to come your son asks you, "What does this mean?" you shall say to him, "By a strong hand the LORD brought us out of Egypt, from the house of slavery.

The principle of the firstborn being dedicated to God was well established in the Old Testament. So was the Passover ceremony. But there were more Passover requirements.

Redemption of the unclean

God's requirement was for every firstborn creature to be devoted to the LORD for his service. However, the donkey was an unclean animal, and what is unclean cannot be presented as a sacrifice to a holy God. Should the donkey merely be allowed to go free from this universal law? Not at all. The omniscient God allows no exceptions to this requirement. The donkey was unclean by birth. It was universally recognized in Israel as an unclean beast. And yet, God required the firstborn of every creature to be dedicated to him. So, how would this problem be remedied? What could make the unclean clean? God did not make an exception; instead, he made a way.

There was absolutely no way of escape from this dilemma except by the substitution of a lamb in place of a donkey. "Every firstborn of a donkey you shall redeem with a lamb." The smaller, innocent lamb would be sacrificed to fulfill God's requirement and make the donkey an acceptable animal. Just as the lamb that was sacrificed on that first Passover night, so too, a lamb could be sacrificed for the least of the animals, the donkey. The key was the substitution of the lamb for the donkey. It foreshadowed the Savior's substitution for lowly people like me.

JESUS WAS GOD'S PASSOVER LAMB

Passover Seder Dish

While visiting a Jewish friend in Israel, I was invited to his home for a Passover *seder* with his family. Each element of the meal was explained to his young children. After a moment of reflection, I asked, "When do we slay the Passover lamb?" The entire family looked at me, dazed and stunned. "Slay the Passover Lamb? We don't do that anymore," replied my friend. Most modern Jews believe that the sacrifices the Jewish people have endured over the years, especially in Jerusalem, have become their sacrificial lamb. Some believe the lamb is the modern State of Israel. "But that was to be an integral part of the Passover feast," I gently questioned, and it was to be "forever, throughout all generations."

What my Jewish friend did not see, and perhaps could not see (2 Cor 4:4), was that the reason Jews no longer slay a lamb at Passover is that Jesus, the real Passover Lamb, was killed at Calvary for every generation. Hebrews 9:12–14 explains:

> "He [Jesus] entered once for all into the holy places, not by means of the blood of goats and calves but by means of his own blood, thus securing an eternal redemption. For if the blood of goats and bulls, and the sprinkling of defiled persons with the ashes of a heifer, sanctify for the purification of the flesh, how much more will the blood of Christ, who through the eternal Spirit offered himself without blemish to God, purify our conscience from dead works to serve the living God.

Understood correctly, the Passover memorial and the need for a lamb to be slain for the people to be acceptable to God both illustrate the truth that Jesus was slain on our behalf to make us acceptable before God. His is the blood on the doorpost and lintel of our lives. We are the unacceptable, unclean humans; he is the perfect, sinless human. It was his death at Calvary and his blood shed there that made it possible for us to stand before God in his righteousness and not our own.

> "All my iniquities on Him were laid, He nailed them all to the Tree;
> Jesus the debt of my sin fully paid, He paid the ransom for me."
> —J. M. Moore

Just as the Passover lamb redeemed the Israelites in ancient Egypt, and just as the lamb was sacrificed to redeem the unclean donkey, Jesus, the perfect Passover Lamb, was slain to redeem us, to make us acceptable to God. That's the story of redemption. God plans to redeem us from an impossible situation by the incomparable sacrifice of his own Son. "For while we were still weak, at the right time Christ died for the ungodly. For one will scarcely die for a righteous person—though perhaps for a good person one would dare even to die—but God shows his love for us in that while we were still sinners, Christ died for us" (Rom 5:6–8).

Although we may rejoice in God's inscrutable plan, we cannot progress without considering the undesirable consequence of not slaying a lamb to make the donkey clean. "If you will not redeem it you shall break its neck," instructs Exodus 13:13 and 34:20. There was an alternative for the Jews who were confronted with the firstborn of a jenny, a female donkey. If they choose not to redeem the animal and make it clean as a sacrifice to God, they must kill the animal instead. That would render the animal useless, and they would gain nothing.

Here's the point

For the unclean animal, the options were redemption or death. There was no third option. The Jews could not simply look the other way. They could not pretend the commandment didn't exist. They could not legitimately deny God's commandment. Their only options were redemption or death.

This is, of course, precisely the same situation we humans find ourselves in. When it comes to the penalty for our sin, as we stand before the judgment bar of God, we cannot simply look the other way or pretend the commandment doesn't exist. We must come to grips with it. It's redemption or death. We cannot deny God's requirement for faith in Jesus as Savior for redemption. Hebrews 10:3–14 sums up God's plan for the sacrifice of his Son:

> In these sacrifices there is a reminder of sin every year. For it is impossible for the blood of bulls and goats to take away sins. Consequently, when Christ came into the world, he said, "Sacrifices and offerings you have not desired . . . in burnt offerings and sin offerings you have taken no pleasure. Then I said, 'Behold, I have come to do your will, O God . . . And by that will we have been sanctified through the offering of the body of Jesus Christ once for all. And every priest stands daily at his service, offering repeatedly the same sacrifices, which can never take away sins. But when Christ had offered for all time a single sacrifice for sins, he sat down at the right hand of God. For by a single offering he has perfected for all time those who are being sanctified.

Free from the law, O happy condition,
Jesus hath bled, and there is remission;
Cursed by the law and bruised by the fall,
Grace hath redeemed us once for all.

—P. P. Bliss (1838–1876)

WHAT ALL THIS MEANS FOR YOU

What redemption means to us is incalculable. But to enjoy it, we must first understand it. Perhaps an illustration will help.

Your father gives you his priceless gold watch, accompanied by a gold chain. It is a family heirloom, passed down to him by his father and his father before him, and so on. You cherish this watch. It's the best gift you've ever received. But life for you has taken many twists and turns, most of them selfish and all of them bad. You enjoyed partying, and that led to alcohol and drugs. Slowly but surely, you were draining your bank account until it was so low you couldn't even buy the necessities of life. Finally, you hit rock bottom.

The only thing of value you had left was that gold watch and chain. You went to the local pawn shop and sold it for pennies on the dollar. The money you received lasted only a few days, and you went to the pawn shop again to see if the pawnbroker would help you. He said he couldn't because the watch had been sold to the man standing over there. When you turned, it was your father, holding the watch. It was yours again. You didn't deserve it, you didn't earn it, you were desolate without it. However, your father repurchased the watch for you, and it was yours again.

That's the picture of redemption. Whether you work in an office building or construction, whether you work from home or are a homemaker, God's redemption through his Son is available to you. God gave humankind the opportunity for eternal life, but we squandered that opportunity. We sold our souls to Satan and joined his rebellion against God. But when Jesus died on the cross, when he shed his blood, you got the opportunity to have your life back again. Like the son with the watch, all you had to do was reach out and take it. The Father did all the work for you. That's the essence of redemption. You lose. Jesus pays. You trust and regain. It's called redemption.

> "The final book of the Bible is, therefore, a fitting end to the story of the fall with its triumphant declaration of full redemption."
> —Anthony L. Chute

The authors of the New Testament unmistakably understood the ransom for our redemption to be the life of Jesus of Nazareth. Australian New Testament scholar Leon Morris affirms, "Paul uses the concept of redemption primarily to speak of the saving significance of the death of Christ."[52]

By dying in our place, Jesus paid the penalty for our sin. He redeemed us, ransomed us, and repurchased us from the consequences of our sin, which ends in eternal death. This was undoubtedly a significant accomplishment on that Friday afternoon when Jesus of Nazareth was nailed to a cross in Ancient Jerusalem. Accomplishments don't get much bigger than this!

There's a sweet and blessed story
Of the Christ who came from glory,
Just to rescue me from sin and misery;
He in loving kindness sought me,
And from sin and shame hath brought me,
Hallelujah! Jesus ransomed me.

—Julia Harriet Johnston (1849–1919)

Chapter 7

Jesus Provided the Basis for Our Forgiveness

The crowd had chanted, "Crucify him, Crucify him." They had ridiculed and taunted him while he hung on the cross. Still, when the crowd was at its worst, Jesus was at his best, praying, "Father, forgive them."

What Forgiveness Is Not
What Forgiveness Is
God Must Atone Before He Can Forgive
Jesus Provided Our Example of Forgiveness
How Can a Righteous God Forgive Unrighteous People?

"To err is human, to forgive, divine." Do you know who said that? It was Alexander Pope, considered the foremost English poet of the early eighteenth century. While what Pope said is both poetic and very meaningful, I like some of the parodies that arise from it, such as:

- "To err is human, but to really foul things up, you need a computer" —Paul R. Ehrlich
- "To err is human. To blame someone else is politics."—Hubert H. Humphrey
- "To err is human, to forgive is against company policy."—Lew Wasserman

Some wrinkles in this quote are more virtuous and more helpful, such as:

- "To err is human. To repeat error is of the Devil."—Seneca the Younger
- "To err is human, to repent divine; to persist devilish."—Benjamin Franklin
- "To err is human, but to persevere in error is only the act of a fool."—Cicero

The horror of crucifixion brings us face to face with the reality of how contemptible our sin must be to a holy God. God cannot be righteous, he cannot be just, he cannot be fair, and do nothing about sin. If we see YHWH, the God of the Bible, as a full-orbed God, a God of love, a God of mercy, a God of justice, a God of wrath, a God of grace, and a God of forgiveness, we will better understand why this full-orbed God does what he does.

The God of wrath, justice, and righteousness must address our sin. He cannot be righteous if he grants us blanket forgiveness. That's cheap forgiveness, and cheap forgiveness is no forgiveness at all. It is worthless. The God of love, mercy, and grace must find a way to address the need for justice. If God says he loves us but does nothing about the Damocles sword of personal sin hanging over us, he is not a God of love.

> "Sincere biblical repentance is as much a work of grace as not sinning in the first place. To err is human, to make progress is divine."—Kevin DeYoung

What does the Bible say about forgiveness, both how God forgives us and how we, in turn, are commanded to forgive others? What God speaks through his Word is remarkably direct. However, let's begin by clearing the air about forgiveness.

WHAT FORGIVENESS IS NOT

There is significant misunderstanding and misinformation surrounding forgiveness today. The Internet is filled with demonstrable ignorance. So, before we consider what forgiveness is, let's think about what forgiveness isn't. Let's clear the clutter of popular beliefs about forgiveness. That way, we'll better understand the biblical message of forgiveness when we encounter it. So, what is forgiveness not?

Forgiveness is not condoning sin.

Forgiveness does not mean you condone an offense against you. To condone sin is to tolerate it, to overlook it, to disregard it. Just as God does not condone our sins, we cannot condone the sins committed against us or our own sins against others. To condone sin is sin.

After David's great sin with Bathsheba, he attempted to cover his sin in multiple ways. Nonetheless, he was unsuccessful. Uriah the Hittite was dead. Bathsheba was pregnant. And David was caught. It appears that David was willing to brush aside the consequences of his sin and would have gotten away with it were it not for one man.

The prophet Nathan went to the king in his palace and told a touching story about a man who had huge flocks, but he took one little lamb from a man when that lamb was all the man had, and he was very fond of it. The prophet then asked David what should be done to such a wrongdoer. An angry David responded, "As the LORD lives, the man who has done this deserves to die" (2 Sam 12:5). Nathan then stuck his finger in David's face and said, "You are the man!" (v. 6).

We can never condone sin. Someone in your family may make wrong choices and thumb their nose at God. They may tell you they never want to see you again. While you must never stop loving them, you must make it clear that you cannot condone their lifestyle choices. God doesn't condone sin, and neither should we. You don't condone sin among those you love to be hard on them; you do it to be honest with them, and with God.

Forgiveness is not the denial of sin.

God cannot forgive us, nor can we forgive anyone who has wronged us, if we deny the need for forgiveness. If we say to God, "I have done nothing wrong; there is nothing to forgive," we cannot expect divine forgiveness. Likewise, if someone has wronged us and we simply deny that anything happened, we should not expect forgiveness. Forgiveness is not denial.

You cannot deny that the omniscient God keeps a record of everything. Cancer does not go away simply if you deny you have it. Something must always be done, or forgiveness can never take place.

Forgiveness is not hiding sin.

God cannot forgive us, nor can we forgive anyone who has wronged us, simply by hiding sin. To be forgiven, sin must constantly be exposed. In the

Garden of Eden, when God asked Adam, "Where are you?" it was because "the man and his wife hid themselves from the presence of the LORD God" (Gen 3:8). God didn't ask, "Where are you?" because he was unaware of their hiding place. He asked about their whereabouts to expose their sin to Adam and Eve. God wanted Adam to admit he had sinned and was hiding from God. Forgiveness is not hiding the wrong someone has done to us. It's bringing it to light and dealing with it biblically.

Jesus' words just after John 3:16 are important. He said, "The light has come into the world, and people loved the darkness rather than the light because their works were evil. For everyone who does wicked things hates the light and does not come to the light, lest his works should be exposed. But whoever does what is true comes to the light, so that it may be clearly seen that his works have been carried out in God" (John 3:19–21).

Hiding sin is never the answer. The truth of Proverbs 28:13 is both for you and those who sin against you. "Whoever conceals his transgressions will not prosper, but he who confesses and forsakes them will obtain mercy."

Forgiveness is not glossing over a sin.

The dictionary defines glossing over something as "masking the true nature" of something or giving "a deceptively attractive appearance" to someone or something. You don't forgive a friend who has hurt you simply by masking that hurt. That never works. If God's forgiveness consists merely of giving "a deceptively attractive appearance" to our sin, we are in big trouble. Dirt swept under a rug eventually finds its way out. Sweeping sin under the carpet is but a temporary solution to a permanent problem. This is why God did something about our sin; he didn't just gloss over it. When someone wrongs us and we sweep that wrong under the rug, we are never truly satisfied, and the bulges in the carpet, however tiny, are a constant reminder that we have not permanently addressed the issue.

Salvation by God is never halfway. Forgiveness of our sin is never halfway. God didn't cavalierly treat our sin. He cut off the head of the snake by sending his Son to be crucified one Friday afternoon in Jerusalem, the Holy City. That's how you take care of sin!

Forgiveness is not forgetting about a sin.

We are all aware of the popular idiom, "Forgive and forget." The *McGraw-Hill Dictionary of American Idioms and Phrasal Verbs* says this idiom means, "You should not only forgive people for hurting you, you should also forget that they ever hurt you." If this weren't impossible, this would sound like good advice. But have you ever forgiven someone and still been unable to forget what they did to you? Of course, you have. Just as it is not human nature to forgive, it is not human nature to forget.

Even when you sincerely forgive someone, it is genuinely challenging, if not impossible, to forget what they did to you. Our minds tend not to forget selectively, and while we forget millions of things in our lifetimes, the things that have hurt us the most are not among them. Nowhere in the Bible does it say, "Forgive and forget." Allow me to repeat: nowhere in the Bible does it say, "Forgive and forget." You can't forget, and God doesn't ask you to. He asks you to forgive. Don't beat yourself up if you cannot forget. It means you're human.

Does God forget our sins?

Doesn't God forget our sins when he forgives them? Psalm 103:12 says, "As far as the east is from the west, so far does he remove our transgressions from us." This sounds promising. Isaiah 43:25 records God's actual words. "I am he who blots out your transgressions for my own sake, and I will not remember your sins." That's even more concrete. Jeremiah 31:34 repeats God's words, "For I will forgive their iniquity, and I will remember their sin no more." There it is in black and white.

But this is the language of a prophet. It's a metaphor, a word picture, not a declaration. It is designed to emphasize God's graciousness and resolve not to hold us liable for the sin he has forgiven. God is omniscient, knowing all things actual and all things potential—past, present, and future. The all-knowing God does not forget anything. What the Almighty was referring to in Isaiah 43:25 and Jeremiah 31:34 is that God no longer holds against us the sins he has forgiven. He doesn't forget the sin; he forgets the need to punish the sin because he has already forgiven us. The heart of God is tender, forgiving our sins. Nevertheless, the mind of God is keen, never forgetting that he has forgiven us of our sin and thus not holding it against us.

When God exposes our sin, it is not to shame us but to forgive us. To properly forgive wrongdoing, God could not deny that it had occurred. He could not hide sin among a different set of trees than the one Adam and Eve were hiding behind. God could not cavalierly sweep sin under the cosmic carpet, nor could he simply forget about sin. God knew that to forgive us, he had to do something about our sin. He knew positive action was required. That positive action occurred at a place called Calvary.

God knows what forgiveness is not. He also knew what it is. The Bible has much to say about God's desire and his ability to forgive us. Here's what we know.

WHAT FORGIVENESS IS

According to *Greater Good Magazine*, "Psychologists generally define forgiveness as a conscious, deliberate decision to release feelings of resentment or vengeance toward a person or group who has harmed you, regardless of whether they deserve your forgiveness."[53] This is a reasonably good definition because it encompasses most of the elements of biblical forgiveness. Let's go to God's Book to find out what genuine forgiveness is.

The Bible is replete with references to forgiveness

Forgiveness is a frequent topic in the Bible. It was a favorite topic of Jesus. The word meaning to "forgive" (Greek: ἀφίημι; English: *aphíēmi*) is found 133 times in the New Testament, almost half [fifty-five times] in the Gospel of Matthew. The word has a variety of meanings, and most of the time it is not translated as "forgive." About two-thirds of the time, it is translated as "to leave," "to walk away," or similar. Matthew 4:11 says after Satan tempted Jesus, "Then the devil left (*aphíēsin*) him." Matthew 4:20 and 22 describe Jesus' call to discipleship of the four fishermen: "Immediately they left (*aphentes*) their nets and followed him. Immediately they left (*aphentes*) the boat and their father and followed him."

However, Jesus had much to say about forgiveness, primarily in our relationship with God and the forgiveness we receive from Him. Still, the Bible does not fail to instruct us about forgiving others, as Table 1 shows.

Table 1: New Testament References to Forgiveness

References to God forgiving us	
New Testament Book	*Scriptures*
Matthew	6:12, 15; 9:2, 5, 6; 12:31, 32; 26:28
Mark	1:4; 2:5, 7, 9, 10; 3:28; 29; 4:12; 11:25
Luke	1:77; 3:3; 5:20, 21, 23, 24; 7:47, 48, 49; 11:4:12:10; 23:34; 24:47
Acts	2:38; 5:31; 8:22; 10:43; 13:38; 26:18
Romans	4:7
2 Corinthians	1:10
Ephesians	1:7
Colossians	1:14; 2:13; 3:13
Hebrews	9:22; 10:18
1 John	1:9; 2:12
References to our forgiving others	
Matthew	6:14, 15; 18:21, 35;
Mark	11:25
Luke	6:37; 11:4; 17:3, 4
John	20:23
2 Corinthians	2:7, 10, 13
Colossians	3:13

Clearly, forgiveness was a hot topic in the New Testament because there was ample sin for God to forgive.

The concept of forgiveness in the word *aphíēmi* is seen nineteen times in Matthew (Matt 6:12, 14, 15; 9:2, 5, 6; 12:31; 18:21, 27, 32, 35). So, how does a word that generally means "leaving" also find meaning in "forgiving"?

WHAT DOES THE BIBLE MEAN BY "FORGIVE"?

The undisputed meaning for "forgive" in the Bible is to release, to let go, or to leave behind (hence the translations related to "leaving"). It means you do not hold a person accountable for the harm they have done to you. You release to God the wrath you have toward that person and walk away free of your burden of anger. Paul taught us, "Dear friends, don't try to get even. Let

God take revenge" (Romans 12:19 CEV). Failure to forgive holds the person wronged in bondage, not the person who did the wrong. God released the wrongs of a rebellious planet and left them all at the cross. That's where genuine forgiveness took root and blossomed.

At its most basic level, the crucifixion of Jesus, which brought our salvation, also brought about forgiveness for our sins. Salvation and forgiveness are often linked in the New Testament (Luke 1:77; Acts 10:43; 13:38; 26:18), as are the shedding of Christ's blood (Matt 26:28; Heb 9:22) and repentance of sin (Mark 1:4; Luke 3:3; 24:47; Acts 2:38). Forgiveness of sin is the divinely designed consequence of redemption by the blood of Jesus.

Colossians 1:13, 14 informs us, "He has delivered us from the domain of darkness and transferred us to the kingdom of his beloved Son, in whom we have redemption, the forgiveness of sins."[54] "As far as the east is from the west, so far does he remove our transgressions from us" (Ps 103:12).[55] Forgiveness was a very significant accomplishment of Christ's death.

FORGIVENESS IS YOURS FOR THE TAKING

Forgiveness is a choice. God chose to forgive us based on Jesus' sacrifice on the cross. We only forgive others when we choose to let go of their offense toward us. If we decide instead to hold onto the hurt they caused us, our inability to forgive soon turns into bitterness. We become receptacles for the vitriol, hate, animosity, and resentment that failure to forgive produces. We all know that bitterness is like acid, doing more harm to its container than to the surface it's applied to. Failure to forgive hurts us more than it hurts the person who hurt us. That's why the Bible often encourages us to forgive others.

> "Most of the ground that Satan gains in the lives of Christians is due to unforgiveness."—Neil Anderson

There is good advice in Proverbs about friends and friendship. "When we please the Lord, even our enemies make friends with us" (16:7). "A truly good friend will openly correct you" (27:5). Proverbs also has much to say about forgiveness between friends. "Making up with a friend you have offended is harder than breaking through a city wall. (18:19). Perhaps the best advice is found in this verse: "You will keep your friends if you forgive them, but you will lose your friends if you keep talking about what they did wrong" (Prov 17:9 CEV).

Even though we grievously sinned against a holy God, the Father did not retain resentment or bitterness toward us. Instead, he let it flow at Calvary, and Calvary makes it possible for us to let go of any resentment or bitterness we have toward God, toward others, or even toward ourselves. When his sinless Son died on the cross for the sins of others, God demonstrated how to forgive. Even God the Son, who was enduring the pain and shame of crucifixion, pleaded with his Father, "Father, forgive (*aphíēmi*) them, for they know not what they do" (Luke 23:34).

When we come to appreciate that God has fully forgiven all our sins, the Holy Spirit will make us spiritually uncomfortable if we choose not to forgive others.

GOD MUST ATONE BEFORE HE CAN FORGIVE

God wants to forgive us of our sins, but first, he must atone for them. That is why the horrible death of Jesus at the cross was necessary. It opened the door for our forgiveness. It was our sin that put Jesus on that cross, not just Roman nails. Every nail driven through his hands and feet was hammered home because of our sin. The pain he endured, the feeling of abandonment, the thirst, and finally his death, all were the result of our sin. God's forgiveness of our sin did not come easily, and it was not cheap. It cost Jesus his life.

> "Without forgiveness, no man is pleasing to God."—John Calvin

Voltaire, the *nom de plume* for François-Marie Arouet, was a French Enlightenment author, historian, and philosopher renowned for his critiques of the Catholic Church and Christianity in general. Voltaire famously suggested God would have to forgive us of our sin, since after all, "that was his job." Is it? Is God under any known obligation to forgive those who have rebelled against him? Why should God forgive an ungrateful creation? Think about it. God doesn't just hand out free forgiveness passes like a get-out-of-jail card. There is a price to be paid before God will forgive our sin, and that price was the death of the innocent Lamb of God, Jesus himself.

It's interesting that the word "atonement" occurs ninety-three times, all in the Old Testament. It is never found in the New Testament. Perhaps that's because the Day of Atonement, which was so prevalent in Old Testament history and culture, became redundant, superfluous, and unnecessary when Jesus made atonement for us through his death. Jesus atoned, recompensed, and expiated our sin when he shed his blood at Calvary, making God the

Father free to forgive our sin because Jesus' personal sacrifice had paid for it. There, at Calvary, Jesus paid a debt he didn't owe, because we owed a debt we couldn't pay.

JESUS PROVIDED OUR EXAMPLE OF FORGIVENESS

As Jesus walked the dusty roads of Galilee and the streets of Jerusalem, paved with Roman stones, he not only taught people to forgive, but also offered forgiveness to those who needed it. One day, while he was teaching in a house in Galilee, suddenly the roof above him began to open up and a man was lowered on his stretcher/bed into the midst of the crowd. The man was paralyzed, and because the crowd was so dense, four of his friends climbed onto the roof and removed some palm fronds and tiles to permit him entrance to Jesus. This is where we pick up the story in Luke 5:20–21.

> On one of those days, as he was teaching, Pharisees and teachers of the law were sitting there, who had come from every village of Galilee and Judea and Jerusalem. And the power of the Lord was with him to heal. And behold, some men were bringing on a bed a man who was paralyzed, and they were seeking to bring him in and lay him before Jesus, but finding no way to bring him in, because of the crowd, they went up on the roof and let him down with his bed through the tiles into the midst before Jesus. And when he saw their faith, he said, "Man, your sins are forgiven you." And the scribes and the Pharisees began to question, saying, "Who is this who speaks blasphemies? Who can forgive sins but God alone?

Who indeed! Maybe that was the point, and the scribes and Pharisees were too dense to see it. It was the issue of forgiveness that first triggered the Pharisees' charge of blasphemy against Jesus.

The issue of forgiveness is something that Christians find most difficult today. It's an issue that must be settled in each of our minds—yours and mine—if we are to live a full-throttled Christian life.

It takes three to forgive

One of Jesus' most poignant teachings was, "If your brother sins, rebuke him, and if he repents, forgive him, and if he sins against you seven times in the day, and turns to you seven times, saying, 'I repent,' you must forgive him" (Luke 17:3–4).

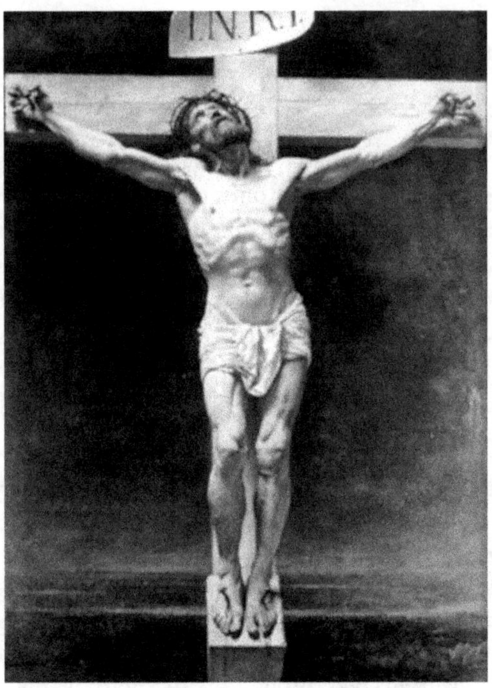

Father, Forgive Them"

You've heard that it takes two to tango. Well, it takes three to forgive. First, there is your brother or sister who sins and repents, or at least they say they do. Second, there is God, who will judge whether or not your brother or sister's repentance is real. That's the responsibility of the all-wise God. That is not your responsibility, but you do have one. Third, your responsibility is to forgive your brother or sister without knowing if his or her repentance is genuine or not. We are not in the business of judging; we are in the business of forgiving.

Your brother or sister, friend or co-worker, has a responsibility, God has a responsibility, and you have a responsibility. Please do not mix them up. This is why understanding forgiveness as a "release" is so important. When someone sins against us, our responsibility is to "release" that sin. To whom? To the person who has offended us? No. We release that person's offense to God and let him deal with it. We would all relieve a great deal of pressure if we would only learn to lay our offenses before God instead of seething about them ourselves.

> "Forgiveness is an unnatural act. You don't find dolphins forgiving sharks for eating their playmates. It's a dog-eat-dog world out there, not dog-forgive-dog."—Philip Yancey

Look, forgiving others is not easy. After all, they offended you in some way. Maybe they told lies about you, bullied you, or slandered you. Whatever that person did, it is not easy for you to forgive them. Nevertheless, there's something worse than forgiving, and that's not forgiving them. If you fail to forgive them, you keep all the bitterness, ill-will, and hatred to yourself. It's bottled up in your mind, driving you crazy. You are a total wreck, miserable. However, the person who offended you is living their best life, totally oblivious to your bitterness. Failing to forgive isn't hurting them at all.

You have to release those feelings to God. You have to give them up. You have to forgive because Jesus commands it, and for your own mental health and well-being. So, if there is someone you need to forgive today, will you do it? Will you say to Jesus, "Lord, take these feelings of hatred from me. I give what offended me to you and release the person who offended me from the consequences of their actions. It's yours, Lord. It's no longer mine." Now, after you have prayed, you must actually—physically and emotionally—do what you've told Jesus you were going to do. That's when you release whatever it is that is destroying your life. You forgive.

The most overwhelming forgiveness of all time

There is, however, a greater example of forgiveness than you forgiving someone who hurt you. Without question, the most profound, most poignant, and most permanent example of forgiveness was demonstrated by Jesus as he hung on Calvary's Cross. There, innocent of any crime himself, having just been spat on, beaten, and bloodied, with a crown of thorns on his head and nails driven through his hands and feet, Jesus pled with his Heavenly Father, "Father, forgive them, for they know not what they do" (Luke 23:34).

"Jesus showed tenderness to the stranger (the widow of Nain) and praised the mercy shown to the Prodigal Son, and to the man beset by thieves on the road to Jericho; it is not surprising then that in his passion Jesus shows forgiveness to those who crucified him."[56]

HOW CAN A RIGHTEOUS GOD FORGIVE UNRIGHTEOUS PEOPLE?

While Jesus provides a stellar example of how we should forgive others, we are still faced with the issue of how a righteous God can forgive his rebellious creation. The fact is, he cannot unless some things happen first. Many of those things are significant accomplishments of Christ's death presented in this book.

The character of God is unfathomable to those who do not know him, and still barely understandable to those of us who do. It is God's stellar character that must hold the line against sin while at the same time showering his love on the sinner. Think about what kind of character can do that.

God is immutable, unchangeable, constant, and always the same in who he is and what he does. God's substance is unchangeable (Ps 102:25–27). He is unchanging in his purpose (Isa 46:10). God is unchanging in his Word (Ps 19:7; 119:86). What God says he will do, you can be sure that he will. When God makes a promise, you can be absolutely confident he will keep it. (Ps 119:89).

The God of the Bible is entirely righteous and just. Righteousness is the quality of being or doing what is right (1 John 2:29). Justice is the quality of being fair (2 Tim 4:8). God always plays fair and does what is right for us and the rest of his creation. "Shall not the Judge of all the earth do what is just?" (Gen 18:25).

God is patient with us

God is merciful and compassionate. "But God, being rich in mercy, because of the great love with which he loved us, even when we were dead in our trespasses, made us alive together with Christ" (Eph 2:4–5). Psalm 103:13 tells us, "As a father shows compassion to his children, so the LORD shows compassion to those who fear him."

Our heavenly Father is long-suffering toward us. Sometimes we are slow learners, and even more often, we are slow to apply what we have learned. But God is patient. He put up with those who provoked him (Exod 34:6; Rom 2:4). He put up with people when they cried, "Crucify him" (Mark 15:14; Luke 23:21; John 19:6). He put up with phony religious leaders when they spit in his Son's face (Matt 26:67; 27:30; Mark 10:34; 14:65; 15:19; Luke 18:32). He put up with Roman soldiers, despite their unbelief (1 Pet 3:20). Why? Because God is love (1 John 4:8,16) and Christ demonstrates God's love for us (Rom 5:6–8). His patience is a by-product of his love.

God's love is universal. He loves everyone regardless of race, creed, or political party. His love is gracious, for he loved us when we were guilty, defiled, and undeserving. God's love is sacrificial, most aptly demonstrated when he gave up his only Son to be crucified on Calvary's Cross. It is the character of his love that enables him to be excessively patient with us.

God had to satisfy divine justice before He could give divine forgiveness

So, how can a God who possesses all these character qualities forgive people who possess few to none of them? God needed no preparation to forgive us, but our relationship with him needed to be changed first. He had to remove the curse on humankind because of sin (Gen 2:15–17). God had to satisfy the need for justice (John 3:36; Rom 1:18; 9:22). He had to place us in a position to be treated as if we were righteous by redeeming us from the marketplace of sin. With these things accomplished on the cross, God was now ready and able to forgive us.

The crowd had chanted, "Crucify him, Crucify him." They had ridiculed and taunted Jesus while he hung on the cross. They stripped him naked to shame him. Everyone mocked him. "Those who passed by derided him, wagging their heads and saying, 'Aha! You who would destroy the temple and rebuild it in three days, save yourself, and come down from the cross!" So also the chief priests with the scribes mocked him to one another, saying, 'He saved others; he cannot save himself'" (Mark 15:29–31). A Roman soldier speared his side all the way to the Savior's heart. Still, God was forgiving, merciful, loving, and pleased with his Son in death. Accomplishments don't get much bigger than this!

There's a wideness in God's mercy,
like the wideness of the sea.
There's a kindness in God's justice,
which is more than liberty.
There is welcome for the sinner,
and more graces for the good.
There is mercy with the Savior,
there is healing in his blood.
—Frederick Faber (1814–1863)

Chapter 8

Jesus Restored Our Severed Relationship With God

The search for significance is the most significant search of humanity. But if our significance is found in insignificant things, our search itself is insignificant.

The Human Need for Significance
We Were Created Significant by God
Our Tragic Loss of Significance
Our Futile Pursuit of Significance
The Consequences of Living Independently of God
The Contrast Between Independent Living and Dependent Living
Reconnecting with God and Finding Significance Again
With Our Significance Returned, How Does the Bible Describe the Christian?
God Blesses Us Now, Not Just In the Future

Presidents do it. Dictators do it. Fathers and mothers do it. Teenagers do it. Do what? They spend their entire lives searching for significance. It is a basic human need to feel significant. We all want it; we all need it.

The dictionary defines significance as "the quality of being important." I would add to that, "the quality of feeling important." Often, people feel significant because of what they do or say, but this can produce a false sense of significance that can be deadly.

People search for significance in some pretty unusual places and some equally unusual ways. To get into the *Guinness World Records* book, Ken Edwards of Glossop, Derbyshire, England, ate thirty-six cockroaches in one minute. Is that significant, or just strange?

In 2017, Ashley Payne of the UK ran the fastest marathon dressed as an elf, in 2 hours 58 minutes and 16 seconds. Isn't that significant?

On November 5, 2007, Jackie Bibby of the U.S. sat in a Dublin, Texas bathtub with a record eighty-seven snakes. Just as an aside, he also holds the record for the most rattlesnakes held in his mouth by the tail (ten). How significant is that?

According to the *Guinness World Records*, here are other significant accomplishments.

- Brazilian Elaine Davidson holds the record for body piercings at 4,225.
- Most eggs crushed with the head (80) in one minute by Ashrita Furman.
- In 2021, Croatian Budimir Šobat held his breath for an astonishing 24 min 37.36 sec.
- Eleven-year-old Fin Keheler allowed forty-three snails to be placed on his face.
- In 2018, Italian Dimitri Panciera balanced a whopping 125 scoops of ice cream on a single cone.
- Ilker Yilmaz, of Istanbul, Turkey, set the distance record at 9'2," for squirting milk from his eye.

People will do the oddest things to feel significant. As of 2017, Ashrita (Keith) Furman has set more than 600 official Guinness records and currently still holds over 200 records, thus holding the Guinness world record for the most Guinness world records. My personal favorite is the head-butt hero, Kevin Shelley. He holds the record for a mind-blowing forty-six wooden toilet seats smashed on his head and shattered in just 60 seconds. That's almost one broken toilet seat every 1.3 seconds! Now that's significant, or is it? How many starving children were fed by Shelley's feat? How did his record lessen the political tensions in the world? Who will spend eternity in heaven because of broken wooden toilet seats? Pause your chuckling for a moment, and think seriously about it.

Unfortunately, most people seeking significance confuse achievement with relevance. In the broader scheme of things, not all achievement is significant. On Tuesday, March 4, 2025, American basketball player LeBron James achieved something no one else has in history. He reached the

50,000-point mark in his basketball career. That's quite an achievement, but is it significant? The sad thing is that, for most, when their achievement is no longer recognized, their significance is no longer recognized either.

THE HUMAN NEED FOR SIGNIFICANCE

You start on the ground floor of your company. You work hard and slowly but steadily begin to climb the corporate ladder. The people in your office begin to realize you will someday run this company, and indeed, you do. After years of hard work and loyalty to your company, you are finally made president and CEO. You are at the pinnacle of your career. You've made it. You're significant.

Mistaken significance

However, over time, your company begins to experience some losses and downturns. The board feels some of the blame falls on you. After a particularly stressful year, you are let go at the annual board meeting. You are no longer the president and CEO. No longer are you at the top of your game. No longer are you even in the game. What made you significant is now gone, and you are disheartened, discouraged, and depressed. All your significance was in your position; now that it is gone, so is your significance.

Alternatively, to paint another scenario, when you were still a preteen, you enjoyed playing football. You and your friends played ball every day after school until your mother called you for dinner. In high school, your skills were sharpened by your coach. Eventually, you became the first-string running back. You were beginning to feel significant. You became a top college prospect, and you had your pick of four or five institutions to attend on a football scholarship. You got a full ride because others thought you were significant. Next stop—the NFL. You had a fabulous career due to your considerable contributions to the team. You won the MVP award twice. That proves you are significant. And then it happened.

You got tackled from behind and came down awkwardly, landing on your knee. What's worse, a massive 300+ pound lineman landed on top of you. You are carted off the field without realizing you would never return. Your career came to an abrupt end. You still have your trophies and your memories, but what you no longer have is your significance. You lost that when you blew out your knee.

These are just two examples of mistaken significance. I'm sure you can think of many more. Many people find their significance in what they can do, the position they have attained, the number of copies their book has sold, the number of people they have working for them, the number of grandkids they have, and so on. However, what happens when they cannot do that anymore, or they spend years writing a book that no publisher wants, or their grandchildren no longer sing, "Over the river and through the woods, to grandmother's house we go." They never visit. They never call. They never text. They are out of your life

Finding significance in insignificance

When you seek your significance in that which does not, cannot last, what happens when your significant thing is gone? How do you handle not being as significant as you once were? For some, all of life's meaning goes out the window, and they abandon themselves to a life of depression.

Athletes yearn to be part of the team again. Corporate CEOs miss hosting the annual Christmas party, where everyone gets bonuses. Grandmas miss seeing their grandkids. For far too many, when the relationship that gave their life significance ends, life is essentially over.

To most people, significance is essential. Nevertheless, they don't know where to find it. The Bible, however, addresses this issue head-on. Let's explore our God-given significance, the heartbreaking loss of it, and how we can regain it through what Jesus accomplished on the cross.

WE WERE CREATED SIGNIFICANT BY GOD

Most have never given it much thought, but one of the significant accomplishments of Christ's death on the cross was to restore significance to us by reuniting our severed relationship with God. Here's why that's important.

God created us with significance. Human beings were the capstone—the crown—of his creation. In all that God created, we were his "pride and joy." Think with me about what made us God's special creation.

People: God's most significant creation

First, we humans were the last of his creation (Gen 1:23–27), his finest work, his *magnum opus*. We were created on the final day of the creation week. That in itself gave us significance. After day 5, Genesis 1:26 says, "Then God said, 'Let us make man in our image, after our likeness.'" Our being created on the final day doesn't mean God finally got it right. Everything he created was already just right. It simply means that God waited until all the pieces were in place and the universe was just right before creating people to enjoy His creation.

The Genesis record of creation builds from day one to day six. In that way, it is similar to Piotr Ilich Tchaikovsky's 1812 Overture. It begins with a whisper. You can barely hear it. Nevertheless, it ends with church bells, a strong-voiced choir, and, if you're enjoying the Boston Pops performance, cannons blasting away. Everything builds to the end.

Creation can also be likened to the William Tell Overture, which sounds like music from a meadow until you hear the Lone Ranger riding over the bluff. Creation builds. Each day is a singular accomplishment, but the most significant accomplishment comes on day six, when, out of the dust of the ground, God created a man—a human being, a person created in the image of the Divine Person. That we were the "final" creation gives us intrinsic significance.

Adam was created from existing material

Second, God used existing material to create Adam. Most theologians understand creation to have been accomplished by fiat. That is, God simply spoke the world into existence. In fact, the Hebrew word for creation (Hebrew: בָּרָא; English: *bârâ'*) means to create by divine fiat. This implies that God needed no outside help in creation. The word *bârâ'* also means God had no material to work with. God just spoke, and there was light. He spoke, and there were fields and forests. By just speaking, unaccompanied by any outside forces, there were animals of all kinds, and there was a planet "just right" for us to live on. All this he accomplished by word of mouth, God's word, from God's mouth. No purchase order was available for the required materials. He spoke, and his creation appeared.

Nevertheless, the creation of the first man was decidedly different. God took a handful of earth and from this raw material, he fashioned his creative masterpiece. Adam and his posterity would forever be reminded, "You are dust, and to dust you shall return" (Gen 3:19). Remember, however, at this point, the dirt of the ground was still pure, undefiled by sin. God used a readily available raw material. However, he took this common material and made with it something decidedly uncommon—a human being. That gave us significance.

Adam was created in God's image

Third, Adam was created in the image of God. This was not the case with the flora and fauna. It was not true of the giraffe, the alligator, or the salmon. It was not true of the mighty sequoia, the velvet rose, or a field of corn. It was only true of humankind. After he had created everything else, Genesis 1:26 informs us, "Then God said, 'Let us make man in our image, after our likeness.'" The next verse reads as history, recording that God did precisely what the Holy Trinity intended. "So God created man in his own image, in the image of God he created him; male and female he created them."

> "Is it not wonderful news to believe that salvation lies outside ourselves"?—Martin Luther

Being made in the image of God does not mean we are divine. It does not mean we will ever become God (or an angel, for that matter). Our image is godlike because we have a spirit that is in tune with God's spirit.[57]

Others may disagree, but I believe this means that, while animals—fish, amphibians, and so on—also have a body, and while breathing animals have a soul (that which animates the body), only humanity has a spirit. It is that spirit that tunes us to God and places us on the same spiritual wavelength as God. It is the spiritual component humans possess that distinguishes us from and sets us above the lower creatures. Lions have a body and soul, but no spirit. Your family pet, which you love dearly, has a body and soul, but no spirit. You and I possess a body, soul, and spirit because we were created in the image of God. That gave us significance.

Adam was also created in God's likeness

Fourth, we were not only created in the image of God, but also in the likeness of God. "Let us make man in our image, after our likeness" (Gen 1:26). Is there a difference between image and likeness, or is it a distinction without a difference?[58] I believe there is both a distinction and a difference. Let me explain.

The words "image" and "likeness" are distinct in the original Hebrew. "Image" is (Hebrew: צֶלֶם; English: *tselem*) while "likeness" is (Hebrew: דְּמוּת; *dᵉmûwth*). The distinction lies in the meanings and uses of the Hebrew words. The word *"tselem"* is used whenever Genesis speaks of man being created in the image of God (Gen 1:26; 27 (twice); 5:3; 9:6). "Tselem" means the exact image, the express image, a spiritual connectivity unique to humankind. Genesis 5:3 also makes a distinction between the image of God and the likeness of God, saying, "When Adam had lived 130 years, he fathered a son in his own likeness, after his image, and named him Seth." That a distinction is made is clear.

The difference appears to be that "likeness" is not as strong a noun as "image." Both "express correspondence to God, [but] 'likeness' indicates that this correspondence is one of similarity, not identicalness."[59] When the Bible writers wanted to express that something was similar to another but not a duplicate of another, they would use the word *d*^{e}*mûwth* (see 2 Kgs 16:10; 2 Chron 4:3; Ps 58:4; Isa 13:4. The prophet Ezekiel uses *d*^{e}*mûwth* no less than sixteen times (Ezek 1:5 (x2), 10, 13, 16, 22, 26 (x3), 28, etc.).

Thus, the language appears to favor the idea that as humans, we were both created in God's image with spiritual connectivity to him, and in his likeness, with similarity to him. Nothing else in God's creation possesses these two qualities, except human beings. That gives us significance.

God breathed the breath of life directly into Adam

Fifth, we were the only creation of God into which the Sovereign God personally breathed the breath of life. Could this just be Hebrew poetry? That's certainly possible, as animals exhibit various breathing patterns depending on their environment. There are aquatic and terrestrial animals, large and small, and each uses a method of breathing adapted to its habitat. Whether through their nose in the middle of their face or gills on their side, all fish, amphibians, reptiles, birds, and mammals "breathe" through interaction with their living environment. When they are born, they draw their first breath from the environment around them, whether it be air or water.

Not so with the first man. After creation, Adam did not inhale a large amount of rarified air in the Garden of Eden. He didn't fill his lungs before exploring the Garden of Eden. Genesis 2:7 records a fascinating detail of creation. "Then the LORD God formed the man of dust from the ground and breathed into his nostrils the breath of life, and the man became a living creature."

This was Adam's first breath, and it was not just a breath of fresh air. This was a breath of God's air. God actually exhaled the breath of life into Adam's nostrils, and the man became a living being. Genesis presents this as fact, not as a metaphor. That gave us significance. This was not done for the great apes or the tiniest puppy. It was not done for Adam's offspring. It was not done for Eve. God breathed only into Adam the breath of life.

> "This is the idea that God, by a direct act, brought into being virtually instantaneously everything that is."—Millard Erickson

However, subsequently, Cain, Abel, Seth, and all the other children would know they were special because they came from Adam, who inhaled the breath of God directly from the mouth of God. This should make you feel pretty significant as well because you first breathed from someone who first breathed from someone who ultimately drew breath from a man whose first breath was from God. Think about it. You are exceptional. In Las Vegas, the expression "I shook Sinatra's hand" was something of a gentlemen's agreement, an unbreakable code between the members of an exclusive group. Well, you are a member of such a group, the human being group, because your first ancestor took his first breath from the mouth of God, which is super special.

God did not create hybrids

Finally, everything in creation was made "each according to its kind" (Gen 1:12, 21, 24, 25). Newborn alligators crack out of their eggs looking exactly like adult alligators, only much, much smaller. Why? Because kind produces kind. The only way kind does not produce after its kind is if there has been a genetic alteration or mutation.

I live in Nebraska. This is a major region for beef and corn production. In fact, in the early summer when the days are hot and rain is likely, I can sit at night out on my deck and listen to the corn grow. That's an exaggeration, of course, but in the days I used to drive every morning some twenty miles into Lincoln to my office and the recording studio, when I went back home at the end of the workday, the corn was noticeably higher than in the morning. Part of the reason is that universities in the Midwest all have an "Ag Department" that constantly works to improve corn hybrids to increase yields. This is when kind reproduces a hybrid type.

Not so in God's creation. All of his creation reproduced "according to its kind," and since we were part of God's special creation and Adam was made in God's image and after his likeness, we were created according to the "God kind." That does not make us God, but it makes us more like God than we are like the great apes or orangutans that were produced "according to their kind." We are God's special creation, made in his spiritual image. Nothing else in the vast creation of God is as close to the heart of God as you and I are. It was our unique relationship with God that gave us significance at creation.

As humans, Adam and Eve enjoyed fellowship with God, a fellowship that no other creation by God enjoyed. The key to Adam's significance was not in his ability or who he was. The sole source of Adam's significance was his unique relationship with God. His connection to God was the key factor in his success. Our relationship with God is what gives us significance as well. As long as that relationship is unbroken, we have an importance that nothing else in the created world can compare.

But Adam and Eve did not enjoy that significance for long.

OUR TRAGIC LOSS OF SIGNIFICANCE

Unfortunately, soon Adam's divine image was tarnished, and his blessed fellowship with God was broken. Genesis 3:1–6 records how Satan, disguised himself in the form of a serpent, came to Eve when she was alone, questioned the veracity of God, and lied about God's intentions for the crown of his creation. Sadly, Eve and later Adam listened to Satan's lies and chose to join his rebellion against God, deliberately disobeying God.

Today, people often disobey God. The rebellion against God is intense and currently overwhelming our society. We live on a sin-cursed planet as a result of Adam's sin and our complicity in his sin. In my lifetime, I have seen my country go from Bible-reading, God-fearing families who never missed church to disintegrated families with foul minds and mouths, tearing down society because they have no moral compass and never attend church.

The interaction of God and Adam

When God confronted Adam and Eve about their sin, he began by asking Adam questions to which the Almighty already knew the answers. "Where are you?" (Gen 3:9). Adam and Eve were hiding because they knew they had sinned and recognized they were naked. That brought them shame. Adam mumbled, "I was afraid, because I was naked, and I hid myself" (v. 10). God had a remarkable comeback. "Who told you that you were naked? (v. 11). Think about it. Who could have told him? There were only Adam and Eve. Actually, nobody had to tell Adam he was naked. Suddenly, he realized it for himself. Before this, apparently, Adam and Eve weren't even cognizant of the fact that they had no clothing.

But the most piercing question from God followed. "Have you eaten of the tree of which I commanded you not to eat?" (v. 11). Adam did next what most men do. Verse 12 records his answer to God's direct question. "The woman whom you gave to be with me, she gave me fruit of the tree, and I ate." How did that answer God's question? It didn't; it was just Adam's way of shifting personal responsibility to someone else. It must have been God's fault because he gave Eve to Adam. Or, it was Eve's fault because she was alone in the garden with Satan. It had to be her.

Nevertheless, Eve was no better. She quickly said, "The serpent deceived me, and I ate." Shift the blame to the snake. Granted, Satan used the serpent for his Trojan Horse entrance into the garden, but both Adam and Eve have now sinned. Both Adam and Eve have, for the first time, recognized that they were naked. For the first time, our first parents felt the pain of shame.

Our first family was kicked out of the Garden of Eden

Shifting the blame did not work. God was not buying their flimsy excuses. Because they were now sinful, God had to remove them from the Garden of Eden lest they eat of the Tree of Life and remain in their sinful state forever. The last two verses of Genesis 3 say, "The LORD God sent him out from the garden of Eden to work the ground from which he was taken. He drove out the man, and to the east of the garden of Eden, he placed the cherubim with a flaming sword that rotated every way to guard the way to the tree of life." God had to drive Adam and Eve from their idyllic home because their sin would taint everything they previously enjoyed. If they ate of the Tree of Life, they would permanently be kept in a sinful state with no redemption, no salvation, and no hope.

Instead of walking in fellowship with God in the cool of this beautiful garden, Adam and Eve were now banished from it. Their closeness to God was disrupted. In siding with Satan and disobeying God, their unique relationship with God was now severed. No more would they enjoy his presence. No more would they live in the warmth of his company. Their relationship was detached, disconnected, and destroyed by their sin. They were now on the outside looking in.

What gave Adam and Eve significance—their unique relationship with their Creator—was now gone. They not only lost their home in Eden, but worse, they had severed their relationship with God, the connection that gave them significance. Ever since, we, the descendants of Adam and Eve, have been doing whatever we could dream up to regain that significance, often in wild and crazy, but always futile, ways.

OUR FUTILE PURSUIT OF SIGNIFICANCE

Our relationship with our Creator severed, we sought significance in other ways. Some looked for it in their position. They became president of something or other. Others sought significance in education. Having that PhD behind their name is what they deem their most important accomplishment. Some people seek significance in their achievements. The *Guinness World Records* features hundreds of people who believed they were "significant," some because they've grown the world's longest mustache or fingernails. But as I said, our pursuit of significance has always been futile.

The wrong source to regain significance

There is a problem with our search for significance. All our attempts to regain our lost significance come from within us. All our attempts are something we do or try to be. But what happens to our significance when we can no longer do whatever it was we thought gave us significance? What makes the president significant after he retires? What makes the PhD significant when her paper is peer-reviewed and found to be inaccurate, inept, or worse, plagiarized? What significance does the *Guinness World Records* holder have when their record is shattered by someone else? What happens when what we relied on for significance is destroyed? The answer is obvious. Our significance is also destroyed. It is gone.

Ultimately, we must conclude that we cannot regain significance by what we do, who we are, or what others think of us. Singer Bobby Darin wrote a song, especially for Frank Sinatra, one line of which reveals, "To say the things he truly feels, and not the words of one who kneels; the record shows I took the blows, and did it my, my way." Once, when I was with a Christian businessman in Cuba, we were talking about his success when he bragged, "I owe a lot of it to the fact that I did it my way." I reminded him that is the national anthem of all the people in hell.

Doing life our way severs our relationship and separates us from God. That's what happened to Adam. When that special relationship is gone, our significance goes with it. Perhaps now we can understand the immortal words of the Bard when he said that life "is a tale told by an idiot, full of sound and fury, signifying nothing." (William Shakespeare, *Macbeth*, Act 5, Scene 5).

I have always said that the search for significance is the most significant search of humanity. But if our significance is found in insignificant things, our search itself is insignificant.

THE CONSEQUENCES OF LIVING INDEPENDENTLY FROM GOD

When our first parents were expelled from the Garden, they had a whole new life. They were independent. Their ties to their Creator were severed, so they were free to do as they pleased. They now had freedom, but soon realized that, while estranged from God, it wasn't what they expected.

Whereas God provided for their every need in the garden, now Adam must work hard, by the sweat of his brow, to till the soil. Adam had to battle weeds, thistles, thorns, and briers. When Eve gave birth, she experienced a level of pain she had never known before. All this came with human freedom and the independence they sought from God. Suddenly, they felt insignificant.

A whole new kind of life

After severing their relationship with God, Adam and Eve did not just have a different outlook on life; they had an entirely different kind of life—life without a connection to their Creator. Before they sinned, they had a dependent relationship with God. That dependence brought bliss, harmony, and an abundance of everything they would need or even desire. Now, they have a completely independent, non-relationship with God, and it's turning out to be a nightmare. They are on their own, free to do as they please, but there is no harmony in their lives and no abundance in their pantry. There is but pain and sorrow. There is everything that life without God brings.

That independence, along with its consequences, Adam and Eve passed on to everyone who followed them biologically. That includes you and me. We are experiencing the same pain of independence from God that Adam and Eve did. We live in a world wholly overrun by sin, sinful people, and sinful ideas. Since we now have no meaningful relationship with God, we have no meaningful significance. We have no sense of purpose. Ecclesiastes 3:11 says that God "has put eternity into man's heart," but men and women have difficulty today finding God's eternity. They are estranged from the God who created them with significance, which means they are also estranged from any real significance.

Sit alone in a quiet place and be honest with yourself. Brutally honest. Where do you get your significance? Is it being a mother, a grandmother, or a supervisor? Is your significance found in your team, on the court, or on the field? Is what you are doing really significant? Does it matter for time?

Does it matter for eternity? Does it matter at all? If you are confronting insignificance, perhaps for the first time, I have good news for you.

The cure for insignificance is not natural; it's supernatural

There is a cure for our tragic loss of significance, but it's a hard pill to swallow. We must admit to many things that, intrinsically, we don't want to admit to and are prone to diverting elsewhere. We must admit we are sinners. We must acknowledge that, whatever else we can do physically or mentally, we are spiritual failures. We must agree that when our dependent relationship with God was voluntarily cut, Adam made a horrible mistake. We must admit that his mistake is our mistake today. We must come clean with God, stop our foolish independence, and rediscover the source of our original significance in the Garden of Eden. We must find a way to restore the relationship that initially gave us significance. Is it even possible?

> "Jesus did not come to Earth to show us the way; He came to be the way."—Woodrow Michael Kroll

We all need to rediscover our significance, not in the things we do or who we have become, but in returning to a dependent relationship with our Creator God. That's the only way possible. This is why St. Augustine said of God, "You have made us for yourself, O Lord, and our heart is restless until it rests in you." Real significance is found only in a restored relationship with our Creator.

THE CONTRAST BETWEEN INDEPENDENT LIVING AND DEPENDENT LIVING

The contrast between those who are still living independently of God, thinking they are creating their own path, doing things their own way, thumbing their nose at God, and those who are enjoying a life dependent on God could not be more striking.

Table 2: What We Are When We Have No Relationship With God

We are	
Separated from Christ	Ephesians 2:12
Aliens from the safety and identity of the people of God	Ephesians 2:12
Strangers from God's covenants and promises	Ephesians 2:12
Hopeless vagabonds with a very dim future	Ephesians 2:12
Darkened in our understanding	Ephesians 4:18
Alienated from the life of God because of this ignorance	Ephesians 4:18
Hard-hearted due to the influence of sin over us	Ephesians 4:18
Mostly callous and always given to sensuality	Ephesians 4:19
Greedy to indulge in every kind of impure living	Ephesians 4:19

However, things are even worse for those who live independently of God. A darker result of independent living is hopelessness.

"No hope." The two most demoralizing words

There are not two more devastating words in any language than the words "no hope." Paul described humankind this way. "Remember that you were at that time separated from Christ . . . having no hope and without God in the world" (Eph 2:12). No relationship with God, no significance. No significance, no hope. Had it not been for what Christ accomplished in his death on the cross, the future would be bleak for all of us.

However, Paul continued in the next verse, "But now in Christ Jesus, you who once were far off have been brought near by the blood of Christ" (Eph 2:13).

> "Growing up a devout Muslim, it took years of investigation for me to realize that the cross of Jesus Christ—the very thing I had thought insulted God's greatness—was the very thing that demonstrates it."—Abdu Murray

Once we were far from God, but because of the blood of Christ shed at Calvary, we have the opportunity to be brought close to him, to have our relationship with God reinstated, and our significance restored.

Once we had a severed relationship, but now, because of the blood of Jesus and his death on the cross, we can have that relationship repaired, restored, reconnected, and renewed, made as good as new.

Once, we were aliens, strangers, and hopeless vagabonds. But with a reconnected relationship with God by faith in the Savior's death, everything is new, and we have become significant again.

When reconnected with God, who we become

When we are in a restored, dependent relationship with the Almighty, things change instantly. Straight from the pages of Scripture come these benefits of a restored relationship with God:

- We are again the finely crafted workmanship of the Creator (Eph 2:8–10)
- We are a saint in the biblical sense of the word (Eph 1:15–18)
- We are again a son or daughter of God (1 John 3:1–2; Rom 8:14–16)
- We are an heir to a fabulously wealthy Father (Rom 8:16–17)
- We are again a special person (1 Pet 2:9–10)
- We are a finely tuned athlete, competing by the rules (1 Cor 9:25; 2 Tim 2:5).
- We are a good soldier in the army of the Lord (Phil 2:25; 2 Tim 2:3–4)
- We are ambassadors for Christ Jesus (2 Cor 5:17–20).

When our relationship with God is restored through Christ's blood, we can again enjoy the benefits of being reconnected with the Almighty.

RECONNECTING WITH GOD AND FINDING SIGNIFICANCE AGAIN

Unmistakably, we humans lost big time when our relationship with the loving God was severed. When Adam and Eve disobeyed God, it was the worst day of our collective lives. Adam represented the entire human race. He acted as the federal head of all the human beings who would follow him. It wasn't just a dark day in history. It was the darkest day.

However, God has promised in his Word that our severed relationship with him can be restored. But how? Again, the Bible provides the answer.

Relying on God to repair our severed relationship

How can we find our way back to God? Honestly, we can't. God is righteous and holy; we are unrighteous and unholy. God is just; we are unjust. We are like oil and water; we just do not mix because God is the epitome of righteousness and holiness, and we are slugs, worms, and wretches, as the old hymn writers liked to say. However, since we could not go to God, God came to us. Jesus, God the Son, came to earth and became human in a unique combination—the God-man. That was God's plan.

Here are the essential points of the divine plan.

- God always has a plan, and his plan to bring us back to significance was a plan he would activate and accomplish all by himself (John 1:1–3, 14; Luke 19:10).
- God's plan would require death for life, because "the life of the flesh is in the blood" (Lev 17:11).
- God's plan has always required the ultimate sacrifice be made to open the door for us to return to a positive relationship with him, a relationship that would restore our significance.
- God's plan would accept nothing less than perfection (Lev 22:18–20; see Mal 1:6–8).

Quality control for his plan required three things from God. First, he would have to devise the plan himself. If we or any other creature lent a hand in coming up with a plan, it would be flawed, spoiled, tainted by sin. Second, he would have to implement the plan himself to ensure it was executed flawlessly. It was the only way. Third, to ensure that a perfect sacrifice would be made to atone for our sin, God would have to offer himself as that sacrifice. There was no other way. Only God could be the perfect sacrifice because only God is perfect in character, thought, and action.

> "Peace on earth, and mercy mild, God and sinners reconciled!"
> —Charles Wesley

Peter reminds us, "You were ransomed from the futile ways inherited from your forefathers, not with perishable things such as silver or gold, but with the precious blood of Christ, like that of a lamb without blemish or spot" (1 Pet 1:18–19).

Perhaps the best part of God's plan to restore our significance is that it would require nothing from us but trust in his Son and his plan. This is the truth expressed by Jesus in John 3:16–18, "For God so loved the world, that he gave his only Son, that whoever believes in him should not perish but have eternal life. For God did not send his Son into the world to condemn the world, but in order that the world might be saved through him. Whoever believes in him is not condemned, but whoever does not believe is condemned already, because he has not believed in the name of the only Son of God."

To God's plan, no additions are needed or accepted. God's plan is not open to suggestion, alteration, or modification. It is a foolproof plan. It's the only plan that will reconnect us with God. It's the only plan that will return us to true significance.

Long before the Garden of Eden was created, long before Adam and Eve sinned in that garden, and long before you drew your first breath or sinned yourself, God already had a plan to save you from your sin. The Passion Week set this plan in motion, and it played out precisely as the eternal God had designed.

Restoring right relationships

In the eternal plan of God, his Son was destined to die on a Roman cross. We must know that the cross is not about establishing religion; it's about restoring a right relationship with our Heavenly Father.

When a woman and her husband have a poor relationship, that isn't good, but it's not eternal. When a daughter has a bad relationship with her parents, it's not fatal. However, when any of us has a broken relationship with our Creator, it's devastating, life-changing, and eternal unless we change.

That change came at a place called Calvary, on a Friday afternoon, when the innocent Jesus of Nazareth was crucified on a Roman cross. By his death, Jesus opened the door to restore our relationship with our Creator God. In restoring a dependent relationship with God, Christ also restored the significance of such a relationship.

As followers of Jesus Christ, children of our Heavenly Father, we are again significant. "In all these things we are more than conquerors through him who loved us" (Rom 8:37). That was a highly significant accomplishment of Christ's death.

WITH OUR SIGNIFICANCE RETURNED, HOW DOES THE BIBLE DESCRIBE THE CHRISTIAN?

Who are you? I don't mean "What's your name," I mean, who are you, really? Are you just a bundle of taste buds, salivary glands, and organs wrapped up in a package of skin, covered with hair (some of you), animated by breath?

Who are you in God's eyes? Who are you since that day you were saved? Who are you for eternity? Let's conclude this chapter by identifying who you are as a new creation in Christ Jesus. You aren't just a do-over. Your name is not Mulligan. You aren't just a sinner saved by grace. When your relationship with God was restored, you became much, much more. Here's what the Bible says about you.

#1. You are a real piece of work.

Please don't misunderstand. I don't say that in a derogatory way, but you are indeed a real piece of work—God's work. That's exactly what Paul told the Christ-followers in Ephesus. Here's what he wrote in his letter to them. "For by grace you have been saved through faith. And this is not your own doing; it is the gift of God, not a result of works, so that no one may boast. For we are his workmanship, created in Christ Jesus for good works, which God prepared beforehand, that we should walk in them."

God didn't save you so you could skip hell. God recreated you, restoring your relationship with him, so you would both be joyful in him and useful to him. As the Master Potter, God has skillfully molded your life to fill a role that he has created just for you, only for you.

In 1970, I moved to France to study at the Université de Strasbourg. It was my senior year in seminary. The classes were all in French from Monday through Friday. That left weekends for trips to Switzerland, Germany, and France. One of my favorite villages in France was Oberbetsdorf (now just Betsdorf), less than an hour's drive north of Strasbourg. In this village, everyone was a potter. I don't mean that was their name; that was their occupation.

Once in Oberbetsdorf, you could walk into a private home, through the house, and out back; you were bound to find a potter or two at their wheels. I was always amazed how they could thump a five-pound block of clay onto the wheel, put some water on their hands, and almost instantly have the makings of a two-foot-high vase. Moreover, when I would ask, they would instantly reduce that tall clay to a flat pot.

This is what God has in mind for us. Once our relationship is restored, we are his workmanship, his lump of clay. He wants us to be willing, to be pliable, so he can shape us for exactly the role he has in mind for us. Let him mold you into whatever he has for you. That way, you can be a real piece of work. You will be significant again.

An Alsatian Woman With Her Pottery

#2. You are a saint.

A Christian is not someone who is forgiven and goes to heaven. A Christian is a person who has become what they were not before. Having our relationship restored with the Heavenly Father makes us saints.

Saints are not dead sinners beatified. Saints are sinners (whether living or dead) whose deepest identity before God has been radically changed forever. When Ananias of Damascus heard that Saul of Tarsus was coming to his house, he prayed, "Lord, I have heard from many about this man, how much evil he has done to your saints at Jerusalem" (Acts 9:13). The "saints" in Jerusalem were the followers of Jesus. They were people who were enjoying their restored relationship with God.

The Apostle Paul traveled heavily throughout Greece and Turkey. Everywhere he went, he preached the Good News of salvation through faith in Jesus Christ. And everywhere he went, he established a church, a group of Christians who met together for prayer, fellowship, worship, observing the ordinances, and the study of God's Word. On two occasions, he returned to those churches to strengthen them. When he could not be there in person, he wrote letters. These letters are the thirteen epistles of the Apostle Paul.

As a Roman citizen, Paul was accustomed to writing letters in the Roman style. As a result, he often addressed these letters to the "saints" living in a specific city or region. Here are some examples:

- Romans 1:7—"To all those in Rome who are loved by God and called to be *saints*"
- Ephesians 1:1—"To the *saints* who are in Ephesus, and are faithful in Christ Jesus."
- Colossians 1:2—"To the *saints* and faithful brothers in Christ at Colossae."
- 1 Corinthians 1:2—"To the church of God that is in Corinth, to those sanctified in Christ Jesus, called to be *saints* . . ."
- Philippians 1:1—"To all the *saints* in Christ Jesus who are at Philippi, with the overseers and deacons."

You don't have to be dead to be a saint. All you need is to be in a right relationship with the God of heaven. The Christians in Rome, Ephesus, Colossae, Corinth, and Philippi could be addressed as saints because they were in the family of God. They were born again and were enjoying the privileges of being saints. People who have come to faith in Christ all over the world are called God's saints, not just the special dead of the Church.

It surprises many people that there were "saints" in the Old Testament as well. They were not followers of Jesus of Nazareth, but they did believe in God's promises and lived their lives accordingly. Therefore, the psalmist said, "Love the LORD, all you his *saints*! The LORD preserves the faithful" (Ps 31:23) and a word of comfort, "Precious in the sight of the LORD is the death of his *saints*. (Ps 116:15).

Some saints you may know are St. Paul, St. Peter, St. James, St. Andrew, St. Bartholomew, St. Woodrow (oh, I like the sound of that), St. John, et al. While Revelation 8:3, 4 mentions the prayers "of" the saints, nowhere does the Bible mention prayers "to" the saints. You don't pray to the saints, you pray for the saints, the living saints. Enjoy being a saint because of your restored relationship with the Father. That makes you special again.

#3. You are a son or daughter of God

For years, Bhumibol Adulyadej was the King of Thailand, and Sirikit was his queen. When Bhumibol died on October 13, 2016, his only son ascended the throne. Vajiralongkorn became king because he was the son of the king.

We, too, are children of the King, but ours doesn't just rule one country. Our King is Jesus, and he is the King of kings (Rev 19:16). We belong to him because we are sons and daughters of God. If your relationship with God has been reconnected through salvation, you are a child of God as well. Read what the Apostle John had to say about being a child of God.

> See what kind of love the Father has given to us, that we should be called children of God; and so we are. The reason why the world does not know us is that it did not know him. Beloved, we are God's children now, and what we will be has not yet appeared; but we know that when he appears we shall be like him, because we shall see him as he is. And everyone who thus hopes in him purifies himself as he is pure (1 John 3:1–3).

The Apostle Paul also refers to us as the children of God.

> For all who are led by the Spirit of God are sons of God. For you did not receive the spirit of slavery to fall back into fear, but you have received the Spirit of adoption as sons, by whom we cry, "Abba! Father!" The Spirit himself bears witness with our spirit that we are children of God (Rom 8:14–16).

Because you are a child of God, you are someone special. Your Father is the God of the universe, the one true God, the God who is love. Enjoy your status as a child of God.

Children of the heav'nly Father,
safely in His bosom gather;
Nestling bird nor star in Heaven,
such a refuge e'er was given.

Neither life nor death shall ever,
from the Lord His children sever;
unto them His grace He showeth,
and their sorrows all He knoweth.

Tho He giveth or He taketh,
God His children ne'er forsaketh;
His the loving purpose solely,
to preserve them pure and holy.
—Carolina Sandell Berg (1832–1903)

But the Bible is not finished describing you once your relationship with God is reconnected.

#4. You are the heir to a fabulously wealthy Father

Being a child of God is not just a status. It is a familial relationship that is to be cherished. Again, the Apostle Paul has something to say about this. "The Spirit himself bears witness with our spirit that we are children of God, and if children, then heirs—heirs of God and fellow heirs with Christ (Rom 8:16, 17).

My earthly father preceded my mother in death. Just before my mother died at age 95, I could see there was a strained look on her face. When I asked what she was so concerned about, she replied, "I have no inheritance to give to my sons." She was worried because, as the wife of a pastor, she was unable to accumulate the wealth others had. She was heartbroken. I explained to her that an inheritance is more than money. As her heir, my brothers and I received a love for the Word that was unexplainable without her. My mother taught "release time" classes in the public school for years. This meant any student who wanted could attend her Bible classes, which were an "unofficial" part of the school's curriculum. She loved the Word and taught it to each of us almost daily, as well as to our children.

My mother had a plush royal blue carpet in her living room. I came into the house one day to find her and two of my small children lying on that carpet. When I asked what on earth they were doing, the kids yelled with excitement, "Grandma is telling us Bible stories. We're Jonah in the deep, blue sea, and Grandma is the whale." That was her legacy. I couldn't have wanted more.

Being the heir of God doesn't often mean we'll be rich, but it does mean possessing things that are more important and more valuable than money. Enjoy being the heir of God and a joint heir with Jesus Christ. What a privilege.

Created with significance. Lost our significance. Restored significance through Calvary. That's God's plan for regaining significance. Don't place your significance in your position, your prominence, or your possessions. All those will change, and one day you will lose them as significance-makers. The only way to regain the significance you had in the Garden of Eden is for the relationship with God that was severed to be reconnected through the blood of Jesus Christ. Stop looking for significance in insignificant places and things. Find true significance in returning to your Lord at the foot of the cross.

An eighth-century Irish hymn, rooted in medieval Celtic Christianity, in small part, captures the close relationship with God that comes with regained significance. Accomplishments don't get much bigger than this!

Be thou my wisdom, and thou my true word;
I ever with thee and thou with me, Lord.
Thou my great Father; thine own may I be,
thou in me dwelling and I one with thee.

Riches I heed not, nor vain, empty praise;
thou mine inheritance, now and always;
thou and thou only first in my heart,
high King of heaven, my treasure thou art.

—Dallán Forgaill (ca. 560—640 AD)

Chapter 9

Jesus Exchanged Our Human Shame for His Divine Glory

At Calvary, Jesus bore the stain of shame because he looked beyond the cross to the joy that awaited him. He did not want the shame. He did not invite the shame. But neither did he avoid it.

What is Shame?
Shame Enters the Human Family
The Shame of Nakedness
The Shame of Crucifixion
The Shame of Nakedness and Crucifixion

The nineteenth-century French sculptor August Rodin is best known for his bronze statue of a man, sitting on a large rock in deep thought and contemplation. It is known worldwide as "The Thinker." Perhaps lesser known is Rodin's marble statue entitled "Eve After the Fall." It depicts Eve recoiling in shame, covering herself, from the consequences of her disobedience to God. She is in despair and ashamed. Rodin appears to have caught the essence of the shame the first family experienced in the Garden of Eden.

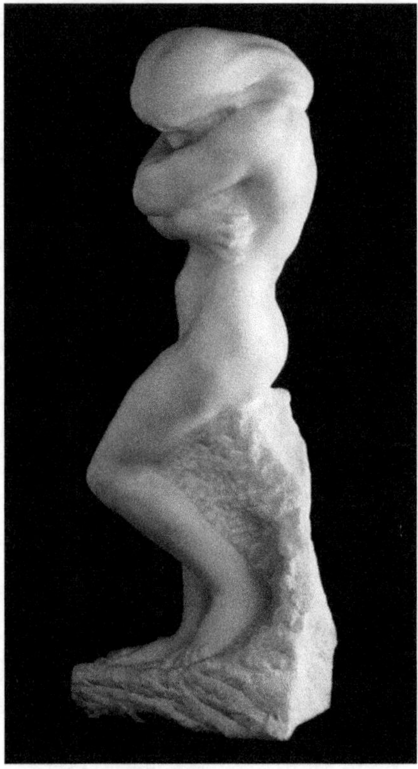

"Eve After The Fall"

The dictionary defines shame as "a painful feeling of humiliation or distress caused by the consciousness of wrong or foolish behavior." In other words, when you act foolishly and humiliate yourself, the result is shame. Synonyms for shame are guilt, remorse, and regret. And then there are the five "d" words describing shame: degrading, demeaning, discrediting, debasing, and dishonoring.

Let's see if we can discover the essence of shame as Rodin did in the original account in the first book of the Bible and the gospel accounts of Jesus' crucifixion.

WHAT IS SHAME?

Before we can explore the shame that Jesus bore hanging for six hours on that cross, we must be certain we understand the meaning of shame. What is it? How do people define it? How does God view it? What do we know of it, and what can we say for sure about it? Shame is an important factor in life. We should at least know what it is.

The psychological definition

According to Brené Brown, a researcher at the University of Houston, shame is an "intensely painful feeling or experience of believing that we are flawed and therefore unworthy of love and belonging."[60] No wonder, then, the last thing we want to do when gripped by shame is talk about it. If we do, others may discover just how horrible we are.

Most psychologists distinguish between guilt and shame. Shame affects who we are; guilt affects what we've done. Shame says, "I'm a bad person," while guilt says, "I've done a bad thing." When Adam and Eve committed the first sin in the garden, I believe they were infected with both guilt and shame. They realized for the first time that they had become sinners and that they had sinned against God. Their consciences told them they had done something wrong. By doing something wrong, they each had become wrong.

Okay, that was fine for our first parents, but what about all their descendants? Does the Bible have anything to say about the shame individuals experienced in both Old and New Testament times? Indeed, it does.

The Old Testament vocabulary of shame

If you think shame was not crucial to Old Testament writers, think again. The Hebrew vocabulary is rich in words often translated as "shame" in English. While there are many, seven words stand out as most frequently found in the text of the Old Testament. Here are the Hebrew words in order of frequency, along with a verse where each is found.

- Hebrew: חָפֵר (English: *châphêr*) has the least usage for the word "shame," just seventeen times. Micah prophesied that God would judge the false prophets and false seers that have led Israel astray. Micah 3:7 records, "the seers shall be disgraced [*bûwsh*], and the diviners put to shame [*châphêr*]; they shall all cover their lips, for there is no answer from God."[61]
- Hebrew: בֹּשֶׁת (English: *bôsheth*) is found twenty-nine times in the Old Testament, translated as "shame." Job 8:22 says, "Those who hate you will be clothed with shame [*bôsheth*], and the tent of the wicked will be no more."[62]

- Hebrew: כְּלִמָּה (English: *kᵉlimmâh*) is the word translated as "shame" thirty times in the Hebrew Old Testament. Psalm 69:19, "You know my reproach, and my shame [*bôsheth*] and my dishonor *kᵉlimmâh*]; my foes are all known to you."[63]
- The Hebrew כָּלַם (English: *kalam*) is used thirty-eight times in the Hebrew Old Testament. Isaiah 50:7 says, "But the Lord GOD helps me; therefore I have not been disgraced; therefore I have set my face like a flint, and I know that I shall not be put to shame [*kalam*]."[64]
- Hebrew יָבֵשׁ (English: *yâbêsh*) is the Old Testament word for "to wither" or "dry up." It appears sixty-seven times in the Hebrew Bible, but in several instances it is translated as "shame." "As a thief is shamed [*bôsheth*] when caught, so the house of Israel shall be shamed [*yâbêsh*]: they, their kings, their officials, their priests, and their prophets" (Jer 2:26)[65]
- Hebrew: בּוֹשׁ (English: *bûwsh*) is the favorite Hebrew word in the Old Testament for "shame," found 100 times in the Bible. Psalm 14:6 notes, "You would shame [*bûwsh*] the plans of the poor, but the LORD is his refuge."[66]

With such rich linguistic choices, it should be unmistakable that the shame, resulting from sin, was serious to God. Combined, these six Hebrew words appear 281 times in the Old Testament, and others appear as well. But let's move on to the New Testament.

The New Testament vocabulary of shame

While there is not the variety of word choices in the New Testament as in the Old, the words "shame" or "to be ashamed" are still found in an assortment of words, the major ones of which are listed below.

- The Greek: αἰσχύνης (English: *aischynēs*) occurs six times (Luke 14:9; 2 Cor 4:2; Phil 3:19; Heb 12:2; Jude 13; and Rev 3:18, with the variation (Greek: κατῃαχύνοντο; English: *katēschynonto*) appearing twice that many times (Luke 13:17; Rom 5:5; 9:33; 10:11; 1 Cor 1:27; 11:4–5, 22; 2 Cor 7:14; 9:4; 1 Pet 2:6; 3:16). "But God chose what is foolish in the world to shame the wise; God chose what is weak in the world to shame the strong" (1 Cor 1:27).
- Other variations of the word also occur as the Greek: αἰσχρὸν (English: *aischron*—1 Cor 14:35) and the Greek: αἰσχύνομαι (English: *aischynomai*—Luke 16:3; 2 Cor 10:8; Phil 1:20; 1 Pet 4:16; 1 John 2:28). "And

now, little children, abide in him, so that when he appears we may have confidence and not shrink from him in shame (Greek: αἰσχυνθῶμεν; English: *aischynthōmen*) at his coming" (1 John 2:28).

- But in the New Testament, other Greek words were also used for shame. Various forms of the root word (Greek: δεικνύω; English: *deiknýō*) are found in Matthew 1:19 (Greek: δειγματισαι; English: *deigmatisai*), Colossians 2:15, Hebrews 6:6, and Jude 7.
- Other verses use (Greek: ὕβρισαν; English: *hybrisan*) meaning "to treat despitefully or shamefully" (Matt 22:6; Luke 11:45, 18:22; Acts 4:5; 1 Thess 2:2).
- When the New Testament writers wanted to communicate shame, they sometimes chose (Greek: ἐντρέπων; English: *entropōn*—1 Cor 4:14; 6:5; 15:34; 2 Thess 3:14; Titus 2:8), a word that can also mean "to regard."
- And (Greek: ἀτιμίας; English: *atimias*), a word meaning shame or dishonor, was also used (Rom 1:26; 9:21;! Cor 11:14; 15:43; 2 Cor 6:8; 11:21; and 2 Tim 2:20). "Now in a great house there are not only vessels of gold and silver but also of wood and clay, some for honorable use, some for dishonorable" (*atimias*).
- Paul and John each chose the word (Greek ἀσχημοσύνην; English: *aschēmosynēn*) for what is unseemly or shameful (Rom 1:27; Rev 16:15).

While the New Testament may not feature the vast variety of Old Testament Hebrew words, as you can see, the New Testament words for "shame" were still quite prolific.

The importance of such a rich biblical vocabulary

So, why do we explore the variety of biblical words for shame? Why is this vocabulary important? Because it gives context. It often differs from the world's definition of what is shameful. Consider Romans 1:26–27. These verses use both *atimiaς* and *aschēmosynēn* to indicate that God finds homosexuality shameful. A majority of people today find it acceptable, even heterosexuals. Words help us distinguish the divine view of what is normal from the human view, which, according to the Bible, is often abnormal.

To avoid shame, many biblically ignorant people today have found ways to mask it. If you introduce positively to the public what God sees negatively and deems shameful, if enough Hollywood stars come out in favor of it, people will successfully mask what God says is unnatural and shameful. We have seen that happen before our very eyes and have normalized it.

It is this rich vocabulary of shame in the Bible that tells us not what we consider shameful, but what God considers shameful. The extensive vocabulary for shame in the Old and New Testaments demonstrates its universality and its importance to God. A holy God will not use shame as a harmful weapon. God doesn't shame us to hurt us but to correct us. He shames us to stop us from continuing down the wrong path, a path that leads us deeper into sin and condemnation. He humbles us to bring us closer to his path and his will. When we are shamed, we are brought closer to him.

"Though they [the unjust] were sharply reproved by him [Jesus], and their errors in principle, and sins in practice, were exposed by him, yet they were not ashamed; such was the hardness and obduracy of their hearts."—John Gill

Armed with the vast vocabulary of shame, we now must explore how shame came to be a common experience for humankind. Why do we feel shame when we do something we know is wrong? How did shame become a human experience?

SHAME ENTERS THE HUMAN FAMILY

Genesis 3 provides the first evidence of shame in human society. After Adam and Eve sinned, the Bible says:

> Then the eyes of both were opened, and they knew that they were naked. And they sewed fig leaves together and made themselves loincloths. And they heard the sound of the LORD God walking in the garden in the cool of the day, and the man and his wife hid from the presence of the LORD God among the trees of the garden. But the LORD God called to the man and said to him, "Where are you?" And he said, "I heard the sound of you in the garden, and I was afraid, because I was naked, and I hid myself." He said, "Who told you that you were naked? Have you eaten of the tree of which I commanded you not to eat?" (Gen 3:7–11).

Any reasonable understanding of this narrative must conclude that after Adam and Eve sinned, they were ashamed of what they did in following Satan's disobedience to God. Before this, there was no reason to hide. Initially, the relationship between God and his first two human creations was flawless. They enjoyed their connection with God and treasured his constant company and watchful eye. Their association with God gave them great significance compared to every other creature in the garden.

Nevertheless, no sooner had Adam joined Eve in rebelling against their Creator God than both of them went into hiding. Why? Because their actions in disobeying God brought about "a painful feeling of humiliation or distress caused by the consciousness of wrong or foolish behavior" (see the definition above). For the first time, the human family experienced what we call shame.

THE SHAME OF NAKEDNESS

The first clue that something had changed in their relationship with God was the discovery that they were both naked. The human body was a beautiful, functional, and incredible creation of God. However, when the guilty pair cut the cord with God and severed their unique relationship with him, suddenly their naked bodies brought a feeling of shame. We should ask why. They were the same bodies as before, but something was different now. Sin had fostered shame. Elsewhere in Scripture, nakedness and shame are associated (see Mic 1:11; Nah 3:5; Rev 3:18).

So ashamed were Adam and Eve that they reacted immediately to their situation. Quickly, the first human pair threw together a fig-leaf covering to conceal their nakedness. It wasn't a good plan, but it was an immediate one. They also attempted to recover from their shame by hiding among the garden's foliage.

When God asked Adam where he was and why he was hiding, Adam responded, "I heard the sound of you in the garden, and I was afraid, because I was naked, and I hid myself" (Gen 3:10). Sin brought shame, and shame brought evasive action to avoid having to deal with it.

> "If you would understand the depth of human guilt, you must look at the cross. If you would see the awful sinfulness of sin, you must look at the cross. If you would understand the need of your own heart, you will see it at the cross. If you ever understand God, you must see him in the cross."—Joe Henry Hankins

The crown of God's creation, Adam, along with his wife, Eve, was now on a downward path. Their sin and consequent shame began in the Garden of Eden. That sin and shame was passed on to Cain, Abel, and their siblings, then to Adam's grandchildren and Eve's great-grandchildren, and on down the line of humanity, dominating every day of every living person from day one until one day, one Friday afternoon at Calvary, Jesus "endured the cross, despising the shame" (Heb 12:2).

We still cover our bodies because nakedness stimulates shame.[67] However, when we die, our body "is sown in dishonor; it is raised in glory. It is sown in weakness; it is raised in power. It is sown a natural body; it is raised a spiritual body. The first man Adam became a living being; the last Adam [Jesus] became a life-giving spirit" (1 Cor 15:43–45). Until we receive resurrection bodies—our heavenly and eternal bodies—humans will innately experience the shame of nakedness.

There are, of course, a strange few who attempt to defy their shame, claiming the "body is a beautiful thing" and that it is "an expression of nature." Thus, they choose not to wear clothes (at least on some occasions and in some places) and suppress their feelings of shame. But if they ever put on a piece of clothing, they become hypocrites immediately. Even "dyed in the wool" (no pun intended) nudists wear clothes sometimes, in public venues, at the office, and elsewhere.

THE SHAME OF CRUCIFIXION

Roman crucifixion was a humiliating experience. The Romans intended it to be. The more pain, humiliation, and shame associated with it, the more crucifixion became a deterrent, a disincentivizing tool.

To enhance humiliation and shame, the victim had to carry his *patibulum* to the killing field. It was to enhance shame, the victim was lifted high on his cross so all could watch him die. It was to heighten shame that the crucified person was left on the cross, sometimes for days. The body rotting, the flies buzzing around the victim's body, the birds pecking at his eyes, and wild dogs nibbling at his toes, all were to enhance the shame of being crucified.

Calvary's Cross was the cross of shame

Even more than others, the cross of Jesus was a cross of shame. The Jewish religious leaders of Jerusalem wanted Jesus to be shamed. How dare he pretend to be the Messiah of Israel! He must endure excessive shaming as he was being crucified. The Roman soldiers also wanted Jesus to be shamed.

How dare he consider himself the "King of the Jews." Only Caesar was king, and he was the king of the world.

However, when considering the shame Jesus had to bear, we must remember it was not his cross he was dying on. It was our cross; he died in our place. Jesus bore the debt for our sin, and he paid it with his own blood. That makes what the writer of Hebrews said all the more meaningful.

> Therefore, since we are surrounded by so great a cloud of witnesses, let us also lay aside every weight, and sin which clings so closely, and let us run with endurance the race that is set before us, looking to Jesus, the founder and perfecter of our faith, who for the joy that was set before him endured the cross, despising the shame, and is seated at the right hand of the throne of God (Heb 12:1–2).

Those of us who have received the benefit of Jesus bearing our shame should be very vocal in our praise toward him. No one else would have done this except a loving God. Sing to him, sing praises to him; tell of all his wondrous works! (1 Chron 16:9). Sing to him, sing praises to him; tell of all his wondrous works! (Ps 105:2).

How Jesus endured the shame of the cross

At Calvary, Jesus bore the stain of shame because he looked beyond the cross to the joy that awaited him. He did not want the shame. He did not invite the shame. But neither did he avoid it.

Jesus could look beyond his struggle with God's will in Gethsemane to the joy of completing our redemption. He could look beyond the interrogation by Annas and the hypocrisy of Caiaphas to the elation of knowing his blood would cover our sin. He could look beyond Pilate's indecision and the terrible beating he would receive from the Roman soldiers to provide for our salvation. He could look beyond the pain of the cross, the degradation of the cross, and the shame of the cross, to the joy he would experience once he returned to the right hand of his Father in triumph over Satan and sin.

Table 1 represents four occurrences of crucifixion in which the actual numbers of the dead are revealed.

Table 1: Crucifixion's Ghastly Numbers

Name	*Crucifixion Atrocities*
Darius	The Persian king impaled 3,000 men after he captured Babylon.
Crassus	The third member of the First Triumvirate, alongside Julius Caesar and Pompey, he crucified 6,000 rebels from the Third Servile War along the Appian Way, from Capua to Rome.
Varus	Roman general Publius Quinctilius Varus crucified 2,000 Jewish rebels in Jerusalem.
Herod	In 4 BC, Archelaus's troops slaughtered 3,000 Jewish rebels in Jerusalem
Caesar	Augustus boasted that he had captured and crucified 30,000 runaway slaves.

Jesus endured the shame and suffering of crucifixion because he knew there was something more. Something that would take away the shame of being crucified in public. Jesus knew that something awaited him that would shove all that into the dustbin of history. There was joy in his future.

THE SHAME OF NAKEDNESS AND CRUCIFIXION

The shame of nakedness was bad enough. The shame of crucifixion was even worse. But the combination, hanging naked while being crucified, was the worst. As he was crucified, Jesus "endured the cross, despising the shame" (Greek: ὑπέμεινεν σταυρὸν καταφρονήσας αἰσχύνης). Everybody despises shame. It's built into who we are. Everyone is ashamed of their nakedness. That's built into our nature as well. Nevertheless, at Calvary, hanging naked on that Roman cross, Jesus obediently took our shame, the scourge of human shame from Eden until now, and dutifully shouldered it just as he dutifully shouldered our sin. Jesus put shame in its place.

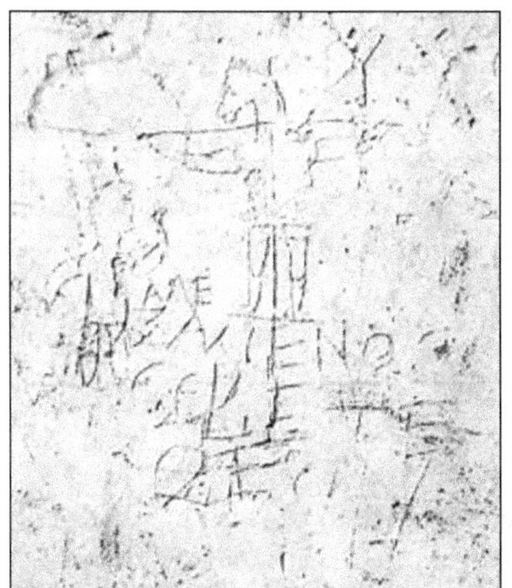

In 1857, Christian art historian Raffaele Garrucci noticed some graffiti scratched in the plaster of a wall in the Domus Gelotiana, a house that had been unearthed on Rome's Palatine Hill. Roman Emperor Caligula had acquired the house for his imperial palace. The small graffito discovered by Garrucci is old and faded, and the original design (left) is now almost invisible unless enhanced (right). The image appears to depict a human figure affixed to a cross, but it has a man's body and a donkey's head. Beneath the cross, written poorly in very crude Greek, is an inscription that reads, "Alexamenos worships [his] God." The majority of scholars believe the figure on the cross is Jesus. If it is, this may be the earliest surviving depiction of Jesus of Nazareth and his crucifixion.

Was Jesus naked on the cross?

Raymond C. Brown asks the question that Bible study groups and Sunday school classes have debated for decades, centuries, and even longer. "Did the Romans make a special concession to the Jewish horror of nudity (*Jub* 3:30–31; 7:20) and allow a loincloth to be used"?[68] Was Jesus naked on the cross, or was he allowed to keep on a loincloth for modesty? As you have noted, I have repeatedly referred to Jesus hanging naked on the cross. The debate will continue, of course, but here is what we know from the literary sources available to us.

Among early portrayals of the crucifixion, such as the Alexamenos Graffito and several of the gems carved with an image of Jesus on the cross, he was depicted naked. The fifth-century ivory box in the British Museum and the cypress door of Santa Sabina in Rome both depict Jesus with a loincloth. Book one in this series, *Roman Crucifixion and the Death of Jesus*, addresses these antiquities more completely.

> "Crucifixes always give Jesus a loincloth, but in reality, Roman crucifixion was designed to be as gruesome, humiliating a death as possible. The condemned were stripped naked in order to die with as little dignity as possible."—John Kubasak

For the first millennium of its existence, the Christian Church did not trumpet the humanity of Christ for apologetic reasons. He had been the victim of the most shameful death. Some of those who opposed him charged that Jesus was nothing but a religious charlatan. As a result, for the first couple of centuries, the church used the sign of a fish, an anchor, the Chi-Rho, or other symbols of the faith more than the cross. These Christ-followers were not ashamed of their Master, but they constantly lived under the threat of a Roman sword. They had to meet in secret until Constantine legalized Christianity in the empire. It was centuries more that the crucified Christ was nearly always depicted with a loincloth covering his human manhood.

Looking at a first-century cross with twenty-first-century eyes

We tend to view everything we read in the Bible through twenty-first-century lenses. But this does a disservice to the writers' words and their intent in the Scriptures. This is true of Jesus' crucifixion. We view him hanging on the cross through the lens of our contemporary standards of modesty. But modesty was never an immovable standard.

Christians have found the idea of Jesus being crucified naked so repulsive, so unappealing that we have often allowed our hearts to overrule our heads. The evidence available to us seems to lead to the conclusion that Jesus was naked on the cross. That said, there has been no consensus among early Christian or Jewish writers about whether or not Jesus was allowed to wear a loincloth at his crucifixion. But for the Roman soldiers of the first century, our standards of modesty today were of little concern.

Modern depictions versus modern scholars

Today, modern films, paintings, and other depictions of Jesus on the Cross feature a loincloth due to our standards of modesty and morality, at least as they apply to Jesus. That is typical iconography. However, take away today's standards, and you are left with the standards of the ancient Romans and how they treated the slaves they crucified. Crucifixions were not about modesty; they were about shame. The more shame they could heap on the crucified, the better, and crucifying a person naked only added to their shame. Since the days of Adam and Eve, shame has always been a part of nudity.

Larissa Bonfante, Professor Emerita of Classics at New York University, where she taught for almost four decades, confirms, "Nakedness, especially male nakedness—the exposure of the intimate 'private parts'—expressed slavery, loss of control, helplessness, dependence, deprivation, humiliation, and mortality. To lose the protection of one's clothing was shocking and shameful."[69]

Martin Hengel, in his classic work on crucifixion, attests to the fact that the crucified were naked. He says, "By the public display of a naked victim at a prominent place—at a crossroads, in the theatre, on high ground, at the place of his crime—crucifixion also represented his utmost humiliation."[70]

Conservative scholar Darrell Bock agrees. "Soldiers cast lots for Jesus' clothing, leaving Jesus to hang naked, the most shameful of conditions, on the cross."[71]

Josephus also speaks of those who were to be executed being naked when they were killed. When Cherea and Lupus were being led to the killing field, "Lupus laid his garment aside, and complained of the cold" (*Ant.* 19.4.5).

Christian sources about crucifying victims naked

Some of the early Church Fathers also appear to suggest that Jesus was completely naked when crucified. For example, Melito, the second-century bishop of Sardis, in his book *On the Pasch 97; SC 123.118*, wrote in his sermon on the passion of Christ, "His body naked [was] not even deemed worthy of a clothing that it might not be seen. Therefore, the heavenly lights turned away and the day darkened in order that he might be hidden who was denuded upon the cross."

> "The Sovereign has been made unrecognizable by his naked body, and is not even allowed a garment to keep him from view."
> —Bishop Melito

People of the second century had witnessed manifold crucifixions. This is how Melito knew the victims of crucifixion were executed without clothing. Church Fathers such as John Chrysostom and Ephraem the Scythian, however, reluctantly agree with this view. Others of the Fathers depict Jesus as retaining the loincloth, and the *Acts of Pilate* 10:1 speaks of Jesus with a loincloth after his outer garments were divided among the soldiers.

Dionysius of Halicarnassus wrote of a Roman citizen who ordered one of his slaves to be put to death. Speaking of the walk on the Via Dolorosa in Jerusalem as a parade of punishment designed to demean the slave, Dionysius wrote, "The men ordered to lead the slave to his punishment, having stretched out both his arms and fastened them to a piece of wood which extended across his breast and shoulders as far as his wrists (the *patibulum*), followed him, tearing his naked body with whips" (Dionysius of Halicarnassus, *Roman Antiquities*, 7.69.1–2). This means the slave was exposed in ways that would have been indecent and utterly shameful. At least Matthew 27:31 tells us that Jesus retained his clothes on the Via Dolorosa. "And when they had mocked him, they stripped him of the robe and put his own clothes on him and led him away to crucify him."

St. Augustine suggests that the purpose of crucifixion was to inflict as much pain and shame as possible while prolonging death (*Tractate* 36.4 [John 8:15–18]). In addition to Dionysius of Halicarnassus, we know victims were crucified naked from passing references by Valerius Maximus (*Facta* 1.7.4).

Jewish sources about crucifying victims naked

In ancient Judaism, shame was also a part of executions. Many rabbinic texts record evidence of crucifixion. Some mention the dripping blood of a crucified person (*m. Ohol.* 3:5; *t. Ohol.* 4:11; *b Nid.* 71b) or the use of a nail from a crucifixion as an amulet or magical charm (*m. Sabb.* 6:10; *y. Sabb.* 6:9; *b Sabb.* 67a). The *Mishnah* refers to the ancient Jewish collections of rabbinical traditions from the time of Christ up to the end of the second century AD. The tractate *Sanhedrin* of the Mishnah records the rabbis discussing how executions ought to be carried out and whether the victim should be naked or not.

The *Mishnah* (*Sanhedrin* 6:3) records three opinions held among the rabbis. They were:

A [When] he was "four cubits [six feet] from the place of stoning, they removed his clothes";

B "In the case of a man, they cover him up in front, and in the case of a woman, they cover her up in front and behind," the words of R. Judah;

C Sages say, "A man is stoned naked, but a woman is not stoned naked."

These represent three different Jewish traditions, as taught by the revered rabbis. Two out of three claim that a man was executed naked among his Jewish countrymen. If the Jews even stripped themselves naked, why would we think the Romans would practice greater modesty than the Jews? There is no evidence that the Romans ever did.

While the Rabbinic tradition was to disdain crucifixion as a penalty for the Jews,[72] the rabbis indeed accepted it as a Roman practice. Many rabbinic accounts involving crucifixion viewed the Roman application of the penalty as "a just punishment for evil men."

Rabbi Simon bar Abba said in the name of Rabbi Johanan, "Is it not so that the Holy One, blessed be he, punished the wicked ones in Gehinnom only naked?" *Esther Rabbah* 3.14 is also in the context of nakedness. Mishnah *Sanhedrin* 6:3 specifies that "the clothes should be removed only at the place of execution, not on the way there."

In Judaism, standards of modesty were significantly higher than those of the Greeks and Romans. Nevertheless, the custom was to stone a naked person to death as a part of shaming the person. In Roman custom, when the malefactor arrived at the cross, he was stripped naked, and what clothes he had were divided among the soldiers, usually a unit of four soldiers with a centurion as the leader, making five.

You may ask, "Why would Roman soldiers want the second-hand clothes of slaves and others of the outcast class"? It's a reasonable question, but I've never encountered anyone who has addressed it in their commentaries or writings. So why would the soldiers divide the clothing of the crucified? Each of the Gospels clearly indicates they did (Matt 27:34; Mark 15:24; Luke 23:34; John 19:24). The Bible doesn't answer this question, but common sense might. I don't believe the Roman soldiers would or could use such clothes for themselves. The Roman government provided soldiers with clothing. Their outer clothes were Roman-issued uniforms, and a *subligaculum* was worn as an undergarment.[73]

Still, Roman soldiers could find use for used clothing, even from victims of crucifixion. Soldiers didn't always take what they wanted from the peasants they ruled. Sometimes, even the most basic pieces of clothing were welcomed by people experiencing poverty in exchange for clandestine goods or services to the Roman army. While the soldiers did not need the clothes of the crucified, they knew they could trade them for forbidden or prohibited items. Outer garments could be sold for some extra cash or used to settle a debt. Enslaved people and peasants who were crucified did not wear *haute couture* or high-end fashion. Still, resourceful soldiers could always find a way to profit from their victims' clothes.

Death by crucifixion at times came quickly, but often didn't come for days. There, the crucified would hang naked, the object of jeering and ridicule, insects alighting in their mouth, eyes, and open wounds, unable to remove them. While hanging naked on their crosses, the crucified were exposed to the elements, unable to eat or drink. It was terrible to witness, even worse to experience.

> "The key to breaking the power of pride-fueled shame is the superior power of humility-fueled faith in the work of Christ and the promises of Christ."—Jon Bloom

The erosion of shame

Today, it is impossible to imagine how shameful it was to die on a Roman cross. We do not blush or hide our faces when we speak of Jesus' cross. Today, the cross is more likely to be hanging on a wall or around someone's neck on a chain than it is to be a symbol of Jesus' ghastly death. It was the Savior who emptied this unspeakable form of execution of its shame.

More than that, today we don't even blush at semi-nudity, let alone full nudity. It's on the TV, in the movies, and on computer screens all the time. Scantily-clad actors and actresses are featured in films and even commercials. Today, we see actors in commercials wearing little or nothing at all. We hear commercials about subjects we used to never talk about in public. Living in our sinful world has desensitized us to how God views the heinousness of sin. Shame has been dreadfully eroded in society today. Nevertheless, we must never forget that for us, Jesus "endured the cross, despising the shame."

This is not to say that Jesus took our shame from us. He did not. We still find shame in many of our actions and words. We still clothe ourselves. We still experience that painful emotion of guilt. We do things that we regret afterward. However, we no longer have to live in shame. We do not have to allow shame to overwhelm us.

At Calvary, Jesus bore the stain of shame because he looked beyond the cross to the joy that awaited him. We must do the same. We don't face the intensity of shame Jesus did at Calvary, but whatever shame we face in this world cannot compare with the joy that awaits us in heaven. The ability to look beyond today to what lies ahead, to take shame off the table, is a significant accomplishment of Christ's death. Accomplishments don't get much bigger than this!

Stretched on the cruel tree,
and fastened by my sin—
Lord, at thy cross, with shame, I see
how guilty I have been.

Oh, how this crimson tide
o'erwhelms my soul with shame!
within thy bleeding wounds I hide:
wilt thou, Lord, own my name?

—Anonymous

Chapter 10

Jesus Provided the "Good News" of the Gospel Story

The good news gets even better. The gospel invitation is open to everyone. It's not for the elite, a special class of people, a particular race, or religion. No, this is an open invitation to you, to me, to everyone.

What is the Gospel?
Biblical Examples of "The Good News"
There is Good News for Everyone
Responding to the Good News

There is one major accomplishment of Christ's death that we hardly ever think about. While this book has focused on the theological achievements of Jesus Christ at Calvary, there is one accomplishment that is more practical, more universal, and more exciting than the others. It's the accomplishment that Jesus provided the good news of the gospel story. In fact, his death and resurrection are the central story of the gospel. He is the good news.

The word "gospel" (Greek: εὐαγγέλιον; English: *euangelion*) means good news. This noun is found no less than seventy-seven times in the New Testament,[74] along with the verb (Greek: εὐαγγελίζω; English: *euangelízō*) another sixty-one times.[75] In these 138 occurrences, the noun and verb for good news are used to demonstrate the importance of what Jesus' death accomplished at Golgotha's killing field.

Without his willingness to die for us and without his miraculous resurrection on the third day, there would be no good news for humankind. We would all be headed for the long, dark night of eternity. That's just how important the gospel message is and how necessary it is for us to receive it.

Table 1: Stylistic Similarities in the Pauline Epistles

Feature	*Scriptures Where Found*	*Comments*
Paul	Rom1:1; 1 Cor 1:1; 2 Cor 1:1; Gal 1:1; Eph 1:1; Eph 1:1; Phil 1:1; Col 1:1; 1 Thess 1:1; 2 Thess 1:1; 1 Tim 1:1; 2 Tim 1:1; Titus 1:1; Phlm 1:1.	Every one of Paul's epistles begins with "Paul." It was the Roman style of letter writing to start with the sender's name.
Apostle, Servant, Prisoner	*Verse 1*—Rom1:1; 1 Cor 1:1; 2 Cor 1:1; Gal 1:1; Eph 1:1; Phil 1:1; Col 1:1; 1 Tim 1:1; 2 Tim 1:1; Titus 1:1; Phlm 1:1.	All but 1 and 2 Thessalonians identify the writer in verse 1 as "Apostle," "Servant," or "Prisoner."
Letter Recipient	*Verse 1*—2 Cor; Eph; Phil; 1 Thess; 2 Thess; Phile. *Verse* 2–1 Cor; Gal; Col; 1 Tim; 2 Tim; Titus 1:4; *Verse 7*–Rom.	The recipient of the letter (e.g., "unto the saints at Ephesus") usually occurs in verse 1 or 2.
Grace and Peace	*Verse 1*—1 Thess; *Verse 2*—2 Cor; Eph; Phil; Col; 2 Thess; 1 Tim; 2 Tim; *Verse 3*—1 Cor; Gal; Phlm; *Verse 4*—Titus; *Verse 7*—Rom.	"Grace and Peace" was a standard greeting in the Roman Empire. The Pastoral Epistles vary this saying, "Grace, Mercy, and Peace."
Grace to you	Rom 16:24; 1 Cor 16:23; 2 Cor 13:14; Gal 6:18; Eph 6:24; Phil 4:23; Col 4:18; 1 Thess 5:28; 2 Thess 3:18; 1 Tim 6:21; 2 Tim 4:22; Titus 3:15; Phlm 1:25.	"Grace unto you" always occurs in the complimentary close of the letter, at the very end.
Amen	Rom 16:27; 1 Cor 16:24; 2 Cor 13:14; Gal 6:18; Eph 6:24; Phil 4:23; Col 4:18; 1 Thess 5:28; 2 Thess 3:18; 1 Tim 6:21; 2 Tim 4:22; Titus 3:15; Phlm 1:25.	"Amen" is not found in some translations, e.g., CSB, GNT, NIV, NLT, RSV, etc., because of manuscript restrictions.
All Scripture references are taken from the King James Version of the Bible.		

WHAT IS THE GOSPEL?

When writing his epistles to churches or individuals, Paul adhered to the everyday letter-writing style of the Roman Empire of his day. Whereas we place our name or signature at the end of a letter, the Romans put it first. So in every one of the thirteen recognized Pauline epistles, the first word is always "Paul."[76] This is followed by an identification of the writer, such as "an apostle of Jesus Christ." Then comes the typical greeting "grace and peace" (except for Galatians, Paul's most stern epistle). From here, the letters often address questions or issues that have arisen within the churches.[77]

Table 1 above provides an evaluation of the style of writing used by the Apostle Paul. You cannot help but notice the similarities between his letters. The most doctrinal of Paul's letters is the epistle to the Romans. It also contains the New Testament's best definition of the gospel, the good news. Romans 1:1–7 is the longest sentence in the Bible. Here, Paul deviates from his usual practice of giving his name and position, followed quickly by "grace and peace." In Romans, the phrase "grace and peace" is not found until verse 7. Why did Paul diverge from his common writing practice in the book of Romans? He had a good reason.

Notice how well verses 1 and 7 fit together in Paul's regular literary pattern. "Paul, a servant of Christ Jesus, called to be an apostle, set apart for the gospel of God, which he promised beforehand through his prophets in the holy Scriptures. To all those in Rome who are loved by God and called to be saints: Grace to you and peace from God our Father and the Lord Jesus Christ" (Rom 1:1, 2, 7). It makes sense. It's his typical pattern in the other letters.

Inquisitive minds want to know why this modification in Romans. Paul so slavishly used the letter-writing style common in first-century Rome, why change here? Let's investigate further.

The longest sentence in the Bible

First, read Paul's first sentence in his letter to the Romans:

> Paul, a servant of Christ Jesus, called to be an apostle, set apart for the gospel of God, which he promised beforehand through his prophets in the holy Scriptures, concerning his Son, who was descended from David according to the flesh and was declared to be the Son of God in power according to the Spirit of holiness by his resurrection from the dead, Jesus Christ our Lord, through whom we have received grace and apostleship to bring

> about the obedience of faith for the sake of his name among all the nations, including you who are called to belong to Jesus Christ, To all those in Rome who are loved by God and called to be saints: Grace to you and peace from God our Father and the Lord Jesus Christ.

After reading these verses, you almost want to say, "Whew!" If you have counted them, you know there are 132 words in this sentence in English. There are fewer in the Greek language, topping off at ninety-three words. Nevertheless, there is no other sentence in the Bible that comes even close to the record Paul set in Romans 1:1–7.

So, what caused Paul to deviate from his usual practice? Look carefully. It was that phrase "the gospel of God" at the end of verse one. Not found in the greetings of any of Paul's other letters, in his deepest epistle, the one that tackles more theological issues than any other, Paul must have decided it was time he defined what he meant by "the gospel."[78] How he defined it is both beautiful and profound. Let's dissect what Paul said in his gospel definition. Here are the key elements:

- *The gospel was "promised beforehand through his prophets."* Paul was saying the gospel came right out of the Old Testament. It was preannounced by the Old Testament prophets from Genesis 3:15 to Malachi 4:2 (see Mark 1:1–3). By quoting the Old Testament sixty-one times in his letter to the Romans, Paul indicated to the Jews that their Scriptures spoke of Jesus Christ and the gospel story. They only needed eyes to see it.
- *The gospel is a part of "the holy scriptures."* This means the story of the gospel is a part of Holy Writ. It is a seminal part of God's inspired revelation. The gospel story comes from God himself as Paul declared, "All Scripture is breathed out by God and profitable for teaching, for reproof, for correction, and for training in righteousness, that the man of God may be complete, equipped for every good work" (2 Tim 3:16, 17).
- Now Paul gets down to the nitty-gritty. *The gospel story is "concerning his Son."* Nothing could be clearer. The gospel concerns God's Son, Jesus Christ. You can preach from the poetic books, the historical books, the gospels, or the epistles, but until you come to Jesus, you have not come to the gospel. You can talk about God's love, his kindness, or his providence, but until you come to Jesus, you have not come to the gospel. The gospel is "concerning his Son," Jesus Christ, and no one or nothing else.

- *The gospel is the story of Jesus' entitlement* to be called the "King of the Jews," as Pilate had inscribed on the *titulus* board above Jesus' head on the cross. Jesus "was descended from David according to the flesh." Jesus' lineage comes down from King David of Israel through both the families of Joseph and Mary. He is in the line that produces the Messiah, the Savior, the King of kings, and Lord of lords. He is rightly positioned by God the Father to be all of those for us.
- *The gospel may use his genealogy to prove he was descended from David,* but no genealogy or anything else was needed to prove Jesus' deity. Paul says Jesus "was declared to be the Son of God." Paul felt no need to prove Jesus was God's Son. Jesus was simply "declared" (Greek: ὁρίσθέντος; English: *horisthentos*).[79] to be the Son of God. You may choose to prove Jesus' human identity, but you do not have to prove his deity. You declare him to be what God the Father said he is, the Son of God.

> "The real truth is that while Jesus came to preach the gospel, his chief object in coming was that there might be a gospel to preach."
> —Robert William Dale

We aren't finished yet. Paul's description of what the gospel is continues in verse 4.

- *The gospel is endowed with divine "power according to the Spirit of holiness."* Later in this first chapter, Paul declared, "For I am not ashamed of the gospel, for it is the power of God for salvation to everyone who believes, to the Jew first and also to the Greek" (v. 16). The Holy Spirit played an active role in the gospel, beginning with the conception of the baby Jesus, the gospel personified (Luke 1:35), and continuing with the affirmation that Jesus is God's Son (Matt 3:16, 17; Mark 1:10; Luke 3:22; John 1:32), guiding us to understand actual gospel truth (John 14:17, 26; 16:13), and empowering us to spread the gospel in Jesus' name (Matt 28:19; Acts 1:8).
- *The gospel story is not complete; it does not end with Jesus' crucifixion.* Any idea that the gospel was accomplished solely by Jesus' death leaves out a crucial element of the story. Paul told the Corinthians, "For I delivered to you as of first importance what I also received: that Christ died for our sins in accordance with the Scriptures, that he was buried, that he was raised on the third day in accordance with the Scriptures" (1 Cor 15:3–4). There it is! The full gospel. Everything there is to the

gospel. The story consists of Jesus' death, burial, and resurrection. In Romans 1:25, Paul confirmed that Jesus "was delivered up for our trespasses and raised for our justification." The account of the one who died on the scandalous cross and rose again from the sealed tomb—that's the gospel story.

"But though we, or an angel from heaven, preach any other gospel unto you than that which we have preached unto you, let him be accursed" (Gal 1:8).

"God forbid that I should glory, save in the cross of our Lord Jesus Christ, by whom the world is crucified unto me, and I unto the world" (Gal 6:14).

BIBLICAL EXAMPLES OF THE GOOD NEWS

Perhaps the best way to illustrate the importance of the good news is to let the Bible authors tell us what they knew of the gospel and what it meant to them. I have listed these Scripture references in categories for greater clarity. The list is super-abundant.

The preaching of the gospel

- Mark 16:15, "Go into all the world and proclaim the gospel to the whole creation."
- Acts 8:25, "They returned to Jerusalem, preaching the gospel to many villages of the Samaritans."
- Romans 1:15, "So I am eager to preach the gospel to you also who are in Rome.
- Romans 15:20, "I make it my ambition to preach the gospel."
- 1 Corinthians 1:17, "For Christ did not send me to baptize but to preach the gospel, and not with words of eloquent wisdom, lest the cross of Christ be emptied of its power."
- 1 Corinthians 9:16, "Woe to me if I do not preach the gospel!"
- 2 Timothy 2:8, "Remember Jesus Christ, risen from the dead, the offspring of David, as preached in my gospel."

The power of the gospel

- Mark 12:24, "Is this not the reason you are wrong, because you know neither the Scriptures nor the power of God?"
- Luke 4:36, "For with authority and power he commands the unclean spirits, and they come out!"
- Romans 1:16, "For I am not ashamed of the gospel, for it is the power of God for salvation to everyone who believes, to the Jew first and also to the Greek."
- 1 Corinthians 1:17, "For Christ did not send me to baptize but to preach the gospel, and not with words of eloquent wisdom, lest the cross of Christ be emptied of its power."
- 1 Corinthians 1:18, "For the word of the cross is folly to those who are perishing, but to us who are being saved it is the power of God."
- 1 Thessalonians 1:5, "Our gospel came to you not only in word but also in power and in the Holy Spirit and with full conviction."
- 2 Timothy 1:8, "Share in suffering for the gospel by the power of God."

The propagation of the gospel

- Mark 13:10, "And the gospel must first be proclaimed to all nations."
- Mark 16:15, "Go into all the world and proclaim the gospel to the whole creation."
- Acts 1:8, "You will be my witnesses in Jerusalem and in all Judea and Samaria, and to the end of the earth."
- Romans 15:19, "From Jerusalem and all the way around to Illyricum I have fulfilled the ministry of the gospel of Christ."
- 2 Corinthians 10:16, "So that we may preach the gospel in lands beyond you."
- Galatians 2:5, "The truth of the gospel might be preserved."
- Revelation 14:6, "An eternal gospel to proclaim to those who dwell on earth, to every nation and tribe and language and people."

The redeeming faith in the gospel

- Mark 1:15, Jesus said, "Repent and believe in the gospel."
- 1 Corinthians 4:15, "I became your father in Christ Jesus through the gospel."
- 1 Corinthians 15:1, "Now I would remind you, brothers, of the gospel I preached to you, which you received, in which you stand."
- 2 Corinthians 9:13, "They will glorify God because of your submission that comes from your confession of the gospel of Christ."
- Ephesians 1:13, "You heard the word of truth, the gospel of your salvation, and believed in him."
- Ephesians 3:6, "Partakers of the promise in Christ Jesus through the gospel."
- 2 Thessalonians 2:14, "He called you through our gospel, so that you may obtain the glory of our Lord Jesus Christ."

The finale for those who do not believe the gospel

- Matthew 7:13, "Enter by the narrow gate. For the gate is wide and the way is easy that leads to destruction, and those who enter by it are many."
- Romans 10:16, "But they have not all obeyed the gospel. For Isaiah says, 'Lord, who has believed what he has heard from us?'"
- Galatians 1:7, "There are some who trouble you and want to distort the gospel of Christ."
- Galatians 2:14, "I saw that their conduct was not in step with the truth of the gospel."
- 1 Thessalonians 1:7–8, "When the Lord Jesus is revealed from heaven with his mighty angels in flaming fire, inflicting vengeance on those who do not know God and on those who do not obey the gospel of our Lord Jesus."
- 1 Peter 4:17, "What will be the outcome for those who do not obey the gospel of God?"
- Revelation 20:15, "And if anyone's name was not found written in the book of life, he was thrown into the lake of fire."

Living the life of the gospel

- Acts 20:24, "If only I may finish my course and the ministry that I received from the Lord Jesus, to testify to the gospel of the grace of God."
- 1 Corinthians 9:23, "I do it all for the sake of the gospel."
- Philippians 1:3–5, "Your partnership in the gospel from the first day until now."
- Philippians 1:12–13, "What has happened to me has really served to advance the gospel."
- Philippians 1:27, "Let your manner of life be worthy of the gospel of Christ."
- Colossians 1:23, "If indeed you continue in the faith, stable and steadfast, not shifting from the hope of the gospel that you heard."
- 1 Thessalonians 2:8, "We were ready to share with you not only the gospel of God but also our own selves."

Obviously, from the diversity evident in these verses, the gospel was an essential part of the New Testament. You cannot tell the Jesus story without telling the gospel story.

Jesus and the gospel

- Matthew 9:35, "And Jesus went throughout all the cities and villages, teaching in their synagogues and proclaiming the gospel of the kingdom."
- Romans 1:1, "Paul, a servant of Christ Jesus, called to be an apostle, set apart for the gospel of God."
- Romans 15:16, "A minister of Christ Jesus to the Gentiles in the priestly service of the gospel of God."
- 2 Corinthians 4:4, "The light of the gospel of the glory of Christ, who is the image of God."
- Ephesians 3:6, "The Gentiles are fellow heirs, members of the same body, and partakers of the promise in Christ Jesus through the gospel."
- 2 Thessalonians 2:14, "To this he called you through our gospel, so that you may obtain the glory of our Lord Jesus Christ."

- 2 Timothy 1:10, "Which now has been manifested through the appearing of our Savior Christ Jesus, who abolished death and brought life and immortality to light through the gospel."

The four evangelists, the writing apostles, and the first-century church in general believed the good news with every bone in their bodies. They were all in. They were willing to give their lives to see the gospel spread to their friends and family, their neighbors, and people across the known world they would never meet. Many of them did give their lives for the sake of the gospel. Paul said, "We had boldness in our God to declare to you the gospel of God in the midst of much conflict" (1 Thess 2:2; see also Col 1:24; Heb 10:32; 1 Pet 2:14, 15).

These saints knew that faith in the gospel message sets people free from the bondage of sin. They knew that "if anyone is in Christ, he is a new creation. The old has passed away; behold, the new has come" (2 Cor 5:17). They knew that, "in Christ Jesus you are all sons of God, through faith (Gal 3:26) and that, "in Christ Jesus, you who once were far off have been brought near by the blood of Christ" (Eph 2:13).

These early Christians believed that "the peace of God, which surpasses all understanding, will guard your hearts and your minds in Christ Jesus" (Phil 4:7). Everyone in the early church truly believed it was God "who saved us and called us to a holy calling, not because of our works but because of his own purpose and grace, which he gave us in Christ Jesus before the ages began" (2 Tim 1:9).

When someone came to faith in Christ Jesus, everything changed, and they knew it. This was because of the power of the gospel. The gospel is "good news." The gospel is God's story. But more than anything, the gospel is "the power of God for salvation to everyone who believes" (Rom 1:16).

But the good news gets even better. The gospel invitation is open to everyone. It's not for the elite, a special class of people, a particular race, or religion. No, this is an open invitation to you, to me, and to everyone.

THERE IS GOOD NEWS FOR EVERYONE

First-century Christians believed that the message of the gospel extended to everyone. In Matthew 22, the gospel of Jesus Christ is likened to an invitation, sent by God, inviting people to a great wedding feast. However, the invitation to the feast is, in reality, an invitation to trust Jesus Christ as Savior. It's an invitation to consider the facts of the "good news," change your mind about God and his Word, repent of your sin, and ask God to turn your life around forever.

The invitation to trust Jesus as Savior is open to anyone and everyone. Not all will receive this gracious invitation, of course, but it is a general call extended to all, including you and me.

Table 2: The Universal Invitation to Come to the Savior

"Whoever" Passages	Mark 16:16; Luke 18:17; John 3:15–18; 3:36; 4:14; 6:35, 37,47, 54, 56, 57, 58; 7:38; 8:12: 11:25; 12:24, 44, 46; 15:5; Rom 9:33; 1 John 4:15; 5:10; 5:12. "Truly, truly, I say to you, whoever hears my word and believes him who sent me has eternal life. He does not come into judgment, but has passed from death to life." (John 5:24).
"Anyone" Passages	John 6:51; 7:37; 8:51; 8:52; Rom 8:9; 2 Cor 5:17; 1 John 4:8; Rev 20:15. "I am the door. If anyone enters by me, he will be saved and will go in and out and find pasture" (John 10:9).
"Everyone" Passages	Matt 7:21; 10:32; Luke 6:47, 48; John 1:9; 4:13, 14; 6:40; 11:26; Acts 2:21, 39; 2:39; 10:43; 13:39; Rom 1:16; 10:4, 11; Eph 3:9; Col 1:29; Heb 2:9; 1 John 5:1; 2 John 1:9; Rev 13:8. "For everyone who calls on the name of the Lord will be saved" (Rom 10:13).
"All" Passages	Matt 11:28; Luke 13:3, 5; John 1:7; Acts 17:30; Rom 3:21–23; 5:18; 6:10; 8:14, 32; Gal 3:26; Col 2:13; 1 Tim 2:3, 4, 6; 4:10; Titus 2:11. "And I, when I am lifted up from the earth, will draw all people to myself" (John 12:32).

Whether or not anyone responds, it is evident that, because of his sovereign grace, God is calling all to repentance. The invitation is stated too many times for us to miss it. "The Lord is not slack concerning his promise, as some count slackness, but is longsuffering toward us, not willing that any should perish but that all should come to repentance" (2 Pet 3:9 NKJV).

God's invitation in the Old Testament

Even though there was no gospel story until the preaching of Jesus, Old Testament prophets nevertheless conveyed hope in God. Deuteronomy 4:29 reminds us, "You will seek the LORD your God and you will find him, if you search after him with all your heart and with all your soul." In David's prayer of thanksgiving that the ark of the covenant had been safely brought to Jerusalem, the king sang, "Seek the LORD and his strength; seek his presence continually!" (1 Chron 16:11).

Isaiah, Israel's foremost and favorite prophet, advised his people to, "Seek the LORD while he may be found; call upon him while he is near; let the wicked forsake his way, and the unrighteous man his thoughts; let him return to the LORD, that he may have compassion on him, and to our God, for he will abundantly pardon" (Isa 55:6, 7).

The command to seek the Lord was a popular one in the Old Testament (see 1 Chron 16:10; 22:19; 2 Chron 11:16; 12:14; 14:4; 15:12, 13; 6:12; 20:3, 4; Pss 34:10; 77:2; 105:4; Prov 28:5; Isa 51:1; Jer 50:4; Hos 3:5, 6; 10:12). Not just God's people Israel, but all of us are advised to seek the Lord. No one is left off God's guest list. Everyone is welcome, and everyone has an opportunity to respond to the gospel invitation, just as the evangelists, the apostles, and the thousands who came to faith in Christ did, recorded in the book of Acts. For us, the good news is that the gospel invitation is still open to you and me, and that it's still valid.

RESPONDING TO THE GOOD NEWS

However, the gospel is just an announcement, a revealing of the good news. By itself, it doesn't bring us into the family of God. Hearing the story of Jesus' crucifixion and resurrection provides you with the facts of the gospel, but hearing the facts is insufficient to save you. The engineers at NASA or SpaceX can know all the facts of how to return a man to the moon, but lunar landings are based on actions, not facts. Facts are not enough; you need faith in the facts to set in motion the events that lead to your salvation.

It takes a positive response to the announcement of good news, not just the announcement alone. A positive response includes giving mental assent to the facts of the gospel (Acts 16:14) as expressed in 1 Corinthians 15:1–4. To give assent to these facts is to acknowledge their truthfulness.

Becoming a follower of Jesus Christ is not an irrational leap into an undefined pit of faith. No, it is a thoughtful and deliberate response to understanding the facts of the "good news." Our salvation comes by trusting (Eph 2:8–10) that at Calvary's Cross, Jesus died so we could live, providing us with the possibility of new life "in Christ." Facts are important; in fact, they are essential. But it is faith that saves us.

Faith that saves

Salvational faith is faith in Christ Jesus as the only Savior this world will ever have. It is a faith in Jesus' atoning work on the cross (John 1:12). Historically, we have been rebellious toward God, even hostile toward him and the things of God. We thought the gospel message was foolish and laughed at those who believed it. But now, having believed in the truthfulness and reliability of the gospel, our minds are changed, our hearts are changed, and our directions and attitudes toward the Almighty are changed.

The kind of faith that saves is infused with repentance (Luke 13:3; Acts 17:30; 20:17–21; 26:19–20; 2 Pet 3:9). To repent comes from the Greek word μετάνοια (*metanoia*), meaning to turn 180 degrees, to go back, to change direction. Repentance, in the biblical sense, exhibits a change of mind and attitude toward God and the "good news" of the gospel. Repentance is reflected in genuine faith. Salvational faith is an informed faith in Christ Jesus as the only Savior God has provided for this world. It is a faith in Jesus' atoning work on the cross (John 1:12). It is God's gift to us (Eph 2:8).

> "Faith is not belief without proof, but trust without reservation."
> —Elton Trueblood

However, there is more. As an Evangelical scholar, I believe salvation is by grace alone, through faith alone, in Christ alone. Nevertheless, the faith that saves us from eternal damnation is not shallow or hollow. Salvational faith is a reasonable faith, a faith based on the facts of the "good news."

Salvational faith is also not a general faith. Saying you believe in God or Jesus is a general faith, but it's not a salvational faith. Believing that Jesus died in your place, placing your complete trust and confidence in what he accomplished at Calvary to save you, that's salvational faith.

The "good news" invitation is open to all; still, each individual must respond in faith to it. The gospel is sufficient for everyone, but it is effective only for those who genuinely come to faith in Christ. Failure to believe the "good news" is bad news (see 2 Thess 1:5–9). This is why the Apostle Paul lamented, "Woe to me if I do not preach the gospel!" (1 Cor 9:16).

If you have read the news on your phone or watched it on television, you know today's world is a mess. Almost 100 percent of reporting is bad news. A society like ours, which is sinful, always produces bad news. However, putting the "good" back into the news was a significant accomplishment of Jesus' death. Accomplishments don't get much bigger than this! For that, we must all be grateful.

My faith has found a resting place,
Not in device or creed;
I trust the ever-living One,
His wounds for me shall plead.

I need no other argument,
I need no other plea,
It is enough that Jesus died,
And that He died for me.

—Eliza E. Hewitt (1851–1920)

Chapter 11

Jesus Defeated Satan in His Long War With God

This is good news. Satan has been defeated. Every skirmish we have with him today is one further reminder to him, and to us, that he may win a battle here and there, but the long war with God is already lost.

The Battle's Soldiers and Generals
The Battles Satan Keeps Losing
The Battle of the Garden of Eden
The Battle of Evil Queen Athaliah
The Battle of Jeconiah
The Battle of King Herod the Baby Killer
The Battle of the Wilderness
The Battle of Gethsemane
The Battle of Calvary
The Battle of the Empty Tomb
The Battle of Armageddon
The Battle of Gog and Magog

Do you know anything about what has come to be known as "the forgotten battle"? Even many Canadians are not familiar with it. The Battle of the Scheldt was a series of military operations during World War II from October 2 to November 8, 1944. It mainly involved the First Canadian Army, with assistance from British and Polish units. It was fought to clear German forces from the Scheldt River in northern Belgium and southwestern Netherlands. This would give the Allies access to the water and the port of Antwerp. The Allies faced a severe challenge. The battle was bloody and grueling, and the Canadians took heavy losses. Still, it is called "the forgotten battle" because many do not even remember this strategic battle of the war.

Another strategic battle is currently underway that most people are unaware of. We rarely know it and even less see it, but there is constant warfare all around us. The reason we often do not know or see the battle is that it is essentially a spiritual one. The Apostle Paul's closing counsel to Jesus' followers living in and around ancient Ephesus was:

> Finally, be strong in the Lord and in the strength of his might. Put on the whole armor of God, that you may be able to stand against the schemes of the devil. For we do not wrestle against flesh and blood, but against the rulers, against the authorities, against the cosmic powers over this present darkness, against the spiritual forces of evil in the heavenly places" (Eph 6:10–12).

The devil's "schemes" (Greek: μεθοδείας; English: *methodeias*) are indisputably tricky.[80] This word is used only one other time in the New Testament when Paul describes why equipping the saints for the work of the ministry is so important. "So that we may no longer be children, tossed to and fro by the waves and carried about by every wind of doctrine, by human cunning, by craftiness in deceitful schemes (*methodeias*)" (Eph 4:14).

Like the Battle of the Scheldt, this battle is often fierce. However, unlike the Battle of the Scheldt, the victory in our battle has never been in doubt. "But thanks be to God, who gives us the victory through our Lord Jesus Christ" (1 Cor 15:57). "That is what Christ came to do—take that weapon out of Satan's hand," says Pastor John Piper.

> To do this, Christ took our sins on himself and suffered for them. When that happened, they could be used no more by the devil to destroy us. Taunt us? Yes. Mock us? Yes. But damn us? No. Christ bore the curse in our place. Try as he will, Satan cannot destroy us. The wrath of God is removed. His mercy is our shield. And Satan cannot succeed against us.[81]

This is good news. Satan has been defeated. Every skirmish we have with him today is one further reminder to him, and us, that he may win a battle here and there, but the long war with God is already lost.

THE BATTLE'S SOLDIERS AND GENERALS

First, we must identify the combatants in Satan's war with God. On the side of the "good guys,"[82] is YHWH, Jehovah, or Yahweh—the Creator God, the Sovereign God, the only God. This is the God of Israel, the God of the Bible.

In King Solomon's prayer of dedication for the dazzling Temple he had constructed, he addressed God saying, "O LORD, God of Israel, there is no God like you, in heaven above or on earth beneath, keeping covenant and showing steadfast love to your servants who walk before you with all their heart" (2 Chron 6:14).

With the prayer of King Hezekiah, some 250 years later, the language was much the same. "And Hezekiah prayed before the LORD and said: 'O LORD, the God of Israel, enthroned above the cherubim, you are the God, you alone, of all the kingdoms of the earth; you have made heaven and earth'" (2 Kgs 19:15). The God of heaven is the Commander of the side of good.

There is only one God

Most educated people are familiar with the more famous pantheon of Greek gods and the names the Romans gave to them, found here in parentheses: Zeus (Jupiter); Poseidon (Neptune); Aphrodite (Venus); Artemis (Diana); Dionysus (Bacchus); Ares (Mars); Eros (Cupid), and so many more. Nevertheless, the Romans went even further by adopting the cult of emperor worship.

The beginning lines of Henry Fairfield Burton's journal article, "The Worship of the Roman Emperors" in *The Biblical World* state, "The impulse that led to the deification of the Roman emperors came from the East. The Pharaohs and the Ptolemies, Lycurgus and Lysander of Sparta, and Alexander the Great were worshipped as divinities both while living and dead."[83] Thus, even Emperor Tiberius, who is perhaps best described as "a dirty old man," was worshipped by the Romans as a god.

Muslims also believe there is but one true God. In the Muslim religion, God is referred to as Allah, which is the Arabic word meaning "the God." Allah is the proper name of the One True God, understood to be singular, immortal, the all-powerful, all-wise, infinite God who is the creator and sustainer of the universe. In Islamic thinking, nothing in heaven or on Earth deserves worship except Allah.

In Hinduism, the general name for God is *Brahma.* The name of the divine essence within us is *Atman.* They are the same, infinite, and eternal. Buddhists do not limit themselves to one god but believe in *Devas* and

Brahmas [heavenly beings], *Nagas* [snake gods], Kinnaras [half-human, half-bird], Garudas [giant birds that are enemies of the Nagas], and *Dharmapala* [the guardians of Buddhism].

Shintoism has over 300 *Kami* (gods), among them *Amaterasu* (the Sun goddess), *Uzume* (the goddess of dawn and revelry), *Fujin* (the god of the wind), and *Hachiman* (the god of war).

The God of the Bible is very different from these. While many pagan gods are mentioned in the Bible, there was only one divine being who was truly God. The God of heaven has a personality. He is not stone or word. He is a spirit who is aware of who he is (John 4:24; Ex 3:13–15; Isa 44:6–8). He is a God who can choose what he will do and direct his affairs (Rom 11:33, 34; Eph 1:11). The God of the Bible is a moral God who can discern between good and evil. "The eyes of the Lord are in every place, keeping watch on the evil and the good" (Prov 15:3). He is a God of reason (Isa 1:18). His intelligence and understanding are far superior to human intelligence (Isa 55:8, 9). The God of the Bible is presented as the sole God, the God of Creation, the God of Abraham, Isaac, and Jacob, the exclusive God, as indicated in Table 1.

Table 1: The Exclusivity of the God of the Bible

"I am God Almighty."	Gen 35:11
"I am God, the God of your father."	Gen 46:3
"O LORD, God of Israel, there is no God like you."	2 Chron 6:24
"Be still, and know that I am God."	Ps 46:10
"I am God, your God."	Ps 50:7
"Declares the LORD, and I am God."	Isa 43:12
"I am the first and I am the last; besides me there is no god."	Isa 44:6
"Is there a God besides me? There is no Rock; I know not any."	Isa 44:8
"I am the LORD, and there is no other, besides me there is no God."	Isa 45:5
"Surely God is in you, and there is no other, no god besides him."	Isa 45:14
"And there is no other god besides me, a righteous God and a Savior."	Isa 45:21
"For I am God, and there is no other."	Isa 45:22
"I am God, and there is no other."	Isa 46:9
"I am God, and there is none like me."	Isa 46:9
"I am God and not a man, the Holy One in your midst."	Hos 11:9

God is the Five-Star General of his army. He is the Master and Commander, the leader of the troops, and his troops are the angels who did not join Satan's rebellion, as well as all men and women, boys and girls, who have demonstrated faith in Jesus as Savior and walk with him daily. The writers of the Bible often mention the qualities that good soldiers must possess to be ready for battle each day (Matt 11:28–30; Luke 14:27; Rom 12:1–2; Gal 2:20; Eph 2:8–10; 6:10–20).

Satan: the archenemy of the exclusive God

Satan's long war with God began when his pride got the best of him. He wanted to be God. If Ezekiel's lament over the King of Tyre is a veiled reference to Satan, as many believe, then we know some things about Satan's position, his desires, his policies, and his staggering fall. Read Ezekiel 28:12–19.

Satan becomes a fallen angel

Sometime in the distant history past, Satan grew weary of being the best and the brightest of God's angels and developed ambitions to replace YHWH as the Supreme God of the universe. If Isaiah 14:12–15 is a poetic reference describing Satan, as it appears to be, then we have another written account of what caused Satan to fall from his vaunted position in the heavens.

> How you are fallen from heaven, O Day Star, son of Dawn! How you are cut down to the ground, you who laid the nations low! You said in your heart, "I will ascend to heaven; above the stars of God I will set my throne on high; I will sit on the mount of assembly in the far reaches of the north; I will ascend above the heights of the clouds; I will make myself like the Most High." But you are brought down to Sheol, to the far reaches of the pit.

Certainly, Satan had an "I" problem. Notice it in Isaiah 14:12–15.

"*I* will ascend to heaven."
"*I* will sit on the mount."
"*I* will ascend above the heights of the clouds."
"*I* will make myself like the Most High."

Satan also had an ambition problem. Ambition is good. The world would never advance without ambition. However, the ambition to have what you are not supposed to have, or to be what God never intended for you to be, really isn't ambition. It's sin! Satan's "I will" statements all represent willful ambition, but this ambition was willful sin! He was rebelling against God's authority, as well as God's being.

Table 2: Satan's Pride and Position in Ezekiel 28

Satan's heart was proud.	v 2
Satan said, "I am a god, I sit in the seat of the gods."	v 2
Satan was privy to every secret of God.	v 3
Satan's wisdom had made him extremely wealthy.	v 4
Satan had to gather gold and silver into his personal bank.	v 4
Satan was a master of commerce.	v 5
Satan made his heart like the heart of a god.	v 6
Satan was the "signet of perfection."	v 12
Satan was both exceedingly wise and handsome.	v 12
Satan had full access to the Garden of Eden.	v 13
Satan held an exalted position, "an anointed guardian cherub."	v 14
Satan was placed by God on the holy mountain.	v 14
Satan walked among the stones of fire.	v 14
Satan was blameless in all his ways.	v 15

THE BATTLES SATAN KEEPS LOSING

In Satan's long war with God, there have been some close calls. These have been skirmishes in which we could have lost the war, and probably would have, in the words of Martin Luther, "Were not the right Man on our side, The Man of God's own choosing: Dost ask who that may be? Christ Jesus, it is he; Lord Sabaoth his name, From age to age the same, And he must win the battle."

Some of the critical battles in Satan's long war with God are investigated here. As you know, war is composed of many small battles, but winning the small battles brings you victory. We cannot examine all of life's secondary battles here, but we can explore the major ones.

#1. The Battle of the Garden of Eden: Genesis 3:1–6, 15 Adam and Eve sinned. God provided. Satan lost.

This is the first battle involving the human race in Satan's long war with God. We all know the story. Satan disguised himself as a snake, a charmer, who deceived Eve. He got Eve to question God, and every time we doubt what God has said, we open ourselves to a frontal attack by Satan.

> Did God *actually* say, "You shall not eat of any tree in the garden"? Well, of course, he did. Check the record. "And the LORD God commanded the man, saying, 'You may surely eat of every tree of the garden, but of the tree of the knowledge of good and evil you shall not eat, for in the day that you eat of it you shall surely die'" (Gen 2:16–17).

Eve ate the forbidden fruit. She disobeyed. Adam soon followed. In choosing to disobey God, they followed Satan, the archenemy of the Almighty. They believed the devil over God. They joined the wrong team, followed the wrong Commander, volunteered for the wrong army, and the consequences were severe. We have been battling Satan ever since because of it.

Table 3: Satan's Pride and Downfall in Ezekiel 28 Continued

Satan's action	*Verse*
Satan became filled with violence	v 16
Satan had sinned against the holy God	v 16
Satan was kicked out of "the mountain of God" by God	v 16
Satan was destined to be destroyed by God	v 16
Satan no longer walked among the stones of fire	v 16
Satan's heart became proud because of his beauty	v 17
Satan's wisdom became corrupt	v 17
Satan was "cast to the ground" by God	v 17
Satan was exposed as a fraud before kings	v 17
Satan was guilty of a multitude of iniquity and unrighteousness	v 18
Satan became as useless on Earth as ashes	v 18
Satan was appalling to everyone on Earth	v 19
Satan would come to a dreadful end	v 19
Satan would one day be no more	v 19

When Adam and his wife saw they were both naked, they hid from God. In a vain attempt to cover their nakedness, they hurriedly sewed together some leaves from a fig tree. Fig trees are plentiful in the Middle East, and their leaves are large compared to other leaves (4–10 inches in length; 3–7 inches in width). This was not exactly *haute couture*, but they thought it did the job. It did not. The purpose of the leaves was to cover their sin, not just cover their bodies. That is precisely what atonement does; it covers our sin. But Adam and Eve used the wrong fabric for their clothing. God has always required a blood sacrifice to cover our sin, and there was no bloodshed in the plucking of some leaves from the fig tree.

Imagine sitting by a quiet stream, under the shade of a leafy tree, eating fresh fruit from the trees all around you. It's Eden, the most idyllic place possible. God has confronted Adam and Eve, but they have not yet been disciplined. Suddenly, the sweet sounds of the singing birds were interrupted by a blood-curdling shriek. It was the squeal of an innocent animal being killed by God to provide Adam and Eve with skins for clothing to hide their nakedness properly. It was the first death in an innocent world, and it was necessary to cover the sin of Adam and Eve.

Had God not provided through the death of that animal, Satan would have won this battle. However, he did not, because of God's provision. That provision cost Adam and Eve nothing but was costly to the animal God had to slay. The same is true with the sacrifice of Jesus Christ at Calvary. God provided the perfect sacrifice in his Son. His innocent blood was shed to cover our sin. Satan thought he had won, but he was the loser, and he lost this first skirmish involving the human family. There would be others.

#2. The Battle of Queen Athaliah: 2 Kings 11:1–3, 12 Evil Queen killed the royal line. Josiah was saved. Satan lost.

Everybody loves a grandmother. Grandmothers are God's gift to us to provide the world with sweetness, love, and apple pie. Nevertheless, there was one grandmother in Israel's history who was less than sweet and loving. Here's her story.

> Now when Athaliah the mother of Ahaziah saw that her son was dead, she arose and destroyed all the royal family. But Jehosheba, the daughter of King Joram, sister of Ahaziah, took Joash the son of Ahaziah and stole him away from among the king's sons who were being put to death, and she put him and his nurse in a bedroom. Thus they hid him from Athaliah, so that he was not put to death. And he remained with her six years, hidden in the

> house of the LORD, while Athaliah reigned over the land (2 Kgs 11:1–3).

When Jehu assassinated King Ahaziah, the slain king's mother saw an opportunity for a power grab. She killed all the royal family who were in line for the kingship and then inserted herself as queen. God did not anoint her, nor was she a godly woman. Amid this slaughter, Jehosheba, the sister of the now-dead King Ahaziah, took one of Ahaziah's sons, named Joash, and hid him in her chambers, where she knew Athaliah would not look for him. For six years, the only living heir of Ahaziah was secretly hidden in the palace.

In the seventh year, Jehoiada the priest brought out the young Joash, and the people crowned him as their king, the rightful heir to the throne. When Athaliah heard about it, she screamed, "Treason. Treason." But the treason was committed by Athaliah, the wicked queen, who was put to death for her treason.

Two key takeaways from this biblical account are essential.

First, when 2 Kings 11 states that Athaliah "arose and destroyed all the royal family," we are not referring to strangers. We are talking about her own grandchildren. This wicked grandmother killed her grandchildren, every last one of them she thought, so they would not challenge her for the throne.

Secondly, had Aunt Jehosheba not hidden Joash, he would not have been able to sit legitimately on the throne later, which would have meant the royal line of David would have been snuffed out, along with the hopes of a Messiah and any claim of Jesus to the throne of David. The battle of the Athaliah affair was a close call, but Satan was defeated once again.

#3. The Battle of Jeconiah: Jeremiah 22:24–30; Matthew 1:16 The Royal line was cursed. Jesus spared the curse. Satan lost.

First Chronicles 3:10–16 records all the male descendants of Solomon. These descendants would become Jewish kings. You will recognize some of their names: Rehoboam, Abijah, Asa, Jehoshaphat, Jehoram, Ahaziah, Joash, Amaziah, Uzziah, Jotham, Ahaz, Hezekiah, Manasseh, Amon, Josiah, Jehoahaz, Jehoiakim, Jehoiachin, and Zedekiah. The next-to-last king, Jehoiachin, is sometimes referred to in the Bible as Jeconiah or Coniah, a shortened form akin to a nickname.

Nevertheless, there was a problem with Coniah. He was a wicked king, so wicked that God spoke in unusually harsh terms against him. Jeremiah 22:24 says, "As I live, declares the LORD, though Coniah the son of Jehoiakim, king of Judah, were the signet ring on my right hand, yet I would tear you off." You can almost feel God's righteous anger against the excessive sins of this man, a man who is the legal ancestor of King David.

Table 4a: Satan's Long War with God

Major Skirmishes of the Old Testament		
Reference	*Skirmish*	*Result*
Gen 3	Temptation in Eden	Satan wins, but God promises a seed
Gen 6	Entire world corrupted	The whole world needs a Savior
Gen 21	Abram's wife is barren	Isaac is born; God's promise fulfilled
Gen 37	Jacob's family is starving	Joseph saves Jacob's line
Exod 3	The Jews are enslaved in Egypt	God raises Moses as a deliverer
Exod 12	Egypt's firstborn are slain	The Jews are spared; Passover instituted
1 Sam 16	God's choice of David as king	David was anointed as Israel's future king
1 Kgs 1	Adonijah grabs the royal throne	Solomon is crowned the legitimate king
2 Kgs 11	Athaliah usurps the royal throne	Joash becomes Ahaziah's rightful heir

However, it gets worse. Not only does God display his anger at sin, but he also places a curse on Coniah and his descendants. This curse was irreversible. Here's how the Prophet Jeremiah recorded it. "Thus says the LORD: 'Write this man down as childless, a man who shall not succeed in his days, for none of his offspring shall succeed in sitting on the throne of David and ruling again in Judah'" (Jer 22:30).

What does this have to do with Jesus? Everything. Jesus is in the line of David, and God's irrevocable curse prohibits anyone in David's line after Coniah from prospering on David's throne. Said differently, to sit on the throne of David, the king had to be a direct descendant of David through his son Solomon. However, anyone born into the line of Solomon after King Coniah could not successfully sit on the throne of David.

You can see the difficulty. You had to be a descendant of Coniah to be king, but if you were a descendant of Coniah, you were cursed and would never prosper as Israel's king. That's a colossal problem. Nevertheless, people of faith have learned that God is always bigger than our problems. He had already dealt with this obstacle.

There are two genealogies of Jesus Christ. The one in Matthew 1 traces Jesus' ancestors down from Abraham to Joseph, "the husband of Mary." This is the legal line. The other in Luke 3 traces his genealogy from Mary back to Adam. These two lines intersect at King David. However, while Matthew 1 connects Jesus to David through David's son Solomon, Luke 3 connects him through David's son Nathan. This is critical because of the curse of Coniah.

Joseph did not father Jesus, but Jesus legally became his son when he married Mary. So, while Jesus is in the royal line of David through his legal father, Joseph (Matt 1:1–16), he is in the biological line of David through Mary, his mother (Luke 3:23–38). It was the legal line through Coniah that was cursed. No blood descendant of Coniah could ever sit on the throne of David, but remember, Jesus is not a blood descendant of Coniah, because he was not biologically the son of Joseph. The curse cannot apply to him.

Jesus is both the legal heir to the throne of David through Solomon, the king's son, and the physical heir through Nathan, the king's son. The blood of David coursed through Jesus' veins, but the blood of Coniah did not. Satan thought he had God trapped, but again he came out the loser in this and every other battle in his long war with God.

#4. The Battle of King Herod the Baby Killer: Matthew 2:1–18
The Bethlehem boys are killed. Jesus escaped. Satan lost.

Herod the Great was Rome's choice to be the client king of the Jews. He was allowed to remain in power as long as Judea was economically, politically, and militarily subordinate to Rome.[84] When the magi came from the East seeking the one who was born King of the Jews, Herod must have said to himself, "*I thought I was the King of the Jews*!" Herod's suspicion and jealousy were piqued, and he plotted to kill this "pretender" to the throne.

After the Magi visited the Christ child in Bethlehem, they were warned in a dream not to return to Herod and tell him where this royal child was living. When Herod discerned they were not returning to Jerusalem, he decided to kill this young would-be king. However, since he could not identify who the child was, Herod ordered every young male child, two years of age and under, in the little town of Bethlehem to be killed. Matthew 2:16 tells us this is precisely what happened. Herod sent his soldiers to Bethlehem, and in one night they slaughtered dozens and dozens of innocent babies, snatching them from their mothers' arms and slitting their throats.

Had Joseph and Mary still been residing in Bethlehem at the time, their young infant boy Jesus would have been among those slaughtered by Herod the Great. Satan would have won the war. There would be no perfect sacrifice to die at Calvary, no Messiah for the Jews, and no Savior for the world. However, God is always a step ahead of Satan. Matthew 2:13–15 records:

> Now when they [the magi] had departed, behold, an angel of the Lord appeared to Joseph in a dream and said, "Rise, take the child and his mother, and flee to Egypt, and remain there until I tell you, for Herod is about to search for the child, to destroy him." And he rose and took the child and his mother by night and departed to Egypt and remained there until the death of Herod.

By the time Herod, Satan's minion, was killing infant boys in Bethlehem, Jesus was already on his way to Egypt and safety. Satan loses again.

#5. The Battle of the Wilderness: Matthew 4:1–11 Satan unsuccessfully tempted Jesus. Satan lost.

It worked on Eve, so why not try it on Jesus? However, with Jesus, Satan was up against God himself, and the results would be much different. When Satan tempted Eve, he implanted doubt into her mind about what God had said (Gen 3:1). After Jesus was baptized by John the Baptist in the Jordan River, the Holy Spirit immediately led Jesus to the wilderness area between the Jordan and Jerusalem. There, Jesus was alone, and there Satan approached him in an attempt to thwart the plan of God.

After Jesus had been alone in the wilderness for forty days and forty nights, fasting the entire time, he was hungry—any person would be. Satan saw his opportunity. The devil said to Jesus, "If you are the Son of God, command these stones to become loaves of bread." This question is in the same subjunctive mood used to describe hypothetical or non-real actions or situations.

Satan said, "If you are the Son of God," not "since you are the Son of God." He tried to introduce doubt in the Savior's mind about his true identity, but it didn't work. Jesus answered Satan by quoting the Scripture. "Man shall not live by bread alone, but by every word that comes from the mouth of God" (Deut 8:3). Satan failed, but he did not give up.

Next, he escorted Jesus to the Holy City and placed him on top of the pinnacle of the Temple, where the distance from the Temple wall to the ground below was the greatest. Again, a comment in the subjunctive mood: "If you are the Son of God, throw yourself down, for it is written, 'He will command his angels concerning you,' and 'On their hands, they will bear you up, lest you strike your foot against a stone.'"

Satan knew enough to quote Psalm 91:11, 12 to Jesus. But again, he failed as Jesus responded, "Again it is written, 'You shall not put the Lord your God to the test.'" With a curse of disgust, the devil lost again.

Undaunted, Satan tried one more time to foil the plan of God. He took Jesus to a high mountain, presumably overlooking the city of Jericho in the Jordan Valley. The devil pointed to all the land from the north in the Galilee and to the south, the Dead Sea, and beyond. He pointed out the mountains of Transjordan and the desert beyond them. He said to Jesus, "All these I will give you, if you will fall down and worship me."

However, Jesus was not falling for anything. Can't you hear Jesus saying, "I already own all of that." Satan could not give what did not belong to him. Satan had nothing to entice Jesus with, nor did he have anything to offer Jesus that did not already belong to the Godhead. Three temptations. Three failures. You would think by now Satan would be tired of losing, but not a chance.

#6. The Battle of Gethsemane: Matthew 26:36–45 Jesus bowed to the Father's will. Satan lost.

The Garden of Gethsemane was not just a skirmish; it was a major battlefield. Like Marathon, Hastings, Waterloo, or Gettysburg, Gethsemane will be remembered as a decisive battle that sealed the fate of war.

It was here that Satan had his best opportunity to turn Jesus away from the cross and change the outcome of his long war with God. If the devil could just get Jesus to succumb to the human dread of a horrible death, if he could get the Master to renege on his eternal agreement to be the sin-bearer, that would be the end of God's plan for our salvation. All Satan had to do was convince Jesus that the personal cost to him was too great and that Jesus should pack it in and return to Galilee.

Satan saw signs everywhere that this was his best chance to defeat the Son of God. However, he must also have seen signs that this could be his last chance. What he threw at Jesus in the garden was more than any human could bear. Matthew 26 is an example of how the Gospels record Jesus' struggle at Gethsemane. Consider these phrases:

Jesus "began to be sorrowful and troubled" (v. 37)

"My soul is very sorrowful, even to death" (v. 38)

"Jesus 'fell on his face and prayed'" (v. 39)

"My Father, if it be possible, let this cup pass from me" (v. 39)

> "My Father, if this cannot pass unless I drink it . . ." (v. 42)
>
> "He prayed for the third time, saying the same words again" (v. 44)

From the perspective of a physician, Luke 22 gives these additional details about the stress Jesus was under in Gethsemane:

> "And there appeared to him an angel from heaven, strengthening him" (v. 43)
>
> "And being in agony, he prayed more earnestly" (v. 44)
>
> "His sweat became like great drops of blood falling down to the ground" (v. 44)

There was a cosmic struggle going on here. This was the classic battle of the wills—three of them. It was Satan's will to get Jesus to avoid the cross. It was the will of the Father to execute his eternal plan for our salvation. And it was Jesus who must choose to yield to the devil's will or maintain his commitment to do the will of the Father. We can be grateful that even during the heat of this battle of the wills, Jesus affirmed, "Abba, Father, all things are possible for you. Remove this cup from me. Yet not what I will, but what you will" (Mark 14:36).

Satan saw his best chance to keep Jesus from the cross slipping through his fingers. If Jesus did not cave to the devil's ploy here, there was little to stop the march toward Golgotha, and Satan knew it.

#7. The Battle of Calvary: Luke 23:1–49 Jesus died to pay for our sin. Satan lost. Big time.

There was no chance Jesus would be acquitted at Caiaphas's trial. After all, the religious leaders of Jerusalem had been attempting to kill Jesus for some time (John 5:18; see also Matt 26:1–4; Mark 14:1; Luke 22:2; John 7:1, 19, 20, 25; 8:37, 40). They had pre-determined that it was in their best interest for Jesus to die (see John 11:45–53). They had prejudged the Nazarene as guilty. All they needed was to conduct a trial. The verdict was already inevitable.

The Jewish religious leaders were hell-bent on crucifying Jesus. That was the last thing Satan wanted, but he still held on to hope. The last chance for any governing authority to stop the crucifixion of Jesus belonged to the Romans. When Jesus was sent to Pontius Pilate, you can imagine the look of concern on the devil's face.

However, Pilate's reputation was as a cruel, uncaring tyrant. Imagine the sigh of relief Satan breathed when Pilate did not automatically verify the findings of the Sanhedrin and simply sentence Jesus to death by crucifixion.

Every time Pilate made a statement to the effect that he found no reason to punish Jesus, let alone kill him, a devilish grin must have appeared on the devil's face.

However, when the Jewish leaders wore Pilate down, threatening to accuse him of not being a friend of the emperor, Pilate gave in. Here, another will emerged in the battle of wills. It was the will of Caiaphas. It was the will of the Sanhedrin. It was the will of the unhinged and agitated Jewish mob crying for Jesus' crucifixion. Luke 23:25 says, "He delivered Jesus over to their will." The will of the corrupt religious leaders held sway that day. Jesus would go to the cross as they willed. Although no one realized it at the time, he would go to the cross as God willed.

> When Jesus said, "It is finished," the payment for sin was complete,
> When Jesus said, "It is finished," it meant Satan's sure defeat.
> When Jesus said, "It is finished," the angels sang a song so sweet,
> When Jesus said, "It is finished," it meant a death he'd never repeat.

When Jesus said, "It is finished," bowed his head, and gave up his spirit, many watching him die were deeply saddened. His mother watched the life of her firstborn ebb away. His beloved disciple watched his best friend die. Other faithful women who had followed Jesus from Galilee were saddened too, but none was sadder than God's primary nemesis, who was watching the events of Calvary the closest. No one was more disappointed on that dark Friday afternoon than was the devil.

Table 4b: Satan's Long War with God

Major Skirmishes of the New Testament		
Reference	*Skirmish*	*Result*
Matt 2	Herod kills Bethlehem's boy infants	The Holy Family escapes to Egypt
Matt 4	Satan tempts Jesus in the wilderness	Jesus resists Satan's three temptations
Mark 14	Jesus struggles in Gethsemane	Satan fails to thwart God's will
John 19	Satan must stop Jesus' crucifixion	Jesus' shed blood provides salvation
Luke 24	Satan must keep Jesus in the tomb	Jesus rises victorious over Satan
Rev 19	Satan battles at Armageddon	The King of Kings defeats Satan
Rev 20	Satan battles at Gog and Magog	Jesus defeats Satan for good

The last person who wanted to see Jesus die was Satan. Some may think Satan would rejoice at the death of Jesus, but he did not. He could not. Satan did not want Jesus to die at Calvary because that would mean the old snake had failed to thwart the eternal plan of God for our redemption. It would mean he had lost the biggest battle in the war to date. The opportunities for him to frustrate God's plan were rapidly diminishing. Satan could feel the end was nearing. He was now fighting his antepenultimate battle.

#8. The Battle of the Empty Tomb: Matthew 28:1–6. Jesus conquered the power of death. Satan lost again.

Satan thought he had one last chance to impede God's plan. That would be to deny the resurrection of Jesus Christ. If Satan could not keep Jesus *from* the cross, maybe he could keep him *in* the grave. He was running out of options. The devil had to make this work.

Each of the four evangelists records the earth-shaking events of early Sunday morning, the morning of the resurrection. Here is how Matthew describes it:

> Now after the Sabbath, toward the dawn of the first day of the week, Mary Magdalene and the other Mary went to see the tomb. And behold, there was a great earthquake, for an angel of the Lord descended from heaven and came and rolled back the stone and sat on it. His appearance was like lightning, and his clothing white as snow. And for fear of him the guards trembled and became like dead men. But the angel said to the women, "Do not be afraid, for I know that you seek Jesus who was crucified. He is not here, for he has risen, as he said. Come, see the place where he lay. Then go quickly and tell his disciples that he has risen from the dead" (Matt 28:1–7).

No matter how you look at it, Jesus' resurrection from the dead was a severe blow to Satan. He had failed to keep Jesus from the cross, and now Satan has been unable to keep him from rising from the dead. Perhaps Satan has begun to question the wisdom of his rebellion so long ago. Every time he battled his Creator, the devil lost. However, there would be yet another battle to defeat God. Nevertheless, Satan had to wait millennia for this battle.

#9. The Battle of Armageddon: Revelation 19:11–21. Jesus rides from heaven in victory. Satan loses again.

The interpretation of the book of Revelation is problematic. Since it is apocalyptic, focusing on future events, several interpretations are possible for what is recorded in the Apocalypse. Some believe these events have already occurred in the first-century Roman Empire (the Preterist view). Some hold that Revelation is just a narrative of the cosmic struggle between good and evil (the Idealist view). Others view the events of Revelation as aligning with general history rather than with specific events or individuals (the Historical view). Many believe the events of Revelation 6–22 are yet future (the Futurist view).

Since I do not find anything in the first century or any other era of history that even comes close to the cataclysmic events recorded in the book of Revelation, I understand these to be yet future events. If they are in the future, are these actual events or symbolic events? Indeed, there is a great deal of symbolism in the Apocalypse. However, with so many references to specific places, numbers, and people, I think it is better to understand the general structure of this final book of the Bible as filled with literal, future events.

If this understanding is correct, our planet awaits God's judgment. It is a time of incredible wars, tribulation, and famine, followed by astonishing peace and stability, then another incredible war, and finally eternity. It is to the events immediately preceding eternity that Satan's bloody battle, his penultimate or next-to-last battle, will be fought. Here is how the Apostle John recorded what God revealed to him on the Island of Patmos.

> Then I saw heaven opened, and behold, a white horse! The one sitting on it is called Faithful and True, and in righteousness he judges and makes war. His eyes are like a flame of fire, and on his head are many diadems, and he has a name written that no one knows but himself. He is clothed in a robe dipped in blood, and the name by which he is called is The Word of God. And the armies of heaven, arrayed in fine linen, white and pure, were following him on white horses. From his mouth comes a sharp sword with which to strike down the nations, and he will rule them with a rod of iron. He will tread the winepress of the fury of the wrath of God the Almighty. On his robe and on his thigh he has a name written, King of kings and Lord of lords. And I saw the beast and the kings of the earth with their armies gathered to make war against him who was sitting on the horse and against his army. And the beast was captured, and with it the

> false prophet who in its presence had done the signs by which he deceived those who had received the mark of the beast and those who worshiped its image. These two were thrown alive into the lake of fire that burns with sulfur. And the rest were slain by the sword that came from the mouth of him who was sitting on the horse, and all the birds were gorged with their flesh.

I have included nearly all of Revelation 19 because this passage describes what is commonly known as the Battle of Armageddon. In this battle, the bloodiest battle of Satan's long war with God, Satan is once again defeated. His two Tribulation Period accomplices, the Beast and the False Prophet, are thrown alive into the Lake of Fire (Rev 19:20), but not the devil himself. However, his fate awaits him.

#10. The Battle of Gog and Magog: Revelation 20:7–10. Jesus is victorious again. Satan loses the final battle.

We come now to the final battle in Satan's long war with God. In the drama that is the end times, we last saw Satan awaiting God's judgment. Revelation 20:1–3 details that judgment.

> Then I saw an angel coming down from heaven, holding in his hand the key to the bottomless pit and a great chain. And he seized the dragon, that ancient serpent, who is the devil and Satan, and bound him for a thousand years, and threw him into the pit, and shut it and sealed it over him, so that he might not deceive the nations any longer, until the thousand years were ended. After that, he must be released for a little while.

John says Satan was bound, thrown into a bottomless pit, and sealed for a thousand years. Beyond these three verses in Revelation 20, we really know very little about this "bottomless" pit except that it had no bottom. Now think for a moment. Satan is bound. If this is literal, he is cast into this bottomless pit that is then sealed. What does the devil do for a thousand years in a pit that has no bottom? He does the only thing he can do. Presumably, he falls. It's a long fall. It's a thousand-year fall. Satan being cast into the bottomless pit effectively restrains his ability to wage war with God for a millennium.

Nevertheless, there is more to the story. Revelation 20 continues, "And when the thousand years are ended, Satan will be released from his prison and will come out to deceive the nations that are at the four corners of the earth, Gog and Magog, to gather them for battle; their number is like the sand of the sea" (Rev 20:7, 8).

After a thousand years in the pit, Satan will be released. By now, you would think he would know better, but he does not. Immediately, he is up to his old tricks again. He attempts to deceive the entire inhabitants of the Earth and gathers them into one final fling, one last battle in his long war with God. Gog is the name of a man, apparently a general of the armies of a place called Magog. These names are also mentioned in the prophecy of Ezekiel 38–39, but Ezekiel was speaking of another battle, not the final one described in Revelation 20. Ezekiel's battle involves armies from the north, whereas Revelation's battle involves a war by all nations.

The Book of Revelation employs Ezekiel's prophetic imagery to depict the ultimate, climactic battle of history. This battle is the final showdown at the end of this age between good and evil, and good ultimately prevails.

> "And they marched up over the broad plain of the earth and surrounded the camp of the saints and the beloved city [Jerusalem], but fire came down from heaven and consumed them, and the devil who had deceived them was thrown into the lake of fire and sulfur where the beast and the false prophet were, and they will be tormented day and night forever and ever" (Rev 20:9, 10).

God is profoundly patient with sinners. He has been warning us that there is a price to pay for living a sin-filled life. He has often told us in his Word that the price is death and hell. Ever since Genesis 3:15, God has been encouraging us to take the straight and narrow path, to enter by the narrow door, to abandon our foolish sin, and fall before him in repentance. Nevertheless, we have consistently refused. Today, the world laughs at those who live righteously. For those who laugh, God has given them plenty of time to trust him. He has been promising that one day he would say, "Depart from me, you cursed, into the eternal fire prepared for the devil and his angels"(Matt 25:41). Well, in this final battle of the long war, God keeps his promise, as he always does.

It's over. It's finally over. All those years, Christians have questioned whether or not God was really in control because they saw so much evil in the world, and now they know. God was in control the whole time. Those who have cursed God and lived their lives as if there were no God, now know. God hasn't forgotten their sin. Judgment Day for the wicked earth has arrived.

But other things are over, too. God promised, "He will wipe away every tear from their eyes, and death shall be no more, neither shall there be mourning, nor crying, nor pain anymore, for the former things have passed away" (Rev 21:4). It's over. It's all over. No more tears to wipe from your eyes. No more grandparents dying with Alzheimer's. No more mourning the loss of your child in a tragic car accident. The crying that seemed to come so often in this life is gone. Completely gone. No more visits to the doctor to adjust your pain meds. There is no more pain. Hallelujah! It's gone. It's all gone. Everything sin tainted in this world is gone. Everything sin harbored in your life is gone. It's all gone.

This is another accomplishment of Jesus on the cross. He soundly defeated the devil at every turn, in every battle, as Table 5 summarizes.

Table 5: Summary of Satan's Long War With God and the Devastating Results

The Battle	*Scripture*	*Comments*	*Results*
Garden of Eden	Gen 3:1–6,15	Adam & Eve sin; God provides	Satan defeated
Athaliah	2 Kgs 11:1–12	Queen killed royal line; Josiah saved	Satan defeated
Jeconiah	Jer 22:24–30	Royal line cursed; Jesus line spared	Satan defeated
Herod the Great	Matt 2:1–18	Bethlehem boys killed; Jesus spared	Satan defeated
Wilderness	Matt 4:1–11	Satan unsuccessfully tempted Jesus	Satan defeated
Gethsemane	Matt 26:36–45	Jesus bowed to the Father's will	Satan defeated
Calvary	Luke 23:1–49	Jesus died to pay for our sin	Satan defeated
Empty Tomb	Matt 28:1–6	Jesus conquered death	Satan defeated
Armageddon	Rev 19:11–21	Jesus rides from heaven in victory	Satan defeated
Gog and Magog	Rev 20:8	Jesus victorious again	Satan defeated

CONCLUSION

In this book, "What Jesus' Crucifixion Accomplished For Us," I did not intend to create a theological textbook. That's apparent from reading it. I have shied away from some of the more popular or perhaps more potent aspects of Christian theology and concentrated on those theological issues that relate specifically to Jesus' crucifixion, death, and resurrection.

I have looked at the crucifixion through the eyes of a wonderer. That's why, among the accomplishments of Jesus' crucifixion, I have included Chapter 9, Jesus Restored Our Severed Relationship With God. In Chapter

11, Jesus Provided the "Good News" of the Gospel Story. And in Chapter 12, Jesus Defeated Satan in his long war with God. These are not typical subjects in most theological textbooks. There are accomplishments at Calvary that we don't often think of, and there are many more. When he was crucified in our place on Calvary's Cross, Jesus accomplished much more than we realize until we sit at his feet in heaven as our Savior-Teacher. Accomplishments don't get much bigger than these!

Although you've come to the end of this book, you have not come to the end of thinking about the accomplishments of Jesus. Take some time today to jot down all the things you can think of that Jesus accomplished at Calvary. Take all the time you need. Come back to your list often. I think you will be pleasantly surprised at the results.

"He, who is witness to all this, says, 'Yes, I am coming very quickly!' 'Amen, come Lord Jesus!'" (Rev 22:20 JBP).

A mighty fortress is our God,
a bulwark never failing;
our helper he, amid the flood
of mortal ills prevailing.

For still our ancient foe
does seek to work us woe;
his craft and power are great,
and armed with cruel hate,
on earth is not his equal.

Did we in our own strength confide,
our striving would be losing,
were not the right Man on our side,
the Man of God's own choosing.

You ask who that may be?
Christ Jesus, it is he;
Lord Sabaoth his name,
from age to age the same;
and he must win the battle.

—Martin Luther (1483–1546)

Chapter 12

Jesus Did Something Spectacular on the Third Day

Jesus' crucifixion set the stage for his resurrection. Without the resurrection, his crucifixion would be incomplete. Without the crucifixion, there would be no need for the resurrection. They can never be separated.

Jesus' Resurrection Was Not a Surprise to Him
Jesus' Resurrection Should Not Have Been a Surprise to His Disciples
Jesus' Resurrection Was Unique Among Biblical Resurrections
Jesus' Resurrection Secured Our Justification
Jesus' Resurrection Is Important to Everyone

While the series *CRUCIFIXION: A Multidisciplinary Investigation of the Death of Jesus of Nazareth* encompasses seven volumes, and if you have read the first five volumes in this series, you have already read 1,361 pages related to Jesus' crucifixion, this final chapter of book number six adds another critical aspect of the death of Jesus. It's his resurrection from the dead.

Some things just belong together. I'm talking about ham and eggs, chips and salsa, macaroni and cheese—you get the idea. When combined, some foods complement each other, making them more enjoyable. That's the way it is with music. If you are as old as I am, you know that apart, two guys named Phil and Don may not have made it, but put them together and you get the Everly Brothers. Where would Art Garfunkel be without Paul

Simon? You may not be familiar with Bill Medley or Bobby Hatfield, but put them together and you have the Righteous Brothers. I know; I'm showing my age. Are you into country music? How about Brooks and Dunn or Big and Rich? And then there is that *Wicked* pair, Cynthia Erivo and Ariana Grande. One is good; two are better.

That's the way it is with the crucifixion. By itself, it is one of the most critical events in history. However, couple the crucifixion with Christ's resurrection, and you absolutely have the most crucial tandem of events since the creation of the world. The crucifixion and resurrection belong together. For men and women, one is good; two are better. Let's investigate the resurrection in light of the crucifixion.

JESUS' RESURRECTION WAS NOT A SURPRISE TO HIM

The crucifixion was quite a letdown. Those who hated the Messiah were pleased, saying, "*I'm glad that's over with and we've silenced another false Messiah.*" Caiaphas and the Sanhedrin were saying, "*We finally killed that pesky Jesus of Nazareth.*" Pontius Pilate said to himself, "*I don't need all that drama. The man may have been innocent, but that's all behind us now.*" Most of Jesus' followers were saying, "*They actually crucified him. The Messiah is dead. What do we do now*"?

Put yourself in the place of Peter, James, Andrew, and the rest of the disciples. They were stunned. When the time came for them to stand up for their Savior, they all ran. Only John is mentioned by the gospels as being at Calvary's Cross. The rest of the disciples were in hiding. They cannot believe what happened on that dark Friday. They sought safety in numbers, so by Sunday morning, they had huddled together when the news came that the tomb was empty and Jesus was alive again.

> "Together with His atoning death and the shedding of His blood, our Lord's resurrection is the keystone of the Christian faith."
> —Floyd H. Barackman

Not everyone was surprised at the resurrection. God the Father, God the Son, and God the Holy Spirit were not surprised. Why was Jesus not surprised that he would rise from the dead on the third day? It was the plan. Everything was going according to plan, God's eternal plan. (Eph 1:3, 8–10).

Colossians 1:18,20 reminds us, "For in him [Jesus Christ] all the fullness of God was pleased to dwell, and through him to reconcile to himself all things, whether on earth or in heaven, making peace by the blood of his cross."

Paul wrote in 1 Corinthians 15: 20–22, "But in fact Christ has been raised from the dead, the firstfruits of those who have fallen asleep. For as by a man came death, by a man has come also the resurrection of the dead. For as in Adam all die, so also in Christ shall all be made alive."

God's predetermined plan

God's determination that Christ Jesus should suffer for the sin of all people was not a vague, indistinct objective that would leave much to coincidence or the vacillating will of human beings. No, the eternal plan of the Godhead for our salvation arose from his determinate counsel (Greek: ὡρισμενῃ hōrismenē), such counsel that defined the time, place, participants, and circumstances of Jesus' crucifixion. Nothing was left to chance. There was nothing cavalier about the events of that Passion weekend. From God's perspective, everything was going according to plan, his eternal plan.

Table 1: Translations of "determinate counsel"

Version	*Translation*
NIV	"handed over to you by God's deliberate plan"
CSB	"delivered up according to God's determined plan"
JBP	"put into your power by the predetermined plan"
TLB	"But God, following his prearranged plan, let you use the Roman government to nail him to the cross and murder him."
KJV	"being delivered by the determinate counsel"
RSV	"delivered up according to the definite plan"
NET	"handed over by the predetermined plan"
NKJV	"delivered by the determined purpose"
GNT	"In accordance with his own plan, God had already decided that Jesus would be handed over to you."
NRSV	"handed over to you according to the definite plan"
MSG	"following the deliberate and well-thought-out plan of God"

You have to be impressed with the variety of ways "determinate counsel" is translated in these modern translations: determined plan, deliberate plan, definite plan, predetermined plan, well-thought-out plan, and more. It's as if the translators had a Greek thesaurus and consistently repeated the idea that God had a plan from the start for Christ's crucifixion and resurrection.

John Wesley believed that the apostle anticipated an objection here. The world would ask why God the Father permitted his only Son to be treated so inhumanely. Surely the omniscient God knew the hearts of wicked men and what they would do to Jesus. Surely the omnipotent God had the power to prevent the beatings, bloodshed, and crucifixion. So, why didn't he?

Of course, God knew what wicked men would do. Genesis 6:5 tells us, "The Lord saw that the wickedness of man was great in the earth, and that every intention of the thoughts of his heart was only evil continually." God knew all that those wicked men intended to do to the Savior. And he had the power to scuttle their plans before Jesus was arrested in the Garden of Gethsemane. He knew how brutal the Roman killing squad could be. So why didn't he stop it? How could a loving God do this? The answer is the determined counsel of God's grace, mercy, and love to redeem humankind from eternal death, by the death of his only-begotten Son.

In describing the extraordinary greatness of God, the Prophet Isaiah noted, "Who has measured the Spirit of the Lord, or what man shows him [God] his counsel? Whom did he [God] consult, and who made him understand"? (Isa 40:13, 14). God consulted no one. The Holy Trinity devised the plan for our salvation without any outside involvement or input.

Acts 2:23, 24 records the definitive statement about Jesus' death and resurrection being the eternal plan of the Godhead. In his preaching, Peter accused the Jews, saying, "This Jesus, delivered up according to the definite plan and foreknowledge of God, you crucified and killed by the hands of lawless men. God raised him up."

The power and ability of the Almighty to intercede and stop his Son's crucifixion should be unquestioned. "Your right hand, O Lord, glorious in power, your right hand, O Lord, shatters the enemy" (Exod 15:6). Psalm 147:4,5 indicates, "He determines the number of the stars; he gives to all of them their names. Great is our Lord, and abundant in power; his understanding is beyond measure." "Behold, I am the Lord, the God of all flesh. Is anything too hard for me"? (Jer 32:27).

God knew all about the crucifixion and resurrection. He had the power to stop them, but if he did, we would have no Savior, no salvation, and no sure future.

Jesus was delivered to the enemy

This word "delivered" (Greek: ἔκδοτον; English: *ekdoton*) in "this Jesus, delivered up according to the definite plan and foreknowledge of God" (Acts 2:23) is commonly used for those who are relinquished or delivered into the hands of adversaries. It means Jesus surrendered, was given up to his enemies, reflecting the eternal plan of the immortal God. In God's "well-thought-out plan," he is the Lamb of God, "slain from the foundation of the world" (Rev 13:8).

Should you ask who delivered God's Son for his crucifixion, you must consider the following:

- By the will of the Father, who did not spare him, Jesus was *delivered* to his enemies.
- By his own will, Jesus *delivered* his life to his enemies; no one took it from him.
- Judas, who betrayed Jesus, *delivered* him to his enemies, Caiaphas and the Sanhedrin.
- In choosing Barabbas over Jesus, the Jewish mob *delivered* him to his enemies.
- Pontius Pilate *delivered* Jesus to his soldiers to batter and abuse the gentle Savior.
- The Roman soldiers *delivered* Jesus to the killing squad, who were his visible enemies.
- The killing squad *delivered* Jesus to Calvary's Cross, the divine plan from the start.

It seems certain. No one delivered Jesus to his enemies without the providential oversight of God the Father. None of his enemies did to Jesus anything that was not part of God's eternal plan. The Holy Trinity delivered Jesus from heaven to earth when he "emptied himself, by taking the form of a servant, being born in the likeness of men. And being found in human form, he humbled himself by becoming obedient to the point of death, even death on a cross" (Phil 2:7,8).

> Peter and John, having been released from prison, returned to where some Jesus-followers were gathered and prayed, crying out to God, "Truly in this city there were gathered together against your holy servant Jesus, whom you anointed, both Herod and Pontius Pilate, along with the Gentiles and the peoples of

> Israel, to do whatever your hand and your plan had predestined to take place" (Acts 4:27,28).

Jesus was not surprised by his crucifixion or resurrection. He was quite clear about this tandem of crucial events. He said, "I lay down my life that I may take it up again. No one takes it from me, but I lay it down of my own accord. I have authority to lay it down, and I have authority to take it up again. This charge I have received from my Father" (John 10:17,18). Jesus had both the authority and the ability to lay his life down at the cross and take it up again at the empty tomb. Everything was going according to plan.

JESUS' RESURRECTION SHOULD NOT HAVE BEEN A SURPRISE TO HIS DISCIPLES

The Twelve are often criticized by twenty-first-century preachers for being somewhat dense and slow to adapt. And, to be honest, there is good evidence that was true (see Acts 1:6). But through our two-thousand-year-old eyes, we may not be seeing clearly what it was like to be selected by this Nazarene as a close follower and learner.

Take Levi (Matthew), for example. I'm sure he did not enjoy collecting taxes from his fellow Jews for the hated Romans, but he was making good money, and it was the best job a Jew could get. In many ways, today, it would be your dream job, especially the money part. Working for the government usually meant job security and good pay. Suddenly, this guy comes along, a man you have never met before, and simply says, "Follow me."

What do you do? Do you Google him to learn more about him? You want references. Has he ever written anything? Does he have a record in a Roman prison? Has the Sanhedrin banished him from the Temple? No, Matthew did none of those things, things we might consider standard due diligence today. What did he do? "As Jesus passed on from there, he saw a man called Matthew sitting at the tax booth, and he said to him, 'Follow me.' And he rose and followed him" (Matt 9:9).

A Tomb in Israel With A Rolling Stone

This is repeated again and again with Simon and Andrew (Matt. 4:19–20), James and John (Matt. 4:21–22), Philip (John 1:43–46), and, presumably, the rest of the disciples (Mark 3:16–19). Nevertheless, as month after month of grueling ministry went on, it appeared some of the Twelve were losing some of that "ministry shine." Crowd control was becoming a problem, and the twelve "learners" had to become the twelve "bodyguards." Funds were always minimal. The religious Jews were constantly there to question Jesus' teaching. Men who lived in one town for most of their lives, doing the same job, were now traveling from Galilee to Jerusalem and back, to Sidon and Tyre, and Caesarea in the north of Galilee. Was this life what they signed up for? There is no hint that they ever questioned the Master's teaching, but his tactics may have been a source of question.

The sources of the disciples' lack of understanding

Luke 9:22 chronicles Jesus' words plainly and definitively. "The Son of Man must suffer many things and be rejected by the elders and chief priests and scribes, and be killed, and on the third day be raised." About a week later, Jesus again revealed his future to these twelve followers.

Jesus had just healed a young boy who had an unclean spirit, "But while they were all marveling at everything he was doing, Jesus said to his disciples, 'Let these words sink into your ears: The Son of Man is about to be delivered into the hands of men.' But they did not understand this saying, and it was concealed from them, so that they might not perceive it. And they were afraid to ask him about this saying" (Luke 9:43–45).

One reason these disciples did not understand the prophetic words of Jesus is that God wouldn't let them. Jesus often spoke about himself in ways that both revealed and concealed his identity and the truth he taught. Four times, the disciple John records the concealing of Jesus' identity and purpose, recording, "My hour has not yet come" (John 2:4; 7:6, 30; 8:20; cp. 12:23).

As a God of order, God is also a God of timing. Because Jesus followed God's plan and its timing, he sometimes had to ask others to conceal his identity. Those whom Jesus asked not to reveal himself before his time include:

- Demons and unclean spirits (Mark 1:24; 1:34; 3:12)
- Crowds, especially recipients of healing (Mark 1:43; 5:43; 7:33, 36)
- Disciples (Mark 8:30; 9:9)

When the time came for Jesus to be revealed as Messiah, Savior, and the Lamb of God who takes away the sin of the world, he fully embraced these roles in the public arena.

Another reason the disciples were slow to understand Jesus' prophetic words is that they were twelve flawed men. They were human. Humans often have difficulty understanding what is not that difficult, and these disciples were no different. We don't know all the occupations or walks of life these twelve men came from, but we do know this. At least four of them were fishermen, hard-working men who grumbled about paying taxes to the Romans. Then there was Levi, also known as Matthew. He was a tax collector for the Romans. Socially, these men could not have been farther from the Jews of Jerusalem. Furthermore, one of the men, Simon, was a zealot—a freedom-fighting lawbreaker committed to overthrowing the Roman invaders. Throw these dozen disciples together and you may not have a pot of stew; you may have a WWE WrestleMania event.

There isn't evidence that these men argued often, but there were some notable flare-ups. When Jesus told his disciples that upon his crucifixion these very disciples would scatter and abandon him, Peter answered, "Though they all fall away because of you, I will never fall away. (Matt 26:33). That could not have gone down well among the others.

Mark 10:35–37 is the account of when "James and John, the sons of Zebedee, came up to him and said to him, 'Teacher, we want you to do for us whatever we ask of you.' And he said to them, 'What do you want me to do for you?' And they said to him, 'Grant us to sit, one at your right hand and one at your left, in your glory.'" Again, a request like this cannot have pleased the other disciples, and it certainly did not please the Lord Jesus.

Table 2: Jesus Announces His Death and Resurrection to His Disciples

Scripture	*Announcement*
Mark 9:31	"The Son of Man is going to be delivered into the hands of men, and they will kill him. And when he is killed, after three days he will rise."
John 14:19	"Yet a little while and the world will see me no more."
John 7:33	"I will be with you a little longer, and then I am going to him who sent me.
Mark 8:31	"The Son of Man must suffer many things and be rejected by the elders and the chief priests and the scribes and be killed, and after three days rise again.
John 3:14	"As Moses lifted up the serpent in the wilderness, so must the Son of Man be lifted up."
Matt 20:18,19	"We are going up to Jerusalem. And the Son of Man will be delivered over to the chief priests and scribes, and they will condemn him to death and deliver him over to the Gentiles to be mocked and flogged and crucified, and he will be raised on the third day."
Luke 9:22	"The Son of Man must suffer many things and be rejected by the elders and chief priests and scribes, and be killed, and on the third day be raised."
Mark 10:33,34	"See, we are going up to Jerusalem, and the Son of Man will be delivered over to the chief priests and the scribes, and they will condemn him to death and deliver him over to the Gentiles. And they will mock him and spit on him, and flog him and kill him. And after three days he will rise."
John 8:28	"When you have lifted up the Son of Man, then you will know that I am he."
John 14:29	"And now I have told you before it takes place, so that when it does take place you may believe."

These were just ordinary men who had encountered an extraordinary God-man. When Jesus spoke of his future crucifixion, their minds were elsewhere. That does not excuse them; it just reminds us that, had we been in their shoes, we may not have understood the Master much better.

Jesus' resurrection was unique among biblical resurrections

I live in America. I was born here. Americans have many idiosyncrasies that others do not have. It seems Americans always have to have something or do something that is bigger and better than everyone else. For example, Americans often tip two or three times as much as Europeans, Asians, or Africans. The exception is that Europeans receive a full month's holiday every year, while Americans receive much less. In many areas, we are unique.

The Cambridge Dictionary defines unique as being "the only *existing* one of its type, or special in some way." Jesus' crucifixion was not unusual; thousands of people were crucified during the years of the Roman Empire. However, Jesus' resurrection was certainly unique. Not that Jesus was the only person raised from the dead. He wasn't. The Bible records fourteen individuals or groups who were raised from the dead after dying.

No, Jesus was not the only person to be raised from the dead, but his resurrection was unique nonetheless. Here are some of the ways Jesus' resurrection was a one-of-a-kind.

1. Jesus' resurrection was unique because his resurrection, and his alone, validates that he is who he claimed to be—the unique God-man, the only begotten of the Father, the Lamb who takes away the sin of the world. During Christ's life and ministry, he demonstrated that he was the master of both the physical world (Luke 8:22–25) and the spiritual world (Mark 5:1–20). However, it was his unique resurrection that demonstrated he was the Son of God, a Person of the Holy Trinity, the God who became flesh and lived among us (John 1:1–4,14).

2. Jesus' resurrection was unique because he often predicted it, and it came true just as he said. Jesus often announced that he would die and be raised from the dead (Matt 12:40; John 2:19–22). Among the others whose resurrection is recorded in the Bible, none—not a single one—predicted their crucifixion and resurrection. If others claim they will rise from the dead, all you must do is give them time to be proven misinformed, misguided, and mistaken. Jesus backed up his claim (John 10:17,18; see Table 2).

3. Jesus' resurrection was unique because Old Testament prophets predicted the Savior's resurrection, but only his resurrection. There is not a single reference in either the Old or New Testaments to a prophet predicting the death and resurrection of Lazarus or Jairus' daughter (see Acts 17:1–3). In rising from the dead as he said he would, Jesus' resurrection not only validates his own claims, but also verifies the

truthfulness and accuracy of those prophets who predicted his resurrection (Acts 2:25–28).

4. Jesus' resurrection was unique because, of the fourteen people or groups mentioned in the Bible to have been resurrected, only Jesus rose from the grave, never to die again. While others were resurrected, all but Jesus eventually died again. Neither the Zarephath's son nor the Shunammite's son lived forever. They died a second time. So did Tabitha and Eutychus. None of these people is still alive today, but Jesus is. Jesus rose to life, never to die again (Rom 6:9). Jesus ascended into heaven, never to die again (Acts 1:9–11; Rev 1:17,18). Of all who have lived, died, and lived again, only Jesus will never see the corruption of death again (Acts 13:34).

Table 3: People Raised From the Dead in the Bible

Scripture	*Person Raised*
1 Kings 17:17–22	The Zarephath widow's son
2 Kings 4:18–37	The Shunammite's son
2 Kings 13:20	The man thrown into Elisha's grave
Mark 5:41	Jairus's daughter
Luke 7:14	The young man at Nain
John 11:38–44	Lazarus, Jesus' friend in Bethany
Matthew 27:52–53	Saints at Jesus' crucifixion
Matthew 28:1–6	Jesus Christ
Acts 9:36–42	Tabitha, also known as Dorcas
Acts 20:7–12	Eutychus, at Troas
1 Thessalonians 4:13–18; 1 Corinthians 15:23	The dead saints of the Church
Revelation 11:7–11	The two witnesses
Revelation 20:4	Old Testament saints and martyrs
Revelation 20:5	The wicked

5. Jesus' resurrection was unique because it changed our view of life. The resurrection of Jesus should both strengthen our faith and change our worldview. Because of his resurrection, we are free to contemplate what life is all about and what really matters in life. If Jesus died and rose from the dead for us, shouldn't we be thinking more about having clean hands and a pure heart (Ps 24:3,4) than who sits in the Oval

Office, or how many online followers we have? How are you spending your free time each day? Is it something that reflects Jesus' crucifixion and resurrection, or is it spending hours gaming, gardening, or grunting at the gym? Among all the resurrections in the Bible, only the resurrection of Jesus can change our view of life and prompt us to think about eternity.

6. Jesus' resurrection was unique because he rose from the grave as the Firstfruits. Just as the ancient Israelites offered the first grain of their harvest to God as an act of worship and a guarantee of a future harvest, Jesus' resurrection was the first of millions like it on Resurrection Day. His resurrection is the promise that more are coming (1 Cor 15:20). Jesus led the way to life after death. We Christians believe that God became man, died for our sins, and was resurrected on the third day. We believe the grave could not hold him because "in him was life, and the life was the light of men" (John 1:4). He was the first to rise from the dead, and we will follow him in bodily resurrection.
7. Jesus' resurrection was unique because when he said, "I am the resurrection and the life. Whoever believes in me, though he die, yet shall he live" (John 11:25), he was making no idle claim. Jesus asserted he was the source of both for us—resurrection from our graves, followed by eternal life. Just as there is no resurrection apart from Jesus, there is no eternal life in heaven without him. Jesus bestows his life on all who trust him as Savior so that we can share in his triumph over death (1 John 5:11, 12). None of this is true for any other person who died and was raised from the dead in either the Old or New Testaments.
8. Jesus' resurrection was unique because, when Jesus triumphed over the grave, he provided a glorious victory for every believer. First Thessalonians 4:14–18 records how this will unfold. "For since we believe that Jesus died and rose again, even so, through Jesus, God will bring with him those who have fallen asleep. For this, we declare to you by a word from the Lord, that we who are alive, who are left until the coming of the Lord, will not precede those who have fallen asleep. For the Lord himself will descend from heaven with a cry of command, with the voice of an archangel, and with the sound of the trumpet of God. And the dead in Christ will rise first. Then we who are alive, who are left, will be caught up together with them in the clouds to meet the Lord in the air, and so we will always be with the Lord. Therefore encourage one another with these words."

"Death is swallowed up in victory." No other resurrection provides such a clear blueprint for our resurrection, nor can any other give us this much encouragement.

9. Jesus' resurrection was unique because it impacts our service for the Lord today. Paul ends his writing on death and resurrection with an exhortation. "Therefore, my beloved brothers, be steadfast, immovable, always abounding in the work of the Lord, knowing that in the Lord your labor is not in vain" (1 Cor 15:58). The apostle purposefully links our resurrection with our reward for current service to the Lord, because after we are raised from the dead, we will stand before the Judgment Seat of Christ. "For we will all stand before the judgment seat of God" (Rom 14:10). "For we must all appear before the judgment seat of Christ, so that each one may receive what is due for what he has done in the body, whether good or evil (2 Cor 5:10). Death ends our opportunities to serve Jesus in this life, but resurrection opens our opportunity to be rewarded for that service in eternal life.

10. Jesus' resurrection was unique because it provides the foundation for our faith. Paul writes in 1 Corinthians 15:3–4, "For I delivered to you as of first importance what I also received: that Christ died for our sins in accordance with the Scriptures, that he was buried, that he was raised on the third day in accordance with the Scriptures." The apostle has just defined the gospel and the foundation of our faith—the death, burial, and resurrection of Jesus of Nazareth. Verses 5 and 6 continue, recording "that he appeared to Cephas, then to the twelve. Then he appeared to more than five hundred brothers at one time, most of whom are still alive, though some have fallen asleep." There were numerous witnesses to Jesus' crucifixion, and although no one witnessed his resurrection, there were more than ample witnesses to the resurrected Christ.

Had Jesus' resurrection been like all the others, we would have been robbed of hope, of justification, and of a home in heaven. The crucifixion and resurrection of Jesus are the twin events that secure our salvation and a bright future for all who come to Jesus in faith.

JESUS' RESURRECTION SECURED OUR JUSTIFICATION

Among the many theological concepts discussed in seminary classrooms, theological society meetings, and often in chat rooms, justification is sure to be included. Justification is the divine act by which God acquits all who trust Jesus as their Savior of the condemnation resulting from sin and declares them righteous. Being justified by God is essential because we all lack adequate righteousness to live with a holy God. This is true both because of our original sin (Rom 5:16,18) and the sin we commit daily (Rom 3:9–19).

Being declared righteous is important because we all stand condemned before a holy God. Our original sin and the sins we engage in daily are not just a stain; they are sufficient to earn condemnation by a holy God (John 3:16–18, 36; Matt 7:13–14). To remove this condemnation, we need a perfect sacrifice (Jesus on the cross) and God's acceptance of it (Jesus' resurrection). "It [our faith in Jesus as Savior] will be counted to us who believe in him who raised from the dead Jesus our Lord, who was delivered up for our trespasses and raised for our justification" (Rom 4:24, 25).

Jesus' resurrection secures our justification by God and guarantees our righteousness. If you think about it, that's nothing to sniff at. The twin towers of justification and righteousness stand out in the plethora of gifts a loving God gives to us. Securing our justification means we will never feel the heat of God's wrath. "Since, therefore, we have now been justified by his blood, much more shall we be saved by him from the wrath of God" (Rom 5:9).

> Jesus of Nazareth "was crucified also for us under Pontius Pilate; He suffered and was buried; and the third day He rose again, according to the Scriptures; and ascended into heaven, and sits on the right hand of the Father."—Nicene Creed

God's wrath is rarely the topic of conversation or discussion. It is something a sinful world would rather avoid. But it is real and it is active. Consider what the New Testament says about the wrath of God.

- John 3:36, "Whoever believes in the Son has eternal life; whoever does not obey the Son shall not see life, but the *wrath of God* remains on him."
- Romans 1:18, "For the *wrath of God* is revealed from heaven against all ungodliness and unrighteousness of men, who by their unrighteousness suppress the truth."

- Romans 2:5, "Because of your hard and impenitent heart you are storing up wrath for yourself on the *day of wrath* when God›s righteous judgment will be revealed."
- Romans 3:5, "But if our unrighteousness serves to show the righteousness of God, what shall we say? That God is unrighteous *to inflict wrath on us*?"
- Romans 9:22,23, "What if God, desiring to show his wrath and to make known his power, has endured with much patience *vessels of wrath* prepared for destruction, in order to make known the riches of his glory for vessels of mercy, which he has prepared beforehand for glory."
- Romans 13:4,5, "For he [the one who is in authority] is God's servant for your good. But if you do wrong, be afraid, for he does not bear the sword in vain. For he is the servant of God, an avenger who carries out *God's wrath* on the wrongdoer. Therefore one must be in subjection, not only to avoid *God's wrath* but also for the sake of conscience."
- Ephesians 5:6, "Let no one deceive you with empty words, for because of these things the *wrath of God* comes upon the sons of disobedience."
- Colossians 3:5,6, "Put to death therefore what is earthly in you: sexual immorality, impurity, passion, evil desire, and covetousness, which is idolatry. On account of these, *the wrath of God is coming*."

In summary, we know these things about God's wrath. It is terrible. It is justified. And it is avoided by all who have placed their faith in the Lord Jesus as Savior. Again, Romans 5:9, "Since, therefore, we have now been justified by his blood, much more shall we be saved by him from the wrath of God." This is another reason why the gospel is "good news."

Remember, the tandem of Christ's crucifixion and resurrection constitutes the one-two punch of Christian theology. Not only do they save us from divine wrath, but they also justify us so that we may receive God's righteousness in exchange for our unrighteousness. To be justified means to be made right before God.

Justification is more than a pardon. A pardon implies that you are still guilty of a crime, but you have been exempted from its consequences. You are pardoned. You will receive no punishment, but you still have the stain of your sin on your permanent record. But when God justifies us, he actually regards us as righteous persons. He can do this because he made us righteous, and so he can treat us as righteous once we come to faith in Jesus.

Romans 5:19, "For as by the one man's disobedience the many were made sinners, so by the one man's obedience the many will be made righteous."

1 Corinthians 1:28–31, "God chose what is low and despised in the world . . . so that no human being might boast in the presence of God. And because of him you are in Christ Jesus, who became to us wisdom from God, *righteousness* and *sanctification* and *redemption,* so that, as it is written, 'Let the one who boasts, boast in the Lord.'"

2 Corinthians 5:21, "For our sake he [God the Father] made him [God the Son] to be sin who knew no sin, so that in him [God the Son] we might become the righteousness of God."

Justification demonstrates the great exchange program. God exchanged our sin and unrighteousness for Jesus' righteousness so that we can live boldly for Christ today and, one day, stand in God's presence, fully right with him. What a deal we got, all because of a loving and merciful God. Don't you think it's time we thanked him more? You could do it right now!

JESUS' RESURRECTION IS IMPORTANT TO EVERYONE

When we think about the importance of Jesus' resurrection, we naturally ponder its significance to us as sinners. However, we are not alone in benefiting from the resurrection. Let's now turn to the importance of the resurrection for everyone.

Jesus' resurrection was, first of all, important to him.

Think about it. Before time began, God the Father, God the Son, and God the Holy Spirit devised a plan for our redemption. This included the Garden of Eden and the Garden of Gethsemane. It included the shedding of the blood of an animal (Gen 3:21) and then, ultimately, the blood of Jesus himself (Matt 26:28; 27:4,24,25; Luke 22:20,44; John 19:34; Acts 20:28; Rom 3:25; 5:9; 1 Cor 10:16; Eph 1:7; 2:13; Col 1:20; Heb 9:12–14; 10:19; 13:12; 1 Pet 1:2,19; 1 John 1:7; 5:6; Rev 1:5; 5:9; 7:14; 12:11; 19:13).

God the Father sent God the Son to Earth to do something no one has ever done before or since, that is, to become the inscrutable unification of God and man, the God-man. He came willingly and received the name Jesus of Nazareth. He lived a sinless life, teaching about God's kingdom, healing the sick, and even raising the dead. Then, at God's appointed time,

Jesus died on Calvary's Cross to atone for our sins. There he suffered and died for us.

His resurrection was just as important as his crucifixion, for it was Jesus' resurrection that signaled the Father's satisfaction with Jesus' work on Earth and confirmed the Father's acceptance of his sacrifice. It was as if God the Father was saying, "*Nice job, son. I'm pleased with you and what you've done.*"

Table 4: Scriptures Affirming the Resurrection of Jesus Christ

Scriptures	*Affirmation*
Mark 8:31	"And after three days rise again. And he said this plainly."
Mark 9:31	"And when he is killed, after three days he will rise."
Mark 10:34	"And after three days he will rise."
Mark 14:28	"But after I am raised up, I will go before you to Galilee."
John 11:25	"I am the resurrection and the life."
Acts 1:3	"He presented himself alive to them."
Acts 1:22	"A witness to his resurrection."
Acts 2:24	"God raised him up."
Acts 2:32	"This Jesus God raised up, and of that we all are witnesses."
Acts 4:33	"The apostles were giving their testimony to the resurrection of the Lord Jesus."
Acts 26:23	"Being the first to rise from the dead."
1 Cor 15:3,4	"Christ died for our sins in accordance with the Scriptures, that he was buried, that he was raised on the third day in accordance with the Scriptures."
2 Cor 5:14–15	"Him who for their sake died and was raised."
Eph 1:20	"He raised him from the dead."
1 Thess 4:14	"We believe that Jesus died and rose again."

The resurrection was also important to Jesus because it confirmed to the world that he was who he claimed to be. The Jewish people had looked for their Messiah for hundreds of years. Day after day, they prayed for his arrival, and day after day their prayers went unanswered. One reason was that they were looking for the wrong kind of Messiah. They wanted a mighty warrior, a David-like king to rule over Jerusalem and the rest of his kingdom. Nevertheless, Jesus presented himself as a humble servant, not a flashy warlord. So when their true Messiah came, they did not acknowledge him.

The Apostle John wrote of the Messiah, "He was in the world, and the world was made through him, yet the world did not know him. He came to his own, and his own people did not receive him. But to all who did receive him, who believed in his name, he gave the right to become children of God, who were born, not of blood nor of the will of the flesh nor of the will of man, but of God" (John 1:10–13). The resurrection proved Jesus was Israel's Messiah, for no one ever rose from the dead who never died again. Instead, the Savior ascended into heaven to sit to the right of the Father.

The resurrection of Jesus Christ vindicated him, corroborated his claims, and cemented his body as that of the God-man forever. "For there is one God, and there is one mediator between God and men, the *man* Christ Jesus, who gave himself as a ransom for all" (1 Tim 2:5, 6).

Jesus' resurrection is important to all who have trusted him as their Savior.

When Jesus died and was placed in the tomb of Joseph, he was entering Satan's territory. The devil is associated with darkness (Prov 4:19; Acts 26:18; Eph 6:12; Heb 2:14), and darkness with death (Job 10:21,22; 23:17; Ps 107:10,14; Isa 47:5; Lam 3:6; Nah 1:8), gloom (Job 23:22; 34:22), and punishment (Job 34:22; Eccl 11:8; Amos 5:20; Zech 1:15; Matt 8:12; 22:13; 25:30; 2 Pet 2:4,17; Jude 1:6, 13; Rev 16:10).

The day we trusted Jesus as Savior, our future and eternal residence were changed from hell to heaven. "But you are a chosen race, a royal priesthood, a holy nation, a people for his own possession, that you may proclaim the excellencies of him who called you out of darkness into his marvelous light to open their eyes, so that they may turn from darkness to light and from the power of Satan to God" (1 Pet 2:9).

Just as Peter did, Paul tells us, "He has delivered us from the domain of darkness and transferred us to the kingdom of his beloved Son" (Col 1:13).

Jesus linked our new life to his resurrection. "Because I live, you also will live" (John 14:19). Both the Savior and we benefited from his resurrection.

Because he lives, we are assured of a future inheritance, another blessing we welcomed through Jesus' resurrection from the dead. His resurrection "sealed the deal" related to our glorification and the permanence of our future. "For I am sure that neither death nor life, nor angels nor rulers, nor things present nor things to come, nor powers, nor height nor depth, nor anything else in all creation, will be able to separate us from the love of God in Christ Jesus our Lord" (Rom 8:38, 39).

Jesus' resurrection also quieted his critics.

"What then shall we say to these things? If God is for us, who can be against us? He who did not spare his own Son but gave him up for us all, how will he not also with him graciously give us all things? Who shall bring any charge against God's elect? It is God who justifies. Who is to condemn? Christ Jesus is the one who died—more than that, who was raised—who is at the right hand of God, who indeed is interceding for us" (Rom 8:31–34).

Certainly, Jesus received benefits from his resurrection, but what we received looms so much larger in our minds. We were called "out of darkness into his marvelous light" (1 Pet 2:9). Because of his resurrection, believers "cannot die anymore, because they are equal to angels and are sons of God, being sons of the resurrection" (Luke 20:36). The promise is not that we will not die, but that we "cannot die anymore," meaning after we are raised from the dead, we cannot die ever again.

Friday was a real downer for those first Christians. The hope built during Jesus' years of ministry was all but dashed in six hours on that Good Friday. The crucifixion of Jesus of Nazareth was part of God's plan, but so was his resurrection on Sunday morning. Suddenly, our faith was all about that third day. Perhaps I can say it best this way.

It was Friday.
We call it "Good Friday."
How could it be good, though?
When Jesus was suffering so?

It was Friday.
The Jewish Sanhedrin tried Jesus.
And even though the trial wasn't fair,
The High Priest didn't really care.

It was Friday.
Jesus was found guilty by the Jewish court.
He was spat upon, slapped, and mocked,
Their smug religion clearly had been rocked.

It was Friday.
But the Jews were helpless to take His life.
So Jesus was sent to Pilate's palace,
To face even greater scorn and malice.

It was Friday.
Pilate promptly questioned Jesus.
But nothing unlawful did he learn.
No guilt in Jesus did he discern.

It was Friday.
Pilate heard Jesus was a Galilean.
So off to King Herod, He was sent,
More suffering was all this new site meant.

It was Friday.
Pilate washed his hands of any guilt.
The crowd chose Barabbas over the Savior,
Evil is always what the wicked favor.

It was Friday.
The mob was shouting, "Crucify Him!"
To the truth, their eyes were blind,
Hatred alone was on their mind.

It was Friday.
Along the Via Dolorosa, He went.
This road was Jerusalem's way of sorrow.
It surely meant there was no tomorrow.

It was Friday.
The killing squad nailed Jesus to the cross.
They raised the Savior up on high,
And there they sat and watched Him die.

It was Friday.
"Father, forgive them," were Jesus' words.
At the peak of His suffering, pain, and loss,
He forgave those nailing Him to the cross.

It was Friday.
It was the day the Savior died.
The day the penalty for sin was paid,
The day His body in Joseph's tomb was laid.

It was Friday.
But why do we call it good?
Tragic Friday, torture Friday, trauma Friday
These descriptions we might better say.

It was Friday.
But here's the thing. We call it Good Friday,
Because even though His pain was numbing,
Jesus knew Sunday morning's coming.

It was Friday.
Life may have dealt you unplanned adversity.
But you know for sure you'll be okay,
'Cause Sunday never comes without a Friday.

It was Friday.
Filled with stress is your life and mine.
But we can handle the struggles of today,
Because Sunday's just the third day away.

—WMK

Epilogue

Some people see the death of Jesus of Nazareth as a terrible injustice. Jesus was innocent of any crime. He was falsely accused in a Jewish court and falsely convicted in a Roman one. He did not deserve to die. His crucifixion was the epitome of justice gone awry.

Others view the Savior's death as the meaningless casualty of a misguided Galilean. Had Jesus stayed in his hometown and remained working in his family's workman's shop, had he not had this Messiah complex that pushed him ever forward toward Jerusalem and an inevitable conflict with the Jewish religious leaders, he would never have been crucified at Calvary. His death did not have to happen. He was his own worst enemy.

Still, others see his crucifixion as just another day in the many days of Roman brutality against the Jews. The day Jesus died, morning crucifixions of others likely preceded Friday afternoon. The day before, dozens may have been crucified by the Romans. This one crucifixion, this pathetic Jesus, was just "another day at the office" for the Roman killing squad. There was nothing special about the crucifixion of Jesus of Nazareth. He was crucified in the Roman Empire just like thousands before and thousands after him.

However, the death of Jesus on Calvary's Cross was anything but meaningless or routine, as the preceding chapters have demonstrated. Jesus' crucifixion was not a hapless casualty but a divine appointment, a date with destiny. Arguably, what happened in Jerusalem made that dark Friday history's most significant day, and coupled with his resurrection on the third day, unquestionably the most momentous weekend in the history of humankind. This is not hyperbole; this is the truth. This was not just another crucifixion; this was the crucifixion of "the Lamb of God, who takes away the sin of the world" (John 1:29).

On the day of Pentecost, following Jesus' crucifixion and resurrection from the dead, Peter was preaching to the masses in Jerusalem and said:

> Men of Israel, hear these words: Jesus of Nazareth, a man attested to you by God with mighty works and wonders and signs that God did through him in your midst, as you yourselves know—this Jesus, delivered up according to the definite plan and foreknowledge of God, you crucified and killed by the hands of lawless men. God raised him up, loosing the pangs of death, because it was not possible for him to be held by it" (Acts 2:22–24).

The title of this book is *What Jesus' Crucifixion Accomplished For Us*. Many overlook the point here, such as those who claim his death accomplished nothing or that it only served to display the supremacy of mighty Rome. However, God sees his Son's death differently, and so should you.

Jesus' death glorified God the Father by demonstrating his love, providence, patience, wisdom, sovereignty, and much more. When Jesus died on the cross, it gave us insight into the character of the Heavenly Father. It provided an avenue for us to view the Father through the cross, a perspective lost on most of the world. In Exodus 33:18, Moses begged the Father, "Please show me your glory." God refused, but when Jesus was on the cross, the Father's glory was fully displayed. Jesus' crucifixion revealed the glory of God publicly, which was a great accomplishment.

Jesus' death also fulfilled many Old Testament prophecies, verifying their calling by YHWH. The oldest prophecy of all, given by God when Adam and Eve sinned, was that Satan would bruise the Messiah's heel, but he would crush Satan's head (Gen 3:15). This was fulfilled when Jesus hung on the cross (John 12:31–33). Daniel 9:26 records that the Messiah would be cut off. This perfectly describes Jesus' death (John 11:50–52). The prophet Isaiah predicted that Jesus would be led to his death "as a lamb to the slaughter" (Isa 53:7), which perfectly portrays Jesus' death (1 Cor 5:7; 1 Pet 1:18–20). Reading the prophecies of Isaiah 53 is like reading John 19. Jesus' death fulfilled multiple prophecies that only he could fulfil.

Jesus' death solidified his place in history. His crucifixion is the only one most people can recall. He divides history into the centuries before him and those after him. Jesus' death accomplished the purpose of his incarnation (Luke 19:10). His crucifixion proved that he clearly understood the purpose of his death (Luke 24:44–47). The Son of God left behind all the glorious trappings of heaven, deprived himself, and descended to Earth to become a human being specifically for this day. He "emptied himself, by taking the form of a servant" for this day (Phil 2:7). He became a human being so he could empathize with humans for this day. He was "born in the likeness of men" for this day (Phil 2:7). When he was crucified, Jesus accomplished everything necessary to clear the hurdles on your path back to God.

Nevertheless, some reading this will say to themselves, "Okay, okay. I get it. Jesus suffered shame at the cross, he battled Satan, he endured the wrath of God, but why? Why would God send his Son to Earth? Why would the Trinity's eternal plan call for the Son to suffer so terribly and then die on the cross? Is it possible that Christianity really is a "slaughterhouse religion"? Why would God do this for you and me?

The answer is the four-letter word that changed everything. Calvary was a result of God's love. Our salvation is the result of God's love. Our eternal destiny is the result of God's love.

The love of God differs from our human love. His love is not an affection that is generated by impulse, a sense of pleasure, or infatuation. God's love is intentional love. It is rational love. God loves based on his deliberate choices (Pss 36:10; 78:68; 86:13; 91:14; 130:7; et al.). God doesn't develop a sentimental attraction to us based on our outward appearance or our inner disposition (Deut 7:6–8). God doesn't have to like us to love us. There is nothing about us for a holy God to like. He loves us based on his character and eternal plan. We don't deserve his love. We don't earn his love. However, we can certainly enjoy God's love.

Here are some Scriptures that articulate God's love for us

GOD'S LOVE FOR US

"The LORD passed before him and proclaimed, 'The LORD, the LORD, a God merciful and gracious, slow to anger, and *abounding in steadfast love* and faithfulness, keeping steadfast love for thousands, forgiving iniquity and transgression and sin'" (Exod 20:6,7; Ps 103:17).

"The LORD is slow to anger and *abounding in steadfast love*, forgiving iniquity and transgression, but he will by no means clear the guilty, visiting the iniquity of the fathers on the children, to the third and the fourth generation. Please pardon the iniquity of this people, according to the greatness of your steadfast love, just as you have forgiven this people, from Egypt until now" (Num 14:18,19; see also Ps 103:8; 145:8).

"Let him who boasts boast in this, that he understands and knows me, that I am *the LORD* who practices *steadfast love*, justice, and righteousness in the earth. For in these things I delight, declares the LORD" (Jer 9:24).

"The *steadfast love* of the LORD never ceases; his mercies never come to an end" (Lam 3:22).

"*For God so loved the world*, that he gave his only Son, that whoever believes in him should not perish but have eternal life" (John 3:16; see also Eph 2:4; 1 John 4:9,10,16,17).

"Now before the Feast of the Passover, when Jesus knew that his hour had come to depart out of this world to the Father, *having loved his own* who were in the world, *he loved them to the end*" (John 13:1).

"*God shows his love for us* in that while we were still sinners, Christ died for us" (Rom 5:8).

"I have been crucified with Christ. It is no longer I who live, but Christ who lives in me. And the life I now live in the flesh I live by faith in the Son of God, *who loved me and gave himself for me*" (Gal 2:20).

"In all these things we are more than conquerors *through him who loved us*. For I am sure that neither death nor life, nor angels nor rulers, nor things present nor things to come, nor powers, nor height nor depth, nor anything else in all creation, will be able to separate us from *the love of God* in Christ Jesus our Lord" (Rom 8:37–39).

In the Old Testament, our duty to love God resulted from the Law. Often, especially in Deuteronomy (which means 'second law'), we are commanded to love the Lord our God "with all your heart and with all your soul." In the New Testament, however, duty morphs into delight, and love becomes the proper response for what God has done for us. "So you see, our love for him comes as a result of his loving us first" (1 John 4:19 JBP).

OUR LOVE FOR GOD

"*You shall love the Lord* your God with all your heart and with all your soul and with all your might" (Deut 6:5).

"And now, Israel, what does the Lord your God require of you, but to fear the Lord your God, to walk in all his ways, *to love him*, to serve the Lord your God with all your heart and with all your soul" (Deut 10:12).

"And the Lord your God will circumcise your heart and the heart of your offspring, so that *you will love the Lord your God* with all your heart and with all your soul, that you may live" (Deut 30:6).

"Only be very careful to observe the commandment and the law that Moses the servant of the Lord commanded you, *to love the Lord your God*, and to walk in all his ways and to keep his commandments and to cling to him and to serve him with all your heart and with all your soul" (Josh 22:5; 23:11).

"I love *those who love me*, and those who seek me diligently find me" (Prov 8:17).

"*You shall love the Lord* your God with all your heart and with all your soul and with all your mind" (Matt 22:37; Mark 12:30,33; Luke 10:27).

"*If you love me*, you will keep my commandments" (John 14:15; 1 Cor 8:31; 1 John 5:1–3).

"And we know that *for those who love God* all things work together for good, for those who are called according to his purpose" (Rom 8:28).

"What no eye has seen, nor ear heard, nor the heart of man imagined, what God has prepared for *those who love him*" (1 Cor 2:9).

Because of God's phenomenal love, everything in his plan for our redemption led Jesus to that dark day and the Roman killing field. "And being found in human form, he humbled himself by becoming obedient to the point of death, even death on a cross" (Phil 2:8). Can you imagine? The God who gives us life, the God who is eternal and never dies, this same God became a man so that he could die for us, his life for ours. He came to Earth to die on this dark and somber day.

> How marvelous! How wonderful!
> And my song shall ever be:
> How marvelous! How wonderful!
> Is my Savior's love for me!

But there's more. Yes, Jesus left the glory of heaven to walk the dusty roads of Galilee. Yes, he humbled himself and became a man. And yes, while he was born to die on this day, he would not die by the sword of an adversary. He would not die from a fall off the cliff near Nazareth. No, Jesus came to die on this day, but God's plan was for his Son to die by "death on a cross" (Phil 2:8). It was the cross that would be the implement of Christ's death, but it would be the eternal plan of God that would take him to that cross.

Jesus was born for this day. He lived a life of perfection for this day. The plot of the Jerusalem religious leaders led to this day. Everything in God's plan, everything in Jesus' life, everything the Sanhedrin wanted, was going to happen on this day, a dark Friday in Jerusalem.

> He took my sins and my sorrows,
> He made them his very own;
> He bore the burden to Calv'ry,
> And suffered, and died alone.

Judas Iscariot betrayed Jesus on this day. Jesus was interrogated by Annas and tried by Caiaphas' kangaroo court on this day. He left the Roman prefect Pontius Pilate dumbfounded on this day. Jesus was brutally beaten by the Sanhedrin and then by the Roman soldiers on this day. Jesus was ridiculed by Herod Agrippa on this day. Jesus walked the Via Dolorosa, the 'Way of Sorrows,' on this day.

Furthermore, Jesus died on the cross, accomplishing all that God required to atone for our sin on this day. This was certainly no ordinary day.

This was the day Christ was crucified for us, a day placed on God's calendar in eternity past.

That this day is cemented in history is undeniable. However, for every individual who has drawn a breath, the question continues to be—is this day cemented in your heart? Has the death of the Messiah made any difference in your eternal future? Jesus accomplished everything necessary to open the door for your salvation; have you walked through that door?

Jesus said, "Truly, truly, I say to you, whoever hears my word and believes him who sent me has eternal life. He does not come into judgment, but has passed from death to life" (John 5:24).

You have now heard; have you believed? "If you confess with your mouth that Jesus is Lord and believe in your heart that God raised him from the dead, you will be saved. For with the heart one believes and is justified, and with the mouth one confesses and is saved" (Rom 10:9–10).

Jesus accomplished everything necessary for your salvation, but it is of no avail until you turn from your sin, believe in Jesus as Savior, and walk through that door that opens to heaven. When do you think would be a good time to do that?

How marvelous! How wonderful!
And my song shall ever be:
How marvelous! How wonderful!
Is my Savior's love for me!

—Charles H. Gabriel (1856–1932)

Endnotes

1. Wright, *Cross Accomplish?*, 12.

2. In those versions of the Bible containing the apocryphal books, particularly the RSV and NRSV, the word "atonement" occurs in 1 Macc 1:46–47; 2 Macc 3:33; 12:45; Sir 5:5; 35:3; 45:16, 23.

3. An excellent example of substitutionary death apart from the Bible is Euripides' play called *Alcestis*. A model wife, Alcestis is noted dozens of times in Greek literature. In Euripides' 438 BC play, Alcestis offered herself in place of another. Greek literature is filled with examples of substitutionary deaths, one person dying for another, such as a spouse or a family member.

4. Wright, *Cross Accomplish?*, 22.

5. For a fuller treatment of theories on the atonement, see Phillips, *What is the Atonement?* 39.

6. Wallace and Rusk, *Moral Transformation*, 2011.

7. See the encyclical *Miserentissimus Redemptor* of Pope Pius XI, §6, *Libreria Editrice Vaticana.*

8. Aulén, *Christus Victor*, 20.

9. Aulén, *Christus Victor*, 20.

10. Paleo-orthodoxy holds that the essential theology of the Christian faith can be traced to beliefs prior to the 1054 AD schism between the Eastern Orthodox (Greek and Russian Orthodox, plus others) and the Western Church (Roman Catholic). It also harkens back to the theology of the period before the formal separation of Protestantism from the Roman Catholic Church (the 1517 AD Protestant Reformation) which is described in the Canon of Vincent of Lérins as "*Quod ubique, quod semper, quod ab omnibus*" ("What [is believed] everywhere, always and by everyone").

11. Weaver, *The Nonviolent Atonement*, 2001.

12. Borg, *Heart*, 95.

13. For excellent defenses of the substitutionary view of the atonement and answers to its critics, see Guillebaud, *Why the Cross?*, 146–63; Stott, *The Cross of Christ*, 1986; Jeffery, *Pierced*, 2007.

14. Wright, *Cross Accomplish?* 37.

15. Mathison is a professor of systematic theology at Reformation Bible College in Sanford, FL: *Worldview and Culture*, June 1, 2008.

16. Guillebaud, *Why the Cross?*, 146–63.

17. Chafer, *Systematic Theology*, vol 3, 68.

18. Fosdick, *Dear Mr. Brown*, 136.

19. Harris, 2 Corinthians, vol 2, 679.

20. Phillips, *The View*, 41.

21. A lengthy quote of Jonathan Edwards' notes from his Bible is appropriate here. "What is an argument *ex posteriori* of the devil's having assumed the form of a serpent in his temptation of our first parents, is the pride he has ever since taken of being worshipped under that form, to insult, as it were, and trample upon fallen man. To this purpose, we may observe that the serpent has all along been the common symbol and representation of the heathen deities (*Jul. Firmic. de errore Prof an. Relig.* p. 15). That the Babylonians worshipped a dragon, we may learn from the Apocrypha, and that they had images of serpents in the Temple of Belus, *Diodorus Siculus*, lib. 2. cap. 4. informs us. Grotius, drawing on several ancient authors, has made it appear that in the old Greek mysteries, participants would carry a serpent and cry, "Εὖα," thereby expressing the devil's triumph in the unhappy deception of our first mother. The story of Ophis among the heathen was taken from the devil's assumption of the body of a serpent in his temptation of Eve (Origen, *contra Celsus*, lib. 6). And to name no more what Philip Melanchthon tells us of some priests in Asia is very wonderful, *viz.* that they carry about a serpent in a brazen vessel, which they attend with a great deal of music, and many choruses in verse, while the serpent now and then lifts himself, opens his mouth, and thrusts out the head of a beautiful virgin, (as having swallowed her,) 'to show the devil's triumph in this miscarriage among those poor deluded idolaters' (William Nicolls. *Conference with a Theist*, vol. 1. Los Angeles, Hardpress, 2013).

22. Snakes Top List of Americans' Fears (gallup.com) Gallup Poll, March 19, 2001, Princeton, NJ.

23. The biblical concept of "forever and ever" is generally understood as the time of God's reign over his creation. He reigns "forever and ever." This is designed to show his divine kingdom is "forever and ever." See: (Ex 15:18; 1 Chron 29:10; Pss 10:16; 45:6; 38:14; 145:21; Dan 2:209; 7:18; Mic 4:5; Gal 1:5; Eph 3:21; Phil 4:20; 1 Tim 1:17; 2 Tim 4:18; Heb 1:8; 13:21; 1 Pet 4:11; 5:11; Rev 1:6; 4:9,10; 5:13; 7:12; 10:6; 11:15; 15:7; 22:5, and others).

24. See the review of "The myth of painless childbirth (the John J. Bonica lecture)" by Ronald *Melzack*, in *Pain, 1984 Aug; 19(4):321–337.*

25. It is interesting that at many funerals the priest, rabbi, or pastor will say, "dust to dust, ashes to ashes," which, of course, is not in the text. That phrase comes from the Book of Common Prayer burial service, which reads: 'We therefore commit this body to the ground, earth to earth, ashes to ashes, dust to dust; in sure and certain hope of the resurrection to eternal life.' The biblical text only says "dust to dust," without "ashes to ashes."

26. John Calvin, *Calvin's Commentaries,* 23 vols., Grand Rapids, MI: Baker, 2009.

27. Floyd H. Barackman, *Practical Christian Theology.* Old Tappan, NJ: Revell, 1984, 72.

28. I am especially fond of God's promise that there will be no more pain. I have been in a pain management program for decades. I see a specialist, a pain doctor, once a month. I have been in and out of physical therapy for years. Currently, I take four different prescription pain medicines daily, each of which addresses a different approach to managing my pain. But "manage" doesn't mean eliminate pain; it only means you mask it. However, unlike my pain management, Jesus' death on Calvary's Cross means one day there will be pain elimination, completely and forever. Frankly, I can't wait!

29. Donald Macleod, *Christ Crucified. Understanding the Atonement.* Downers Grove, IL: IVP Academic, 2014, 59–60.

30. Eusebius, *Proof of the Gospel*, translated by W. J. Ferrar. Grand Rapids, MI: Baker, 1981, 11.1.

31. Rod Parsley, *The Cross*. Lake Mary, FL: Charisma, 2013, 66–68.

32. W. G. T. Shedd, *Dogmatic Theology*, vol 2. Grand Rapids, MI: Zondervan, 1969, 469.

33. Homer, *The Iliad of Homer*. Translated by Richmond Lattimore. Chicago: University of Chicago Press, 2011.

34. Donald Macleod, *Christ Crucified. Understanding the Atonement*. Downers Grove, IL: IVP Academic, 2014, 141.

35. Leon Morris, *The Apostolic Preaching of the Cross*, 3rd rev ed, 1965. Grand Rapids: Eerdmans, 1988, 150.

36. H.C.G. Moule, *The Cambridge Bible for Schools and Colleges*. Columbia, SC: BiblioLife, 2009.

37. Charles Harold (C.H.) Dodd, "The Epistle of Paul to the Romans," *The Moffatt New Testament Commentary*. London: Hodder & Stoughton, 1936, 21.

38. Anthony Tyrrell Hanson, *The Wrath of the Lamb*. London: Society for Promoting Christian Knowledge (SPCK), 1957, 109.

39. Peter Taylor (P.T.) Forsyth, *Positive Preaching and the Modern Mind*. London: Forgotten Books, 2012, 356ff.

40. Leon Morris, *The Cross in the New Testament*. Grand Rapids, MI: Eerdmans, 1965, 192.

41. Marcus J. Borg and John Dominic Crossan, *The Last Week: A Day-by-Day Account of Jesus's Final Week in Jerusalem*. San Francisco, CA: Harper San Francisco, 2006, 159ff.

42. Some argue that the word "propitiation" should be translated as "expiation," which would refer to cleansing from sin rather than the appeasement of God's wrath. But these are twin accomplishments of Christ on our behalf. Propitiation refers to Christ's work of satisfying God's righteousness. Jesus paid the penalty that was due because of our sin. With expiation, our sin is removed from us and transferred or imputed to Christ, who suffers on our behalf, in our place. God is satisfied, and our sin is removed, all as a result of the atonement provided by Jesus on the cross. For the use of "propitiation," see Leon Morris, *The Apostolic Preaching of the Cross*—3rd ed. Grand Rapids, MI: Eerdmans 1965, 179–213.

43. John Murray, *The Atonement*. Philadelphia, PA: P&R, 1962, 37.

44. Harry Emerson Fosdick, Dear Mr. Brown (New York, NY: Harper & Row, 1961), 136.

45. Interview by Leif Hansen (The Bleeding Purple Podcast) with Brian McLaren, January 8th, 2006); Part 1: http://bleeding purple podcast .blogspot.com/2006/01/brian-mclaren-interview-part-i.html; Part II: http://bleeding purple podcast. blog spot. com/2006/01/interview-with-brianmclaren-part-ii.html).

46. The Syrians refused, however, to return the body of Mossad agent Eli Cohen who had been hanged in Damascus.

47. Interestingly, almost half of the times *logízomai* is found in the New Testament, it is located in the epistle to the Romans. Even more intriguing, of the twenty-two times the word is found in Romans, fourteen of those are in chapter 4 where Paul is arguing that the faith of Abraham was accounted to him as righteousness.

48. Proof that Abraham did not actually become righteous but was only treated by God as if he were, is the fact that Abraham took Hagar as his second wife. The conflict between her son, Ishmael [representing the Arabic people], and Sarah's son, Isaac [representing the Jewish people], occurred after Abraham demonstrated faith in God (Gen 15:6).

49. Martin Luther, *Werke*. Weimar, Germany, 1883, 5:608.

50. John Calvin, *Institutes* IV.17.2.

51. "Redeem, Redemption" in the *Evangelical Dictionary of Theology,* edited by Daniel J. Treier and Walter A. Elwell. Grand Rapids, MI: Baker Academic, 2017.

52. Leon Morris, "Redemption" in *Dictionary of Paul and His Letters,* edited by Gerald F. Hawthorne, Ralph P. Martin, and Daniel G. Reid. Downers Grove, IL: InterVarsity, 1993, 784.

53. https://greatergoodberkley.edu/topic/forgiveness/definition

54. The phrase "the forgiveness of sins" is an appositive to the phrase "we have redemption," and is placed here to clarify one aspect of our redemption. This is why the KJV adds the word "even" before "the forgiveness of sins," and the Good News Translation adds "that is."

55. Charles Francis Digby (C.F.D.) Moule, "The Christian Understanding of Forgiveness," *Theology* 71 (1968), 435–43.

56. Carrie L. Lewis, "Narrative Insights into the Crucifixion of Jesus in Luke" (23:33–43). (Jesus Christ) *Currents in Theology and Mission,* October 1, 2005).

57. Often, theologians are divided between those who understand our makeup to be body and soul only (dichotomy) and those who believe we consist of body, soul, and spirit (trichotomy). Those who view humans as a dichotomy prefer to describe our makeup as consisting of two elements: material (body) and immaterial (soul or spirit, but not both soul and spirit). I have come to believe that human beings consist of body, soul, and spirit. Many view the soul as the immaterial part of a human being or animal, regarded as immortal, and the spirit as the non-physical aspect of a person, where the seat of emotions, reason, character, and other qualities resides. Like Old King Cole, who was a merry old soul, the word is used to refer to the "person or individual." While the words "soul" and "spirit" often appear to be used interchangeably, that is not always the case.

First Thessalonians 5:23 clearly distinguishes between the body, soul, and spirit. In the benediction to his first letter to the Christ-followers in Thessalonica, Paul wrote, "Now may the God of peace himself sanctify you completely, and may your whole spirit and soul and body be kept blameless at the coming of our Lord Jesus Christ." There will likely never be a consensus on the makeup of human beings on this side of heaven. Each of us must study the Scriptures and come to our own conclusions. I was theologically trained as a dichotomist; Scripture has rendered me a trichotomist.

58. A distinction without a difference is a linguistic or conceptual distinction that is of no practical importance or which has no effect on meaning; a perceived difference where there is no actual difference.

59. Floyd H. Barackman, *Practical Christian Theology.* Old Tappan, NJ: Fleming H. Revell, 1984, 188.

60. Brené Brown, *Rising Strong.* New York: Random House, 2015. Quoted in *How to Listen to Pain,* Greater Good (berkeley.edu).

61. Job 6:20; Pss 34:5; 35:4, 26; 40:14; 70:2; 72:24; 83:17; Prov 13:5; 19:26; Isa 1:29; 24:23; 33:9; 54:4; Jer 15:9; 40:12; Mic 3:7

62. 1 Sam 20:30; 2 Chron 32:21; Ezra 9:7; Job 8:22; Pss 35:26; 40:15; 44:15; 69:19; 70:3; 109:27; 132:18; Isa 30:3, 5; 42:17; 54:4; 61:7; Jer 2:26; 3:24–25; 7:19; 11:13; 20:18; Dan 9:7–8; Hos 9:10; Mic 1:11; Hab 2:10; Zeph 3:5, 19.

63. Job 20:3; Pss 4:2; 35:26; 44:15; 69:7, 19; 71:13; 109:29; Prov 18:13; Isa 30:3; 45:16; 50:6; 61:7; Jer 3:25; 20:11; 51:51; Ezek 16:52, 54, 63; 32:24–25, 30; 34:29; 36:6–7, 1; 39:26; 44:13; Mic 2:6.

64. Num 12:14; Judg 18:7; Ruth 2:15; 1 Sam 20:34; 25:7, 15; 2 Sam 10:5; 19:3, 5; 30:15; Ezra 9:6; Job 11:3; 19:3; Pss 35:4; 40:14; 44:9; 69:6; 70:2; 74:21; Prov 25:8; 28:7; Isa 41:11; 45:16–17; 50:7; 54:4; Jer 3:3; 6:15; 8:12; 14:3; 2:22; 31:19; Ezek 16:27, 54, 61; 36:32; 43:10–11.

65. Gen 8:7, 14; Josh 2:10; 4:23; 5:1; 9:5, 12; 2 Sam 19:5; 1 Kgs 13:4; 17:7; Job 8:12; 12:15; 14:1; 15:30; 18:16; Pss 22:15; 24:15; 90:6; 102:4, 11; 129:6; Prov 17:22; Isa 15:6; 19:5, 7, 11; 30 :5; 40:7–8, 24; 42:15; 44:27; Jer 2:16; 6:15; 8:9, 12; 10:14; 12:4; 23:10; 46:24; 48:1, 20; 50:2, 38; 51:17, 36; Lam 4:8; Ezek 17:9–10, 24; 19:12; 3:11; Hos 2:5; 9:16; Joel 1:10–12, 17, 20: Amos 1:2; 4:7; Jonah 4:7; Nah 1:4; Zech 9:5; 10:5, 11, 17.

66. Gen 2:25; Exod 32:1; Judg 3:25; 5:28; 2 Kgs 2:17; 8:11; 19:26; Ezra 8:22; 9:16; Job 6:20; 19:3; Pss 6:10; 14:6; 22:5; 25:2–3, 20; 31:1, 17; 35:4, 26; 37:19;40:14; 44:7; 53:4; 69:6; 70:2; 71:1, 13, 24; 83:17; 8:17; 97:7; 109:28; 119:6, 31, 36,78, 80, 116; 127:5; 129:5; Prov 10:5; 12:4; 14:35; 17:2; 19:26; 29:15; Isa 1:29; 19:9; 20:5; 23:4; 24:23; 26:11; 29:22; 37:27; 41:11; 42:17; 44:11; 45:16–17, 24; 49:23; 50:7; 54:4; 56:13; 66:5; Jer 2:36; 6:15; 8:12; 9:19; 12:13; 14:3–4; 15:9; 1:13, 18; 20:11; 22:22; 31:19; 48:13, 39; 49:23; 50:12; 51:47, 51; Ezek 16:52, 63; 32:30; 36:32; Hos 4:19; 10:6; 13:15; Joel 2:26–27; Mic 3:7; 7:16; Zeph 3:11; 13:4.

67. Some British researchers conducted a volunteer study to investigate what causes people to feel ashamed when they are naked. The working theory of these researchers was that the shame of being naked was codified in (most) human societies to protect mating pairs. The British team concluded that the natural gregariousness of humans and their need to interact outside the family group, coupled with nakedness, created too many temptations to stray from the mating pair. "That's where our shame of nudity comes in. Over thousands of generations, we've learned that showing off a naked body sends out sexual signals that threaten the security of mating pairs. And we've chosen to agree that that is a bad thing. Shame is the ideal emotion to enforce that code of conduct. Because it feels unpleasant, we avoid it at all costs." Ransom Riggs, "Why Are People Ashamed of Being Naked?" *Mental Floss*, March 11, 2009. When Adam and Eve were ashamed of their nakedness, I wonder who Adam was afraid would steal Eve from him because she was naked?

68. "Leather bikinis." *Living in Roman London*. Museum of London. 18 December 2010.

69. Larissa Bonfante, "Naked and the Nude," *Archaeology Odyssey* 6:1, January/February 2003.

70. Martin Hengel, *Crucifixion*. London: SCM Press, 1977, 87.

71. Darrell Bock, Luke in *Baker Exegetical Commentary*, vol 2. Grand Rapids, MI: Baker Academic, 1996, 1850).

72. For rabbinic opposition to crucifixion as explained in Deuteronomy 21:22–23, see *Sifre Deut*. 221; *b Sanh*. 46b; and *Midr. Tannaim* 132.7.

73. The type of undergarment worn by the ancient Romans was called a *subligaculum*. It was sometimes a pair of shorts or a simple loincloth wrapped tightly around the lower body. This longer form of *subligaculum* had two strings attached to a longer linen cloth that hung down the back over the buttocks. This more extended portion was brought forward and up the front, where it was tied with the strings. Leather *subligacula* have been found in excavations of Roman London ("Leather bikinis." *Living in Roman London*. Museum of London. 18 December 2010).

74. The word εὐαγγέλιον is frequently found in the New Testament: the Gospels (12 times), Acts (2 times), Paul (61 times), Peter (1 time), and Revelation (1 time).

75. Gospels–13 times; Acts–16; Paul–24; Hebrews–2; Peter–3; Revelation–2.

76. Rom 1:1; 1 Cor 1:1; 2 Cor 1:1; Gal 1:1; Eph 1:1; Phil 1:1; Col 1:1; 1 Thess 1:1; 2 Thess 1:1; 1 Tim 1:1; 2 Tim 1:1; Titus 1:1.

77. Rom 1:8; 1 Cor 1:1; 2 Cor 1:8; Gal 1:6; Eph 1;15; Phil 1:12; Col 1:9; 1 Thess 2:1; 2 Thess 2:1; 1 Tim 1:3; 2 Tim 2;8; Titus 1:5; Phlm 8.

78. Paul uses this phrase again in Romans 15:16; 1 Thessalonians 2:2; and 8:9. He also uses the phrase "gospel of Christ" even more times (Rom 15:19; 1 Cor 9:12; 2 Cor 2:12; 9:13; 10:14; Gal 1:7; Phil 1:27; and 1 Thess 3:2).

79. For the use of *horízō*, see also Luke 22:22; Acts 2:23; 10:42; 11:29; 17:26, 31; Heb 4:7.

80. There is significant diversity in translators' selections for this word. Many are familiar with the King James "wiles of the devil," which is also used in the RSV and NRSV. Other examples are: "tricks" (CEV, GNT); "tactics" (HCSB); "methods of attack" (JBP); "strategies and tricks" (LTB); "schemes" (ESV, NIV, NASB); and "strategies" (NLT).

81. John Piper, *The Passion of Jesus Christ*. Wheaton, IL: Crossway, 2004, 96–97.

82. Keep in mind the expression "good guys" is used only as a descriptor of God's children, bearing in mind verses such as Romans 3:10–18 which is a description of the true character of humankind.

83. Henry Fairfield Burton, "The Worship of the Roman Emperors," *The Biblical World*, vol 40, no. 2 (August 1912), 80–91.

84. Stewart Perowne, *The Life and Times of Herod the Great*. New York: Abingdon, 1956.

Bibliography

Andam, Michael. *It is Finished: What Did Jesus Accomplish on the Cross*? Independently Published, 2020.

Anselm of Canterbury. *Why God Became Man. In The Major Works*. Brian Davies and G. R. Evans, eds. New York: Oxford University Press, 1998.

Aulén, Gustav. *Christus Victor: An Historical Study of the Three Main Types of the Idea of Atonement*. Translated by A. G. Herber. Eugene, OR: Wipf & Stock, 2003.

Baker, Mark D. and Joel B. Green. *Recovering the Scandal of the Cross: Atonement in New Testament and Contemporary Contexts*. Downers Grove, IL: InterVarsity, 2003.

Barackman, Floyd H. *Practical Christian Theology*. Old Tappan, NJ: Revell, 1984.

Barclay, William. *Crucified and Crowned*. London: SCM, 1961.

Barth, Karl. *Church Dogmatics*, 4 vols. The Doctrine of Reconciliation. Edinburgh: T&T Clark, 1988.

Bauman, Richard A. *Crime and Punishment in Ancient Rome*. Routledge: London, 1996.

Beilby, James, and Paul R. Eddy, eds. *The Nature of the Atonement: Four Views*. Spectrum Multiview Book, Downers Grove, IL: InterVarsity Academic, 2006.

Benoit, Pierre. *The Passion and Resurrection of Jesus Christ*. New York: Herder and Herder, 1970.

Bird, Michael F. *Evangelical Theology*, 2nd ed. *A Biblical and Systematic Introduction*. Grand Rapids, MI: Zondervan Academic, 2020.

Blinzler, Josef. *The Trial of Jesus*. Westminster, MD: Newman, 1959.

Borg, Marcus J. *The Heart of Christianity*. San Francisco: Harper, 2004.

Borg, Marcus J. and John Dominic Crossan. *The Last Week: A Day-by-Day Account of Jesus's Final Week in Jerusalem*. San Francisco, CA: HarperSanFrancisco, 2006.

Brown, Joanne Carlson, and Carole R. Bohn, eds. *Christianity, Patriarchy, and Abuse*. New York: Pilgrim, 1989.

Brown, Raymond E. *Death of the Messiah*, 2 vols. New York: Doubleday, 1999.

Chapman, David W. *Ancient Jewish and Christian Perceptions of Crucifixion*. Tübingen: Mohr Siebeck, 2008.

Chapman David W. and Eckhard J. Schnabel. *The Trial and Crucifixion of Jesus: Texts and Commentary*. Peabody, MA: Hendrickson, 2019.

Dever, Mark J., et al. *Proclaiming a Cross-Centered Theology*. Together For The Gospel, Wheaton, IL: Crossway, 2009.

Dodd, Charles Harold (C. H.). "The Epistle of Paul to the Romans," *The Moffatt New Testament Commentary*. London: Hodder & Stoughton, 1936.

Eusebius, *Proof of the Gospel*. Translated by W. J. Ferrar. Grand Rapids, MI: Baker, 1981.

Evans, Craig A., and N. T. Wright. *Jesus, The Final Days*. Louisville, KY: Westminster John Knox, 2009.

Forsyth, P. T. *The Cruciality of the Cross*. Carlisle, UK: Paternoster, 1997.

Fosdick, Harry E. *Dear Mr. Brown: Letters to a Perplexed Person About Religion*. New York: Harper and Row, 1961.

Frame, John M. *Salvation Belongs to the Lord: An Introduction to Systematic Theology*. Phillipsburg, NJ: P&R, 2006.

Geisler, Norman. *Systematic Theology*, vol 3. Bloomington, MN: Bethany, 2004.

Grudem, Wayne. *Systematic Theology: An Introduction to Biblical Doctrine*. Grand Rapids, MI: Zondervan, 1994.

Guillebaurd, H. E. *Why the Cross?* London: IVF, 1954.

Hanson, Anthony Tyrrell. *The Wrath of the Lamb*. London: SPCK, 1957.

Heim, S. Mark. "Christ Crucified. Why Does Jesus' Death Matter?" *Christian Century*, March 7, 2001.

Hoehner, Harold W. *Chronological Aspects of the Life of Christ*. Grand Rapids, MI: Zondervan, 1977.

Homer. *The Iliad of Homer*. Translated by Richmond Lattimore. Chicago: University of Chicago Press, 2011.

Humphreys Colin J. *The Mystery of the Last Supper*. Cambridge: Cambridge University Press, 2011

Jeffery, Steve, Michael Ovey, and Andrew Sach. *Pierced for Our Transgressions: Rediscovering the Glory of Penal Substitution*. Wheaton, IL: Crossway, 2007.

Jeremias, Joachim. *Golgotha*. Leipzig: Pfeiffer, 1926.

Kostenberger, Andreas J., L. Scott Kellum, and Charles L. Quarles. *The Cradle, the Cross, and the Crown: An Introduction to the New Testament*. Nashville, TN: Broadman & Holman Academic, 2009.

Lane, William L. *The Gospel According to Mark*. Grand Rapids: Eerdmans, 1974.

MacArthur, John. *The Murder of Jesus*. Nashville: Word, 2000.

Macleod, Donald. *Christ Crucified. Understanding the Atonement*. Downers Grove, IL: IVP Academic, 2014.

Mansfield, Stephen. *Killing Jesus*. Brentwood, TN: Worthy, 2013.

Meier, John P. *A Marginal Jew: Rethinking the Historical Jesus*, vol.1: *The Roots of the Problem and the Person*. New York: Doubleday, 1991.

Morris, Leon. *The Apostolic Preaching of the Cross*, 3rd rev ed. Grand Rapids: Eerdmans, 1988.

———. *The Cross in the New Testament*. Grand Rapids, MI: Eerdmans, 1965.

———. "Redemption" in *Dictionary of Paul and His Letters*. Gerald F. Hawthorne, Ralph P. Martin, and Daniel G. Reid, eds. Downers Grove, IL: InterVarsity, 1993.

Murray, John. *The Atonement*. Philadelphia, PA: P&R, 1962.

Nicholson, William R. *The Six Miracles of Calvary*. Grand Rapids, MI: Discovery House, 2001.

Packer, James I., and Mark Dever. *In My Place Condemned He Stood*. Wheaton, IL: Crossway, 2007.

Pannenberg, Wolfhart. *Systematic Theology*, vol 2. Grand Rapids, MI: Eerdmans, 2013.

Parinni, Jay. *Jesus: The Human Face of God*. New York: New Harvest, 2013.

Parsley, Rod. *The Cross*. Lake Mary, FL: Charisma, 2013.

Perowne, Stewart. *The Life and Times of Herod the Great*. New York: Abingdon, 1956.

Phillips, John. *The View from Mount Calvary.* Grand Rapids, MI: Kregel, 2006.
Phillips, Richard D. *What is the Atonement*? Phillipsburg, NJ: P&R, 2010.
Piper, John. *The Passion of Jesus Christ.* Wheaton, IL: Crossway, 2004.
Ratzinger, Joseph. *Jesus of Nazareth. Holy Week: From the Entrance into Jerusalem to the Resurrection.* San Francisco: Ignatius, 2011.
Reymond, Robert. *A New Systematic Theology of the Christian Faith.* Grand Rapids, MI: Zondervan Academic, 2020.
Ryrie Charles C. *Basic Theology: A Popular Systematic Guide to Understanding Biblical Tr*uth. Chicago, IL: Moody, 1999.
Schnabel, Eckhard J. *Jesus in Jerusalem. The Last Days.* Grand Rapids, MI: Eerdmans, 2018.
Sproul, R.C. *The Truth of the Cross.* Lake Mary, FL: Reformation Trust, 2007.
Spurgeon, Charles Haddon. *Christ's Words from the Cross.* Grand Rapids, MI: Baker, 1981.
Stott, John R. W. *The Cross of Christ.* Downers Grove, IL: InterVarsity, 1986.
Treat, Jeremy R. *The Crucified King: Atonement and Kingdom in Biblical and Systematic Theology*. Grand Rapids, MI: Zondervan, 2014.
Vardaman, Jerry, and Edwin M. Yamauchi, eds. *Chronos, Kairos, Christos: Nativity and Chronological Studies Presented to Jack Finegan.* Warsaw, IN: Eisenbrauns, 1989.
Wallace, A.J., and R. D. Rusk. *Moral Transformation: The Original Christian Paradigm of Salvation.* New Zealand: Bridgehead, 2011.
Weaver, J. Denny. *The Nonviolent Atonement.* Grand Rapids, MI: Eerdmans, 2001.
Wilkinson, John. *Jerusalem as Jesus Knew It.* London: Thames and Hudson, 1978.
Wright, N. T., Simon Gathercole, and Robert B. Stewart. *What Did the Cross Accomplish? A Conversation about the Atonement.* Louisville, KY: Westminster John Knox, 2021.
Zugibe, Frederick T. *The Crucifixion of Jesus: A Forensic Inquiry.* Lanham, MD: M. Evans, 2005.

Subject Index

Name Index

www.ingramcontent.com/pod-product-compliance
Lightning Source LLC
LaVergne TN
LVHW050613100826
845148LV00011B/1574
9798385269594